# Welfare Democracy in Ancient India
## (In Context to Vedik Vangmaya and Manav Dharmashastra)

## Dr. Surabhy Dutt

## Pustak Bharati
## Toronto Canada

**Author :** Dr. Surabhy Dutt

**Book Title :** Welfare Democracy in Ancient India
(In Context to Vedik Vangmaya and Manav Dharmashastra)

**Translator :** Smt. Rupa Srikumar

**Published by :**
Pustak Bharati (Books-India)
180 Torresdale Ave,
Toronto Canada M2R 3E4
email : pustak.bharati.canada@gmail.com
Web : www.pustak-bharati-canada.com

ISBN 978-1-989416-81-5

ISBN : 978-1-989416-81-5

Copyright ©2022

# Dedicated to Nation

शन्तिवा सुरभिः स्योना कीलालोघ्री पयस्वती।
भूमिरघि ब्रवीतु मे पृथिवी पयसा सह।।

# Acknowledgement

My book "Pracheen Bharat Mei Kalayankari Janatantra" in context with 'Vedik Vangmaya and Manusmriti' in Hindi was published in 2015. For quite a while my family, colleagues and friends were insisting on getting my book translated in English with an idea to make this Democratic Political Heritage of India reach more and more people with wider readership as well as giving them an opportunity to experience and understand it with a right approach.

During my search for a translator I was little apprehensive as I wanted to make sure that the spirit of original book remained intact in this translation. I am grateful to Smt. Rupa Srikumar, my friend a Novelist, Poetess and a Hindi Motivator who willingly accepted my proposal and translated book beautifully keeping its content. Smt. Rupa Srikumar has translated various books which includes Shlokas from Charak Samhita, 'Md. Rafi, My Abba' by Yasmin Khalid Rafi, and Vishwadarshan' by Mahatma Ramratna. She has also translated books on Philosophy and yoga etc. from Hindi to English and vice versa.

I am also grateful to Dr. Radha, Administrative Head of Kendriya Hindi Sansthaan, Hyderabad, who was always helpful in typing my chapters of the Book with smile and patience. She had also supported me in compiling the Sanskrit Shlokas in to the book appropriately to give it a final shape.

The co-operation of my family has been an elixir of my life. They have been my support system all through my literary journey. I am also thankful to all the friends and the colleagues for keeping my spirits high.

Vedic literature to me is like a vast ocean and the mantras in it are like priceless pearls has always been a guiding force. The book may not be infallible or absolute but I would like to dedicate my literary endeavours to the Goddess Sharda.

**Dr. Surabhy Dutt**

# From Translator

Welfare Democracy in Ancient India is a treasure house of the pearls of polity, collected from the Vedas. It gives a deep insight into the ancient system of ruling, as propagated by the Vedas, Brahmanas, Upanishads, Manusmriti and other ancient scriptures. Since the Vedas hold good for all times, the tenets of ancient polity hold great relevance for the present modem system of democracy. Since it is our past in whose light the present illumines, so is the welfare democracy based on Dharma propounded by the Vedas, the voice of the divine, is a store house of illumination for the present political systems and democracy. Translating this book, 'प्राचीन भारत में कल्याणकारी जनतंत्र' from Hindi to English, Welfare Democracy in Ancient India', by Dr. Surabhy Dutt, was indeed an enriching experience. Not only is the writer a great political Science scholar, she has an in depth knowledge of the ancient system of polity.

**Smt. Rupa Srikumar**

# Preface

While contemplating over different aspects of Ancient Indian Rule, our mind gets flooded with various thoughts. Such as, what do we mean by ancient India? What is political tradition meant to be, and the most important question is, in modern age, what is the topical relevance and basis of the thought created by India's first and foremost sages.

Generally, ancient India is supposed to be from the Vedic Age to the time of Shukraniti (ethics of Shukracharya). It is the same time duration when priceless scriptures like, Shrutis, Brahman Scriptures, Aranyak, Upanishads infused life into Smritis-Manusmriti and Yagyavalkays Smriti, the great poetic work-Ramayan, The Mahabharat and Nitigranth (Scriptures on ethics), the world famous Chanakyaniti (Ethics by Chanakya) and Shukraniti (Ethics by Shukracharya), were created.

Ancient Indian literature is the collector of those systems, which lent stability to human being's long-lasting relationships. Sages and great brains, incarnated on the Indian soil, were inspired by the noble feeling of human welfare, churned their intelligence, to emanate couplets, that provided the universe with innumerable brilliant formulas for forming, systems of knowledge and science. The main among these formulas are, Dharma, Raj Dharma, Nyaya Dharma of inflicting punishment, duty of adhering to Varna system, ways of conducting the Yagna, self-government, nation's advancement, people's power and the welfare of the world. The ruling system has not been treated as the promoter of one singular ideology or community, but emphasis has been given on formation of a nation with high values. The establishment of a cultured nation has been the endeavor of ancient literature, which is a moralistic gift to the present democratic system. The principles of politics propagated by the Vedic literature rich in culture, civilization, knowledge-science, the Smriti scriptures and scriptures on ethics, contain the philosophy of wholesome development of human life, freedom of thought, people's consent, happiness of the people and the final goal is, attainment of redemption or liberation (Moksha) and bliss, in a very effective and logical way. At various junctures, there is mention of the tradition of a republic, Swarajya, self-government, Sabha-Samiti and many such institutions. Here, are mentioned the ruling systems that existed.

'स्वस्ति साम्राज्यं, भोज्यं, स्वराज्यं, वैराज्यं, पारमेष्ठ्यं, राज्यं, महाराज्यं, अयं, अधिपत्यम्, सामन्तपर्यायि स्तात् सार्वभौमः, सार्वयुष आन्तादापरार्धात् पृथिव्यै समुद्रपर्यन्ताय एकराट् ।'

Each word of the literature of Indian thought is alive. 'न कर्म लिप्यते नरे ।' The word Nar, is constituted with use of two letters na and ra. Which means one who is not indulgent, or who is stoic. In which literature are such priceless thoughts available, where in great deeds are accepted like Yagya, inspiring selfless actions. It has been possible only in the Indian thought. Here is the 18th shloka of Geeta's chapter-

काम्यानां कर्मणा न्यासं संन्यासं कवयो विदुः ।
सर्वकर्मफलत्यागं प्राहुस्त्यागं विचक्षणः ।। 2 ।।

"This means, sanyas or renunciation is not forsaking karma (action) but it is giving up desire. Sacrifice does not mean non-activity but it is non craving for the results thereof."

The one who offers his life in the Yagya for people's good, has been considered eligible to run the ruling system and competent to protect dutifulness. The Veda syas-a'विशि राजा प्रतिष्ठितः' (Yaju 20.9) which means, the King is famous amongst his subjects. 'से विशःक्षेमम् अर्दाधरन्' (Atharva 3.3.5). It means the welfare of the nation and the King is dependent on these different types of people constituting the subjects. The ancient saying declares the royal duty thus-

'न वै राज्यं न राजाऽऽसीन्न च दण्डो न दण्डिकः ।
धर्मेणैव प्रजाः सर्वा रक्षन्ति स्म परस्परम् ।।

(Maha.shan. 53-14)

Only that rule is successful, where the King follows Dharma and the subjects also follow the tenets of Dharma. No one rules the other but foster, protect and are well-wishers for one another. According to the Brihadyaranyak's Kshatrasya Ksharam saying (1.4.14). The ruler who controls Dharma can only bring about the welfare of the entire world. The protection of the nation and culture is possible only by the ruler, who is valiant, rational, dear to the subjects. After seeing the above mentioned, examples of Raj Dharma, to say that politics is not related with Dharma, is the consequence of not understanding completely the national and state consciousness.

The greatest facet of our Indian thought is social balance on economic level and balanced behavior towards wealth, the worldly pleasures. Wealth and worldly pleasures have not been treated as the final goal of life. On attaining both these aims, according to the tenets of duty, there is direction for attaining the final goal of human life-Moksha (Redemption). Thus, accordingly, Dharma is considered as a co-traveler in the journey of life, an individual-society-Kingdom (royal duty) all three have been governed by duty.

Contrary to ancient thought, in all the fields of modern society there is economic predominance. Conduct and ethics are no longer topical, human desires are increasing multifariously hundred times. Along with it a thought is created which is completely in tune with industrialization and free trade. Today human beings are getting enslaved to machines. Individual-society-state, all the three are suffering from instability and imbalance. A kind of restlessness can be experienced. In the changed circumstances, to protect existence, the soul of Indian thought will have to be nurtured, for this soul alone is the primary form of the universal human consciousness.

For maintaining an awakened consciousness, we will have to move in the direction of progress. This is the basic mantra of success.

In the perspective of the present political situation, it would not be an exaggeration to say with full faith, that the first source of knowledge, the Vedas are such a huge ocean of knowledge, containing for everyone, the gem studded teaching to be followed.

The sages of India provided the richest thought to the world and as a consequence of immense practice in depth of human values, set ideals to be followed in for life. After setting these ideals, no higher, more liberal or practical ideals could be found. These ideals or directives of duty are an empowered basis of human character and the ruling system, which enjoys the same place as the eternal truth.

'सो अहम् ब्रह्म' and 'तत् त्वम असि' they are introducers of this truth. In case, we Indians build our present democratic system on the tenets of the law given by our ancient scholars, it will be as fruitful for us as it was in ancient times. There is no doubt that the image portrayed by the ancient motivators of politics of Dharma, ethics, justice, non-violence and brotherhood, were meaningfully assimilated, then the law formed in its ambit, would be helpful in giving a new direction to India to attain its goal. Only following these systems can permeate peace, happiness and prosperity, that the, brains of India had created without an axe to grind, totally selflessly.

Declarations like a 'यतोधर्मस्तो जयः' 'सत्यमेव जयते', 'यतोअभ्युदय निःश्रेयसिसद्धिः स धर्मः 'स्वधर्म निधनं श्रेयः परमधर्मो भयावः'

puts forth before us the fact, that in India, the entire country, the entire ancient thought, upholds that, the foundation pillar for an individual's progress to the welfare of the universe, is formed by Dharma. The welfare democratic form of Indian ruling system, its different aspects, and commitments, must be brought to light. In this reference, the following mantra of Ishavasyopanishad, wishes the divine to express the ultimate truth-

हिरण्मयेन पात्रेण सत्यस्यापिहितं मुखम्।
तत्त्वं पूषन्नपावृणु सत्यधर्माय दृष्टये।। 15।।

The face of the truth is covered with a shining golden rosary. O caretaker, remove the facade of being the wisher of welfare, who is truthful, intelligent, blissful, a storehouse of light, and gives an awesome vision to face truthful Dharma, to enable me view it.

**Dr.Surabhy Dutt**

# Contents

Acknowledgement

From Translator

Preface

1. Central Thought                                          1

2. The Concept of Dharma                                   17

3. Vedic Literature : An Introduction                      39

4. Swarajya in Vedic Literature                            53

5. Rajdharma in Manav Dharmashastra                      126

   Before conclusion                                     195

   Books of Reference                                    199

# Chapter 1
# Central Thought

**Western and Indian Thinkers and Thought**
Today, for all the nations of the world, welfare democracy is a desirable subject, a lovable system and a popular way of administration. All nations claim that in their state, people's welfare is secure and for maintenance of peace a congenial atmosphere exist. But the fundamental question is, are these claims truthful? Though there is a strong desire to lead a mutually peaceful life, the demand for ample protection and security is ever increasing. The main cause of this is defiance of cultural heritage and values in the state administration. A state wherein appropriate measures are not taken to elevate a human mind culturally, is neither capable of promoting welfare in the true sense, nor can it remain stable. There is a constant emphasis on the feeling of oneness and unification as one homogenous entity in our Shrutis and Upanishads. This unification upholds the tenets of equality, good-will, good behaviour, ethical conduct and forbearance. These are the values that conceptualise clearly, the basis of ancient Indian cultural state.

Famous Chinese traveller, Huansang has written in his travelogue Safarnamah (second edition) "The basic foundation of Aryan state management was good behaviour. They were famous for truthfulness, imparting justice and impartiality." Sir Moniar Williams (Elphinstone's History of India folio 199) wrote, "The human approach of Indian countrymen was guided by the main ideal, ' live and let live', it was a great principle and regulation. They were against suicide and killing a human being." Famous ancient educationist, Professor Maxmuller, has refuted India's contribution in polity though, relating it only with spirituality, yet he has accepted that, "Rigveda is the oldest book in the library of mankind." Apart

1

from this, he writes in "India what can it teach us?" that, "If I raise my eyes to look in all the four directions, all over the world, in search of the country, where the Goddess Nature has bestowed her abundant grandeur, valour and beauty, offering it with both hands openly, for having made it, the paradise on Earth, my finger will point towards India. If I ask myself, that we Europeans, who have been nurtured by the Greek, Roman and Jewish thought air sphere till now, can revert to which literature for inspiration, that could cleanse our lives, lead us on the path of progress to expand, to inspire not only our physical body, but also our eternal soul, then also my finger will point towards India. The abundant treasure of the history of mankind is available only in India.

Though, the way foreigners and western scholars have freely praised ancient Vedic verses and literature, yet due to many extenuating circumstances its propagation could not be widespread. Foreign invaders, specially, Islamic invaders destroyed large libraries, cultural spots. The way Nalanda and Takshshila libraries were burnt, is an example of religious bigotry, narrowness of the heart, defiance of art and culture and flagrant disregard of human values. In the fourteenth century, and thereafter, the rulers tried to create the impression that their advent in India was a boon for the Indians, and their knowledge, science, literature and style of living was exemplary. They were the forefathers of administrative system and polity. It resulted in our beginning to imitate western thought process, western administrative forms, western way of life to some extent wilfully, also under pressure. It was an eye opener for Indians, when western scholars sought our ancient scriptures and studied them to put forward their essence. Indian literature was critically appreciated, which included Rig Veda, Samarangan's Sutradhar, Kautilya's Artha Shastra, and many other memorable scriptures. But by the time Indians became aware of their valuable, prestigious literature, it was too late. Social reformers with multi facet brilliance, like

Maharshi Dayanand Saraswati, gave a slogan to Indian culture and civilization, it did bring about some change but the western influence had been so deep, that the new administrative mode adopted was basically not conducive to Indian tradition and individuality.

Another important reason for Indians not adopting their own ancient way of thought, was the language of ancient scriptures being Sanskrit. The entire literature was in Sanskrit script. The knowledge of the mother of all Indian languages, Sanskrit, was limited, so our great literature could not be propagated. 'Curiosity only inspires to learn a language,' this is the reason why, western scholars studied Indian literature, but the viewpoint with which it was studied and the kind of aspersions were cast, can never be accepted. The western way of contemplation from different novel viewpoints, could be useful, but it cannot be denied that it clogged our fundamental thought and awareness. The system of polity laid down in our scriptures got distorted on being influenced by western system. The propagators of western polity adopted a policy infused with partiality against the principles and principle holders of Indian polity, declaring them to be an archaic, trying to uphold their own thought as far ahead of times. Vilobi's book 'Political Theories of Ancient World' and Hegel's 'Philosophy of History' are examples of this app- roach. Paulzenet held that Indian political thought was hazy and opposed to religion as 'ethics' were related to politics. He declared Geeta to be romanticism and Hindus, the most mysterious race on the Earth. He called the state related Hindu concepts ludicrous.

Western thinkers upheld the viewpoint that ancient Indian thinkers instead of solving practical problems, remained caught in communalism and ritualism, therefore, could not in any way contribute to political science. Bloomfield and Maxmuller both singularly analysed the Indian political thought, and propagated to create the confusion, that Indians completely lacked nationalistic fervour. In the 'History of Sanskrit Literature' (page 30-31) Maxmuller has commented, "Indians never had the feeling of nationalism in their mind, never did any Indian's heart throb for the nation's importance....if ever the Indian intelligence independently inclined to move to work, create or establish in any direction, it was the field of religion and philosophy." A similar view has been wilfully presented by Bloomfield in his book,' 'The Religion of Vedas' (page 4-5) "Indians were regulated by religious institutions and in such an organisation, there is no room left for taking interest in the nation or working for the community's development. Consequently, Indian national character became vain." The ancient Indian thought was older and most rich, to be able to remove all these misconceptions. To present the evidence of this truth is, truly necessary.

Plato (428-348 BC), who is considered to be a brilliant philosopher of ancient Greece and in the western tradition was treated as the first and foremost organised political doctrinaire, who in his scriptures 'The Republic', 'Laws' gave expositions on an ideal state, philosophical ruler and justice. Plato's disciple, another Greek philosopher Aristotle, (384-322 BC) who is known as the father of political thought for having created 'Politics.' In the beginning of the modern era, an Italian thinker Machiavelli Niccolo (1469-1527) in his treatise 'The Prince' conceived the novel thought of segregating politics from ethics, which paved way for the birth of a new tendency of diplomatic manipulations in the western world.

Thomas Hobbes (1588-1679), John Locke (1632-1704), J. J. Rousseau (1712-1778), were popular thinkers, known to be the birth giver of the principle of social compromise and established the theory of sovereignty, liberalism and general desires. In this series, Jeremy Bentham (1748-1832) established utilitarianism. A political thinker of the 19th century, J.S.Mill (1806-1873) supported envisaging independence and thought representative democracy to be the best organizational set up. The creator of Communist Manifesto, Karl Marx (1818-1883) was such a famous German philosopher, who opposed capitalism vehemently and while raising a voice against the exploitation of the labourers, brought about the principle of class struggle and 'optimum cost.' Ontonio Gramsci (1891-1937) was an Italian thinker in the first half of the 20th century. He stood for democratisation of institutions in hegemony.

It is essential to mention the time duration of western thinkers writing because, though they have all great thinkers of their times but in the interval between their expositions, along with the description of the essence of thought, many imaginary features appear. Impartial thinking led to getting cut off from values, though political thought is intrinsically related to both facts and values as well. Moreover, it can decisively be accepted by taking into consideration the times and duration of the doctrines of western theorists, that they date subsequent to the works of inspiration of Indian 'Polity' and 'Royal Duty' (Raj Dharma), such as the Vedas, Manusmriti, Chanakya and Shukraneeti, so on and so forth. Moreover, the ancient Indian thinkers established superior values and more progressive organizational set up than the thought perpetrated by the western theorists. An administrative system was developed, that was filled with the great sentiment of people's welfare.

A comparative study reveals that the administrative system of Sparta and Athens were opposed to humanity, were based on communal supremacy. In these states the right to 'visible democracy' and 'citizenship' is said to be restricted to a special class, (the elite and the rich property holders) which is opposed to the basic sentiment of democracy. The basic sentiment means- 'People's wish and their rule.' From this point of view, in the western world, the history of democracy might have begun in the 18th century but it cannot be accepted as the birth giver of 'philosophy of democracy'.

In comparison with Greek thinkers and other western

thought, the ancient Indian thought is wide-spread and all pervasive. The inclusion of its humanitarian concepts indicates a touch of humanity in the ruling administration. The way of working of ancient institutions proves that in India there is no room for uncontrolled, arbitrary rule. There are accounts revealing incidents of election of the ruler on the ground of the attributes and competence of a ruler, which indicates, prevalence of democracy. On a political level desire for people's welfare, gave birth to a democratic system, that is only present today in its developed form.

Ancient Indian thought and Western thought can be compared in terms of 'Royal Duty' (Raj Dharma) and 'Ruling System' (Rajtantra). Vedic verses, Smriti and ethical script-ures specify a specific code of conduct for the king, essential to build a superior nation, that can be termed as 'Royal Duty' (Raj Dharma). The kind of a ruling system that was established in the West, was completely an introduction of a single person's whims and fancies. The king was not people's representative but represented God. He was not only a law maker, but law unto himself. People were answerable to the king and were bound by rules and regulations. The western ruling arrangement was indicative of representation of the king's whims. In the West, there were in fact two ruling authorities, the King and the Clergy. History has many examples of their clashes, that arose due to intervening in each other's area of authority. One such example is Louis XIV, who had declared, "I am the state". This declaration indicative of uncontrolled monarchy. In the Indian thought on the contrary, there was no room for the King's whims and fancies. It was essential for him to respect, authorities on the three Vedas (Triveda), those who had knowledge of Smriti, Brahmins and the opinion of the people, the divine attributes (Indra, Air, Yama, The Sun, The Moon, Fire, Varun and Kubera). The King is directed to invoke the deties, implies that the king was to act in accordance with the times and circumstances, for people's welfare and with the intent to maintain the people in good order. He could punish and impart justice. It is considered natural that the people imitate the King's conduct, for this reason a king who punishes, is also known to be punishable. It would not be an exaggeration to call it a technical scheme of political organization presented by ancient teachers. Consequently, in India, emergence of kingship could not override the spirit of democracy. Mahatma Gandhi reiterated, "I dream of such an independent India, wherein Ram Rajya could be restored."

Readers might wonder, as to what is the relevance of studying ancient Indian system in the present scenario? Society is undergoing a change so fast, that it is difficult to gauge, to what extent is the utility of the ancient system? Reverend readers may accept the submission that 'a political system authenticated, established and floated by Dharma, is to be followed in all ages. As such the principles of Dharma were as unwavering as principles of mathematics.

The present has always been illuminated by the past. We get the main principles of Indian culture and national policy from the ancient times of civilized, cultured India, which possibly did not prevail anywhere else in the world. What has been briefly mentioned in the Vedas, has been explained at length in its subsequent parts and sub-parts, also in the entire ancient literature. In the Rig Samhita, 8th chapter of the 10th mondal, 31 and 32 part, there are two suktas. In the first sukta there are 6 Rig mantras and in the second sukta there are 6 Rig mantras. Both the suktas are related to the prayer for the elected person for coronation as the king. In it the duties of the King, the king's relationship with the people etcetera, have been described.

आ त्वाहार्षमन्तरेधि ध्रुवस्तिष्ठाविचाचलिः ।
विशस्त्वा सर्वा वाञ्छन्तु मा त्वद्राष्ट्रमधि भ्रशत् ।। 10.173.1 ।।

In this mantra Sayanacharya says, "O King! You remain stable, to be the head of the kingdom, the people wish you to

7

head the kingdom."

Today in all the nations of the world, though democracy has been established, this democracy has lost its quality due to being harboured by unqualified, incompetent people and ignorance of majority of the people. It is reduced to be like a monarchy and oligarchy. The administrative arrangement has reached the last stage of anarchy, where the people's repre-senttatives are overpowered by lust-attachments and the mire. For selfish motives and for acquiring ruling power, they resort to snatching and looting, treachery and power misuse. The word 'democracy' has become a decorative commodity. Today on seeing the demand for a world market, even in Communist countries, this word has been accepted as a symbol of capitalistic arrangement.

Ancient India's monarchy was better from the point of view, that it was for people's well-being and people's opinion was paid heed to, which is underlined as a special feature of the modern age democracy. The best way of ruling is considered one, wherein, the people have freedom as human beings and enjoy a right to equality, law has importance and people are given a chance to partake in the administration as per their qualification and competence.

The expositions of the first source of knowledge, the Vedas, contain mantras that sermonize and make it known that the king's obligations were of greater importance, than his rights. For this very reason later, according to the Smritis, poetic works and other religious texts, politics became the royal duty (Raj Dharma). This element regulated various obligations, with an ideological foundation.

In the works of ancient Indian ideologists, the appointment of the king, and circumstances thereof have been described, which throw light on the importance of people's opinion and their concurrence. Western thinkers either intentionally ignored this fact or they committed the error of not being able to understand its spirit. Therefore, they limited ancient thought to only spirituality. Ancient Indian ruling system is full of evidence of a developed administrative system. For instance, there was a very strong and well-formed public opinion. Incompetent and depraved characters, lesser people, had no place in the society. The people elected the one, with high qualities, highly active, mentally and physically competent representatives only. Like modern democratic representatives and candidates, a huge propaganda did not have to be done. They were naturally popular due to their noble deeds, excellent conduct, Intelligence and self-control. These were considered as the operating force in life and the royal administration.

A shloka from Kathopanishad:

आत्मानं रथिनं विद्धि शरीरं रथमेव तु।
बुद्धिं तु सारथिं विद्धि मनः प्रग्रहमेव च।।

(Tritiya Valli-3)

This means, 'the soul is the master of the chariot, body is its chariot, intelligence is its charioteer and mind is its reins. Great thoughts that prompted self-realization and showed the righteous path, are only available in Vedic literature.

In the entire Vedic literature, mantras are available, that give directions for the election of the king by his subjects. (विशः) The subjects elected the king for the reason, that he would redeem them of their problems. The king takes an oath that 'he would protect his subjects, as a matter of duty.' Only with a pure mind, words and deeds was elected as king. Shatpath Brahman, Aittareya Brahman, Manusmriti and Yujnavalkya Smriti have clearly stated that the king must be noble in his conduct, have knowledge of the Vedas, duty-bound and just in case of not fulfilling the vows taken at the time of coronation, the subjects had the right to rebel against a cruel and corrupt king. An ineffective ruler could be deposed by an assembly of ministers appointed by the people. Rebellion and death sentence against king Vena is an example of this practice. King Sagar disowned his son Asamanjas to remain popular among people. Election or opposition of the king was in the arena of people's rights. In the 219th shloka of Manusamhita's 8th chapter, is mentioned:

यो ग्रामदेशसंघानां कृत्वा सत्येन संविदम् ।
विसंवेदन्नरो लोभात्तं राष्ट्राद्विप्रवासयेत् ।।

In the above- mentioned mantra, taking a vow, related to acceptance of the obligation of activities for welfare, has been described. " If a person, while taking his position, takes a vow to protect his village, nation and organization, to the effect, that 'I will work for the welfare and protection of this village, nation, and organization' and after getting it, under the spell of his own selfishness, breaks the vow, behaves contrary to it, in that circumstance, this officer, blinded by selfishness, be extricated from the nation," Likewise, the mantras in Rigveda, confirms that the rule be continued by appointing competent rulers.

आ यद्वामीयचक्षसा मित्र वयं च सूरयः ।
व्यचिष्ठे बहुपाय्ये यतेमहि स्वराज्ये ।। (5.66.6,4)

It means, only that one has the right to be a ruler, competent to carry on the administration of the state, who is pure, sacred, dutiful, impartial, free from desire and is illumined with knowledge of the truth. Another mantra (10.63.13) of the Veda is mentionable.

अरिष्टः स मर्त्तो विश्व एधते प्र प्रजाभिर्जायते धर्मणस्परि ।
यमादित्यासो नयथा सूनीतिभिरति विश्वानि दुरिता स्वस्तये ।।

The said mantra draws a picture of very high standard system of ruling, addressing the scholars, the mantra reiterates-

"O men of pure character ! you rid of all kinds of sinful conduct, illumine a path of exemplary, prudent, dutiful, high conduct. A group of people following such a path can never be defeated. Such a rule always progresses with its subjects in the world."

From the entire descriptions, we have received from scriptures created by ancient thinkers, related to the way of ruling, we come to know that the system of election made it imperative to take into account the opinion and consent of all the subjects, it was mandatory. Only most qualified competent person was elected for coronation for the ruler's position. There are many examples of deposing incompetent ascendants to the throne, in history. Asamanjas, the eldest son of Sagar, a king from the Soorya family, Devapi, the eldest son of an emperor from the Chandra family and Prateek are the ones who were bereft of their royal position, for being egoistic and afflicting cruelty on the subjects. The examples, mentioned above, prove that one flouting his duties, deceiving his subjects, the nation and a self-willed man, was not coronated to the royal position and the subjects also denounced him. Along with the process related to nomination of the king, there is a mention of formation of a Dharma Assembly or Dharma Committee, consisting of ancient thinkers, scholars of Manu Smriti, Chanakyaniti and Shukraniti, disciplinarians, authorities on ethics and good conduct and various specialist. Perusal of descriptions and information available regarding the ancient courts, the court procedures, relationship of witness and evidence, does not leave any doubt, that in the ancient Indian procedure of justice, no meddling with the evidence and effort to suppress truth for upholding falsehood was accepted in any way. Court decisions were taken promptly and a verdict contrary to ethics was a punishable offence. Provisions related to the court's organization and the qualifications of the judges, made in the Smriti and other scriptures of ethics, if compared with the present ethos, were arrived at with more maturity. With this view- point Manu Smriti has been awarded the status of the 'first constitution'. Subsequently, in the thorn plucking research on Chanakya's 'Artha Shastra,' it provides description of law, which is a good example before the modern legal system. In the third provision, 'Dharmastheey' rules applicable on judges and the limits imposed to contain their jurisdiction, reminds us of the present impeachment process. In the present judicial system, the description of judicial investigation and judicial activity bears evidence of its existence in ancient thought:

वेदः स्मृतिः सदाचारः स्वस्य च प्रियमात्मनः ।
एतत्, चतुर्विधं प्राहुः साक्षात् धर्मस्य लक्षणम् ।।

(Manu.2.12)

Whatever is appropriate, according to the Vedas, Smriti, ethics and the spirit, on proving good on these four parameters, after proper perusal and investigation, a just decision be taken, so that the subject's interests are not compromised and impartial justice is bestowed.

In India the present condition of parliamentary rule is deplorable, due to the Executive's unnecessary interference and unregulated behaviour, partial justice has been pushed to the witness box. Constitutional limits are being crossed. Besides, the common people are ignorant of the ways to get speedy justice, causing unfulfillment of the very purpose of judicial activity.

In the ancient sources of the entire Indian thought, there are descriptive accounts of the ruling system, there are innumerable sources of representative institutions. But the one on assembling of Sabha-Samiti is mostly used and is commendable. They have been acknowledged as nation's and United Nation's allied arrangements. In the Sabha there are people's representatives and the Samiti consists of nation's representatives. The word 'Samiti' is formed by combining two words,'sam' and 'iti'. In English Committee appears to be a derivation of San (Com) plus Iti (ittee). (from Vinaykaray Abhinandan scripture) In an intense discussion on composition of the assembly it was said, " An assembly be constituted, with civilized members, possessing knowledge of Trai Vidya (त्रयी विद्या) be able to maintain national importance adhering to the tenets of the scriptures." How does the ancient literature depict the formation of the assembly and the Committee? And what was their role? On this subject, various thinkers have deeply contemplated and described the workings of the system of ruling in great details. Accepting the plant of parliamentary system, the importance of the Assembly Committee, in the year 1985, in the 'Second International Parliamentary Session' held in New Delhi, foreign delegates highly praised the ancient Indian democratic system, in their speeches. Erstwhile President of India, Gyani Zail Singh, in his inaugural speech, emphasizing its importance by saying. "Today in most of the nations of the world, the plant of the parliamentary system that is thriving, the roots of this plant were nurtured in this country's soil. Our sages spread the messages of humanity through the medium of such institutions, which are exemplary for all nations to follow." Stressing on this he also emphasized on following ancient values for establishing international cooperation.

In the Vedas are indicative of a state of thriving democratic institutions like Grahapatya, Ahvaneey, Dakshina-gni and Sabha Samiti, which proves that the Vedic times were the best for organised ruling institutions. True knowledge of national conduct was received by kings through these institutions. Sages who were self-realized, knower of mantras, directed the king to treat the members of the assembly with reverence and the king should take decisions after consulting scholars. Disregard of the senior Assembly members by the king, makes him liable for his own downfall. The Assembly kept an eye on the king's conduct. An unregulated king was considered detrimental to the interest of the subjects and the nation. Pointing to the duties of the members of the Assembly, we have discourses dealing in detail with their attributes, qualifications and obligations in the ancient Indian literature. Materialistic as well as spiritual elevation, was considered a duty by the members of the Assembly who had knowledge of scriptures on justice. The offender of the Assembly rules was punished. In the ancient thought we come across descriptions which indicate that parents keenly made efforts to make their children competent to become members of the Assembly, by gaining knowledge of the Vedic scriptures religious scriptures, Smriti and Niti scriptures, and play important role in forming national policies.

Manusmriti and Yagyavalyay Smriti also hold righteous members of the Assembly and steadfast Council responsible for the stability of the system of ruling. It has been declared that the Council should consist of members who are intelligent, elite, well conducted, sacred in their behavior and the ministers be competent to discharge their obligations and commitments in a commendable way. The members of the Council have been called 'Loksammatah Rajanah' (king by people's consent). This reminds of 'Rajkrit Rajanah' of the Vedic age. The 'loksammat rajanah' were more in numbers. As members of the Council, consulting them and seeking their opinion was mandatory. These 'Lokesammat' king's advise, (who knew Dharma and Artha very well (could be equated with the present time, Working Council, Working Committee or Council of Ministers) could not be criticised by the ruler. The 'Shukraniti' mentions that existence of a strong Council of Ministers, organized to keep a check on the king from becoming self-willed.

The ruling system then bears evidence of appointment of fearless ministers, who could freely advise the king, with the intention to correct his actions. For these ministers promoting the interest of the nation, was treated as their first priority and they were adept in ethical behaviour. Ministers who were ill conducted were not given a place in the Assembly or the Council. The present condition of democracy in India is diametrically opposite to this. The ruling bowl is completely full of Adharma, misconduct and immoral conduct. Criminals, behind the bars dream of becoming people's representatives. Representatives bet on groupism, money-power, and alluring promises. Competence and priority of conduct has vanished. As a consequence of these, unacceptable practices are leading to the failure of democracy.

Today when we view the international scenario, having been placed on the national stage, another truth looms high, that men enslaved by materialism have reduced the life-saving protection of the concepts of humanness, humanity and humanitarianism, to a web of words only. In the 19$^{th}$ and 20$^{th}$ century there began in the West, a thought process and life vision on 'humanitarianism', with a view of wholistic welfare of human beings. Hundreds of philosophers, socialists, politicians established the human honour, redeeming it from all kinds of blind faiths and previous callings, conveyed the message of entering the path of wellbeing. Some stressed on acquiring 'knowledge' and 'ethics' for it. Some thought the need of the hour was the divine and other faiths. Most of them visualised human welfare without all these. The Declaration of Human Rights from an international organisation like the United Nations was prepared and directives were issued to all nations. Non-aligned movements were carried on from time to time to raise a voice for humanity and human rights. After carrying on widespread propaganda on a war footing, in this direction, the incidents related to, discrimination on the grounds of colour, caste, gender, child labour, exploitation of women consistently happened. Children were kidnapped using animals and kept locked up, used for, inhuman, recreational games for tourists, like tying the child up on the back of the camel and then making the camel run, were carried on openly. The reason for all these unethical practices was, a lack of pre-decided and well-arranged national and international parameters and inactivity of the International Court of Justice. If we genuinely want humanness to survive, then we will have to adhere to the values of our ancient rich civilization, culture and literature. We come across the description of the arrangements made in the ancient Indian literature, which enables clearing the path for man's individual and holistic welfare and development. This path holds good for all countries, in all ages, to be adhered to, by human beings at the same time. In it there is no scope for discrimination on account of gender, cast, class struggle violence and inhumanity. India's ancient thought has had in it, human welfare, self- development, flowing all through. Once again with great resolve, intensive effort have to be taken for sending this flow to each human being. Compassion, friendship and the sentiment of world- welfare, have to cross the national boundary, to realize the best, ideal of 'Vasudaiv-kutumbakam' presented, with its root mantra:

सर्वे भवन्तु सुखिनः, सर्वे सन्तु निरामयाः ।
सर्वे भद्राणि पश्यन्तु, मा कश्चिद् दुःख भाग्भवेत् ।।

## Chapter 2
# The Concept of Dharma

The Indian vocabulary word 'dharma' does not have a synonym in any other language or literature. 'Dharma' or duty is motioned, inspired by the knowledge of the history of human beings and contains the society within a well-defined ambit. It is the uniqueness of dharma or dutifulness which bestows importance to motion with containment, progress with obstruction, individual viz a viz the whole humanity. To treat dutifulness or dharma as the basis of human being's effective social organization for peace, in the history of human beings, over a sizeable duration of time, is marked by bloodshed and war-fares, in the name of 'duty' or dharma. There is reference of serving the human beings and that of human sacrifice in the law of duty. Probably all the practices of duty or dharma, considered cruel killing valid. The Vedic law of duty holds cruel destruction as an appropriate act. Islam upholds killings of non-Muslims and even Christianity stands for destruction of enemies. Life and death, abstaining and hoarding, love and malice, are mutually paradoxical and are incorporated in the ambit of dutifulness or dharma. In the entire world if there is one linchpin holding the vast people together emotionally in oneness, beyond the boundaries of countries and time, it is dutifulness or dharma.

In the various time zones known in history, the inspirators of new concepts of duty or dharma, have given different interpretations of what dutifulness or dharma really is. In the process they have complicated its basic meaning thoroughly. The defining words used in the Vedic verses, have been chosen keeping in mind their complete meaning and their potential. As the Vedas are to impart knowledge, Shruti is to be heard and remembered, likewise, the word 'Dharma' or duty has a classic meaning, expresses high values.

**Origin of the word, Dharma**

The origin of the word 'Dharma' is from the letter 'धृ', which means, the one who takes over an obligation. 'आ सामन्तात् धारयति इति धर्मः' thereby meaning, that which upholds all, in totality is 'dharma' or duty. To substantiate, it is said that it holds the entire universe, in the form of cosmic order, it is the eternal truth. It is Dharma or duty that regulates and controls human behaviour. What is outside the ambit of this regulation and control, is unrighteousness. In the Vedas righteous duty or 'purity' from the point of ruling power, is the 'truth', from the point of view of ethical regulation, conception and happiness, it is honey or is called honey like. In a mantra in Rigveda, it is said, 'ऋतेन य ऋतजातो विवावृधे राजा देव ऋतं बृहत्' (9.108.8) "The cosmic order is simply a paramount truth, it is liable for making the universe well organized. People endowed with high qualities are manifesttation of cosmic order." Almost similar, to conception of duty is Tao's concept, 'Man is ruled by Earth, the Earth is ruled by Heaven, the Heaven is ruled by the Tao, Tao is ruled by itself.'[1]

In the Taittiriya Aranyak it is stated that Dharma is the foundation pillar of all cosmic spheres. In this world people seek knowledge and guidance from a person who know thoroughly the 'subject of duty' and is adept in it. It is also mentioned in Manusmriti, 'धर्मो रक्षति रक्षतः' (8.15) meaning thereby, Dharma also protects the protector.

The ancient Indian rulers had a firm conviction, that there is nothing superior to the conception of duty or Dharma. Duty alone was the well- defined driving force of their social and political life. All their work was well governed by dutifulness or dharma and their politics was also based on duty. Not only the king, even the subjects followed the tenets of duty in their personal and social life.

---

[1] Paul Carus, Tao-Te-Ching by Lao Tzu, p. 2, 1913 XXII

Dutifulness or Dharma is an auspicious light within the self, related to it is a mantra worth mentioning as under -

ऋतं तपः सत्यं तपः श्रुतं तपः शान्तं तपो दमस्तपः शमस्तपो।
दानं तपो यज्ञस्तपो भूर्भवः सुवर्ब्रह्मै तदुपास्वैतत्तपः ।।

(Taittiriya Pra.10, Anu.8)

In the mantra duty is referred to as the constant, cosmic order, meaning thereby, the spoken truth. (It has also been called the actual reality). meaning thereby, to hear and adhere to all genre, (quiet) meaning thereby, that which is formulated as, good deeds, to inspire to be dutiful, it has been said earlier, that constant practice of regulated breath, abstinence, charity, rituals before fire, love and devotion is penance.

The chapter 'Shiksha Valli' of Taittiriya Upanishad, ninth and eleventh anuvak, mantra, while giving an exposition on Dharma, conveys, that adhering to the cosmic order, truth and regulated breath ( Dhrit, Satya, Tap and dam) is all that needs to be done. In addition to it, self-learning and listening to discourses, may never be discontinued. The deeper meaning is, that only after self-learning (contemplation on duty or dharma and acquiring knowledge) one should give sermons on duty, and on imparting knowledge, to others. When the Upanishad instructs us to 'speak the truth', 'सत्यं वद' 'follow dutifulness' 'धर्म चर', it applies to those phases of our lives in which we perform our duties to live. These phases are, Brahmacharya, Grihastha, Vaanprastha and Sanyas ashrams. Meaning thereby, members of the four Varnas (Cast), belonging to, the four Ashrams of life, to attain the four fold purpose–education (materialistic and spiritual) and earning wealth, known as 'Artha', leading a conjugal family life, known as 'Kama' and acts of piety, known as 'Dharma' to attain ultimate release, known as 'Moksha' involve an adherence to the prescribed actions, that itself is duty or Dharma.

Swami Dayanand Saraswati in Rigvedadi Bhashya Bhoomika has composed an extremely beautiful mantra on the subject of duty -

i) सत्यं परं परं सत्यं सत्येन न सुवर्गाल्लोकाच्चयवन्ते कदाचन, सतां हि सत्यं तस्मात्सत्ये रमन्ते ।

ii) धर्म इति धर्मेण सर्वमिदं परिगृहीतं धर्मानातिदुश्चरं तस्माद्धर्मे ।

iii) धर्मो विश्वस्य जगतः प्रतिष्ठा, लोके धर्मिष्ठं प्रजा उपसर्पन्ति धर्मेण पापमपनुदन्ति, धर्मे सर्व प्रतिष्ठितं, तस्माद्धर्म परं ।

It means the truth (Satya) is the best, it is the Supreme Creator and redeems, as it only illumines everyone, and the air and other matter are protected by it. Truth (Satya) only emanates from truthful conduct, and gentlemanliness among good people. Truth (Satya) in the form of cosmic order (Dhrit), is truthful speech and conduct. There is no other better parameter for Dharma. In the past the parameters laid down for dutifulness or Dharma, will also hold good in future, as they constitute Dharma. (Thereby meaning that dutifulness is applicable for all times.) Justice, means giving up partiality, adhering to good conduct and abstaining from any misconduct, is dutifulness or Dharma. Only a dutiful soul (one adhering to the tenets of dutifulness or Dharma in conduct) is trusted. Dutifulness makes a human being rid of sins, inspires him to work for the wellbeing of all, hence dutifulness or Dharma is the best concept to be adhered to.

Vedic scholars hold that 'Dharma is that which helps becoming master of self-elevation (Abhudaya) and helps in achieving spirituality (Nishreyas).' On being elevated, deeds for the worldly progress and wellbeing are performed, with highest good in mind, it leads to the progress and well- being in the other worlds also. Thus, Dharma has connection with the worldly aspects and the other worldly aspects of life. Dharma includes those principles, elements, way of living, which enables human beings to develop the highest, honourable, ruling powers to enable make a happy worldly life possible. It also will redeem from the cycle of birth and death, be peaceful for all intent and purpose and happy in attainment of liberation. While explaining the concept of Dharma, in

Mahabharat Shantiparva, Bhishmapitamah says (Mahabharat Shantiparva 109; 10-12), the remedy which leads to the rise (अभ्युदय) and security of human beings, is Dharma. Dharma is competent to provide security to the entire universe. It is omnipresent and omnipotent and does not let a human being fumble from where he is stationed. That which is instrumental in the apparent progress and liberation of living beings, is Dharma.

Most valuable and acceptable definition of Dharma is-

धारणात् धर्म इत्याहु धर्मो धारयते प्रजाः।
यत् स्यात् धारण संयुक्तं स धर्म इत्युदाहृतः।।

(Maha.69.58)

The regulations that stabilize life, are known as Dharma, as the subjects can only be secured by Dharma. It is the key to make human beings well qualified, well organized. The focal point of the entire universe's mobility is Dharma. In fact, conduct and behaviour governed by ethical values is regular practice of Dharma. In the ancient Indian literature, there have been various expositions of Dharma or dutifulness. These expositions reveal the deep, extensive, omni present facet of dutifulness or Dharma.

In the Atharvaveda (12.1.17) it is mentioned, 'पृथिवीं धर्मणा धृताम्'— With Dharma's support the Earth is stable. It has been wished in Yajurveda, (17.67) 'पृथिव्या अहमुदन्तरिक्षमारुहम्' "I may rise from the Earth to the sky, from the sky to the ever illuminated solar zone, may I rise, to attain the eternal blissful astral level (Loka) and the happiness filled light." And it is only possible when our conduct would be dutiful. Vedas wishing for auspiciousness, reiterate, O man you must always progress in life. For the purpose, I invigorate you with power and intelligence, so that you adopt an admirable dutiful, good conduct in your life.

In Taittiriya Aranyak (10.63) are two aspects of the word Dharma- the first one holds that the entire universe is based on Dharma. 'धर्मो विश्वस्य जगतः प्रतिष्ठा।' The other is, that Dharma is the greatest component of the subject's life,- 'तस्माद् धर्म परमं वदन्ति।' mimansak (1.2) and sutra bhashyam (1.2.2) which try to establish that whatever emanates welfare is included in the word Dharma.'य एव श्रेयस्करः स एव धर्मशब्देनोच्यते।' (Mahabharat Shantiparva 109; 10-12)

Evaluators again express their opinions as under-

'आर्ष धर्मोपदेशं च वेदशास्त्रविरोधिना
यस्तंर्केणानु सन्धते स धर्म वेद नेतरः।।

विहित क्रिया साध्यः धर्मः पुंसो गुणो मतः।'

The persons who experiment the duty-based talks of sages, in consonance with the contentions of the Vedic scriptures, they only have knowledge of Dharma, none other. "When a man becomes a master of his attributes by following the prescribed procedure, is upholder of Dharma." The great sage Jaimini through the sutra, 'चोदना लक्षणोऽर्थी धर्मः।' has directed that, 'inspired by the teacher or the Vedas, getting involved in sacred deeds, is practicing Dharma.'

In the said sentences, Dharma is made to be understood, beautifully defined and explained in a way that, it proves the regulations and principles which have the quality to elevate life and maintain it within the limits of honour, is Dharma. It does not have narrowness of relevance to only one country or the feeling of sectarianism. These definitions are valid not only for India, but for the entire universe.

India's rich ancient literature, repeatedly declares in this sentence, 'शृण्वन्तु विश्वे अमृतस्यपुत्राः' (Yaju 11.5) 'वेदोऽखिलो धर्ममूलम्' (Manu 2.6) O, progenies of the nectar, Vedas alone is knowledge, and the entire knowledge is the root of sciences. Each folio of the ancient thought's treasure of knowledge, is beyond regional boundaries, is written for human welfare and universal welfare. The entire Earth is considered one family, noble features like, every body's wellbeing and happiness, make appearance in this literature.

उत्क्रामातः पुरुषमावपत्था मृत्योः पड्वीशमवमुञ्चमानः ।।

(Atharva 8.1.4)

उद्यानं ते पुरुष नावयानं जीवातुं ते दक्षतातिं कृणोमि ।।

(Atharva 8.1.6)

O man! progress, do not deteriorate, break the shackles of death.

O man! See to it that you progress in life, do not degenerate.

I invigorate you with life and strength.

In Yajurveda, conveying a message for every individual, to be active, it has been said that along with the external 'yagya', internal 'yagya' is mandatory. 'यज्ञ' is a wonderful word and act, that is neither found in any other ideology in the world, nor performed. 'यज्ञेन यज्ञं अयजन्त देवाः ।।' (31.16)

'The said Mantra expresses only the sentiment that O human being, by seeing the physical manifestation of Yagya, in the form of fire, ignite within you the spiritual Yagya. The underlying sentiments of Yagya for the performance of an act, only leads to success. The essence of the Upanishads is also as under-

'कुर्वन्नेवेह कर्माणि जिजिविषेच्छतं समाः ।

एवं त्वयि नान्यथेतोऽस्ति न कर्म लिप्यते नरे ।।

(Eshavasya.2)

A human being should wish to live for a hundred years, involved in selfless activity. Doing such activity does not give rise to attachment.

**Dharma in Western Thought**

Western thinkers have presented a different concept of Dharma. Duncan and Derrett[2] treat Dharma not as a concept but a problem. According to them it lacks clarity, is indecisive and undefinable. If an endeavour is made to elucidate it, it will

---

[2] The concept of Duty in South Asia, Ed. by J Duncan M.Derrett, p.xiv

only be entanglement in meaningless arguments. John But on the other hand, and John W. Spellmen[3] in his exposition, accepting the Indian thought says, "good attributes, right action, natural laws, all recognized truths, traditions, ways-customs, law implementations and all related systems to them, come in the category of Dharmas."

In the mantras of Rigveda, Dharma is treated as a (गुह्यनीत) a hidden treasure. It is disguised, hidden and secretive. It is said, 'धर्मस्य तत्वं गुह्याम्' (the element of Dharma is hidden) that is why it ought to be brought to light. Widengrane in his book 'The Region Phynomonology' writes, 'Dharma can only be brought to surface if some argument, conflict or war arises. The root cause of his point of view was the series of events that had taken place then. In the medieval Europe, the supremacy of God and Dharma were experienced only during wars and disputes, winning them was supposed to be duty. For this very reason, Widengrane held, T.B Prat's religions consciousness, in his exposition, 'Man is the controller of destiny' as inappropriate. The Vedic way of dutifulness permits a man, the freedom to work according to his own temperament, mental make-up and feelings. Professor Dunning writes,[4] the ancient Aryans did not keep their politics aloof from dutifulness, philosophy, the atmosphere of investigative evaluation of the elements. Bloomfield has also expressed a similar opinion, while saying, "Right from the time of inception of history, religious institutions assigned honourable limits to the character and conduct of the Indian subjects." On the other hand P. Carpra in 'The Tao of Physics] has written on ancient Indian thought on Dharma.- "The Indian religious thought has connections with that infinite mysterious knowledge, which is proven in debate."

---

[3] John W.Spellmen, Political theory of Anciant India, p.98
[4] Prof. Dunning, A History of Political theories Ancient and medival p. XIX

Most of the Western thinkers hold a viewpoint, that Indian thinkers instead of addressing the actual problems, for solving them, get entangled in religion. As a matter of fact, all these Western scholars have referred to Dharma as the western or English word religion and relate to it as such. For us it is necessary to understand the basic difference between Dharma and religion.

## Dharma versus Religion

What is Dharma? As elucidated in the beginning, that which regulates and controls the entire human behaviour, is dutifulness or Dharma. The conclusions of the entire Vedic literary thought, is given under the title of, 'Dharma versus Religion,' as such, the form of attributes of dutifulness, its indicators, elements, nature, foundation and source etc. have been attempted to be clarified-

## Attributes of Dharma

1) Pervasive 2) regulative 3) director 4) perpetual 5) ethical 6) non-violent

## Features of Dharma

1) Patience 2) Forgiveness 3) Control of senses 4) non-stealing 5) chastity 6) affection 7) increase knowledge 8) education 9) truthfulness 10) non-anger

'धृतिः क्षमा दमोऽस्तेयं शौचमिन्द्रियनिग्रहः ।
धीर्विद्या सत्यमक्रोधो दशकं धर्मलक्षणम् ।।

(Manu.6.92)

## The elements of Dharma

1) Dharma is all pervasive. 2) Dharma is all binding.
3) Dharma is all progressive.

## Nature of Dharma

1) Truth 2) Duty 3) Justice

After reviewing and gaining knowledge of various stances of Dharma, religion will have to be understood. Generally, the modern meaning of Dharma is treated as a synonym of religion. It really is not so. Religion has an institution, post and portfolio. But Dharma cannot be institutionalized or posted with portfolio. Religion is a narrow imaginary concept of Dharma.

## What is Religion

1) Religion has been defined in the form relevant to a sect or community.

2) It sprouts many branches and sub- branches.

## The General active elements of religion

All religious communities accept the existence of three general conditions– 1) God 2) Soul 3) Universe

## The foundation of Religion

Religion is really based on three pillars-

1)      Prayers 2) Activity 3) Symbol and indicators.

It clearly shows that dutifulness or Dharma is extensive, and religion is a narrow imaginary concept of dutifulness. The ambit of dutifulness is not limited, in it naturally, an individual, society, nation and the cosmos are included unimpaired, implicitly. Having realized this difference, it is difficult to accept and adopt the concept of secularism at the state level. In the Indian constitution the way dutifulness or Dharma has been connected to the form of prayer, that is not in conformity with the dutifulness motivated Indian thought. In fact, an arrangement for ruling, devoid of dutifulness, is shallow. This is the reason why the rule of secular India, and its rulers have lost values and conduct. There is no guideline or directive force to monitor their conduct, on the contrary, they have garbed dutifulness with sectarianism and are using it as a pawn to grab political power.

On studying the scriptures on Niti and Smriti, inspired by Vedas and Upanishads, it is learnt that they have laid special stress on the conduct of the rulers and values for ruling. A state that has been called a nation, was not separate from dutifulness but stands testimony to dutifulness. To understand this stance of dutifulness in greater depth, it is necessary for us

to know its extensive investigation and the sources thereof.
## Sources of the Dharma
A shloka from Manusmriti related to Dharma is very well said-

श्रुतिः स्मृतिः सदाचारः स्वस्य च प्रियमात्मनः ।
एतत् चतुर्विधं प्राहुः साक्षात् धर्मस्य लक्षणम् ।। (1.12)

In the said shloka, while describing the source of Dharma, Manu the inspiration of Dharma among humans, says, to test what is falsehood, there are four parameters- Shruti, meaning thereby scripture on dutifulness. Smriti means, that one, which has been there for ever, meaning thereby, superior tradition, the third is good conduct, this implies conduct and thinking of superior men. The fourth parameter is 'स्वस्य च प्रियं आत्मनः' meaning thereby, whatever is dear to the soul, it can also be called the voice of the inner self. Scriptures explaining it say-

सदाचार स्मृतिर्वेदाः त्रिविधं धर्मलक्षणम् ।
चतुर्थमर्थमित्याहुः कवयो धर्म लक्षणम् ।।

In this Shantiparv (259.3), shloka it is said- good conduct, smriti and Vedas are the three foundation stones of Dharma.

Scholars consider mastering the economic goal, as the fourth foundation stone. Likewise, vide Manavdharma Shastra (7.43), Aapstambh Dharma Shastra (1.1.1), Gautam Dharma Sutra (11.19.20), a scholar of Vedas, way of conduct, way of doing things and customs and tradition is termed as dutifulness or Dharma and the original form of its law is called the source. Way of conduct is the prime Dharma, has been corroborated by the following mantra in the Rigveda-

'भद्रं वै वरं वृणते भद्रं युञ्जन्ति दक्षिणम् ।।' (10.164.2)

This means, that a person with immaculate behaviour is suitable to be in the assembly.
## Eternal and continuous Dharma
From a micro and macro viewpoint, Dharma is eternal and continuous as well. It is eternal in the sense that its elements are the same, universal and unchangeable. After intense study of Vedic incantations and deep contemplation on Dharma as

advocated by sages, having been proven on questioning, regulations are presented for all arrangements. It is an ever-developing concept that improves with a person's individual development and maintenance of the social arrangement. In ancient times it was part of the king's duty to maintain high traditions and moral conduct. The religious scriptures make legal arrangements for it. Thus, Shruti, are a moral conduct, declarations of scholars, high traditions, have been named as sources of Dharma or dutifulness (law). Manu opines (2.8), 'शुनिचैव श्वपाके च पण्डितास्समदर्शिनः ।।' meaning thereby, Dutiful is that, which is observed by scholars of the Vedas, and that which is accepted by those souls, who are beyond attachment or contempt, possessors of great qualities. Thus, in all ages, even though the traditions and customs might have undergone change, but the scholars and scrupulous men did not feel uncomfortable with the set norms of dutifulness. The incantation of the Rigveda (4.23.9, 1.123.9), iterate that the foundation pillars of truth (Satya) are strong. 'ऋतस्य दृढ़ा धरुणानि सन्ति।' In the cosmic order (Dhrit) the morning does not vacillate from its place. 'ऋतस्य योषां न मिनाति धामा।'

The exposition of Dharma makes it clear that it is also the law. Law cannot be contrary to extensive dutifulness. Law nurtures, and dutifulness is to be adopted. So, both are synonyms. When law expands, it is to contain the pervasive dutifulness up to its milestone. Scholars of religion have concluded that only those established traditions, way of doing things and customs be made into law which are congenial and purposeful. The question arises that how should the law makers, their decision making authority, on any subject be? Manusmriti states-

वेदोऽखिलो धर्ममूलं स्मृतिशीले च तद्विदाम्।
आचारश्चैव साधूनामात्मनस्तुष्टिरेव च ।।

(Manu.2.6)

All the Vedas are the source of Dharma and the Smriti and politeness of a scholar of the Vedas, is also dutifulness.

28

Likewise, the conduct of noble people and their soul-satisfaction is also the source of Dharma. The complete meaning of this shloka is, those responsible for making plans for performance of duty ought to possess knowledge, knowledge of science and good moral character. A human being's conduct, speech and opinions are an evidence of Dharma, thus, these are the main sources of Dharma.

From the sources of Dharma, this truth is repeatedly revealed that Shruti bears relevance for all times, is eternal, and is the foundation source, and Smriti is the sum up of essence emanated from these principles. That is why it is said, 'Smriti may change, but Shruti will remain permanent'. This way, the two aspects of dutifulness attract attention- Sanatan dharma, which is eternal, and the other is dharma pertaining to the Yuga (age)- which is established in a Yuga and continues.

**Various forms of Dharma**

The pervasive and infinite form of Dharma manifests in various meaningful acts. Its sources reflect that, duty, commitment, justice, tradition, way of doing things and customs, truth, good conduct are the indicators of everyone's elevation. How Dharma is related to its various aspects, is to be brought to light.

**i) Dharma as Duty**

It is very important to pay attention to the fact, that in our thought, instead of rights, the word duty has been used. The source of inspiration of 'dutifulness or Dharma is obligatory', are ancient scriptures. Obligations expect man to lead a regulated life. It is the call of human being's dutifulness or Dharma, that he should observe all the obligations he owes to himself and the society with full commitment. The Manav Dharma Shastra, and the Gita are extensive treatises on dutifulness in the form of obligations. According to Manu (2.2.4,13), each act committed by a human being is based on desire. Dharma is meaningful for those, who are not caught up in desire and money. That is why Manu (2.88.99) further says,

"The way a chariot puller, keeps the horses reign pulled tight, likewise, a human being must have his senses under control." "The end of desire is not its fulfilment, they become more intense like the fire satiated with ghee." In this situation the question arises, what is the dutiful act for a human being? And what are those principles that ought to direct his actions? Bhagvad Gita gives answers to these questions (Cha. 2.47-48,3.19). In it while propagating, action without expecting the desired result thereof, it is said, "an action should not be performed expecting the result thereof. On being devoid of attachment, committing an act with an obligatory feeling, is worthy of praise. The act performed with equanimity is known as 'yoga'." The shlokas of the 18th Chapter of the Gita iterate that the action that is done as a response to the call of Dharma, figures in the righteous category.

'नियतं सङ्गरहितमरागद्वेषतः कृतम्।
अफलप्रेप्सुना कर्म यत्तत्सात्त्विकमुच्यते।' (18.23)
'प्रवृतं च निवृत्तिं च कार्याकार्ये भयाभये।
बन्धं मोक्षं च या वेत्ति बुद्धिः सा पार्थ सात्त्विकी।' (18.30)
'धृत्या यया धारयते मनःप्राणेन्द्रियक्रि याः।
योगेनाव्यभिचारिण्या धृतिः सा पार्थ सात्त्विकी।' (18.33)

These shlokas preach one's own dutiful action. It is also said that Dharma must be prompted by the conscience and a feeling from within. Bhagwat Geeta (18.29-32) mentions three types of conscious intelligence. The first one is an act, in accordance with the scriptures, without pride, far from attachment or malevolence, is performed by righteous intelligence (Satogun). The act that is performed doing hard work, and is prompted by the hope of its fruitfulness by a proud person, is indicative of rajas or passionate intelligence, (Rajogun) and an act that is performed without taking into consideration the consequence, involvement of loss, violence or capacity, only prompted by ignorance, that act is motivated by tamas or inert intelligence (tamogun). Likewise, three types of resoluteness has been described, (18.33-35) righteous, passionate and inert resolutions. It is very clearly discerned by these shlokas, that a person who cannot control his physical, emotional and social needs, he exposes his lowliness. And a person whose tasks are actually inspired by the self within, he alone is governed by dutifulness. Manu (4.158-160) has also reiterated this view through the medium of shlokas that whoever performs the assigned duties, follows the path of dutifulness, leads a happy life. The institution of Varna is a manifestation of the dutiful actions. Each human being must perform great deeds in accordance with his competence to contribute in the organization of the society and place in his own particular caste institution, perform duty as prescribed by the Varna Institution. In the various shlokas of Gita (4.13.18, 41) describing the caste institution, it is clearly stated that it is not birth that determines the varna, but actions performed are decisive.

In Manu Smriti, Mahabharata, and thereafter, Kautilya's Arthashastra, while describing ordinary Dharma (Saadharan Dharma), it said- simplicity, not harming anyone, truthfulness, chastity, kindness, forgiveness, loving justice are ordinary or general tenets of duty for all castes. Patanjali (Yogsutra 2.30) mentions, five Dharma related values, which are non-violence, being truthful, non-stealing, celibacy and non-possessiveness. They expressed that the ordinary Dharma or Manavdharma or is essential for the stability of ethical and social life. This universe endeavours for achieving happiness, and happiness cannot be obtained without giving up bad deeds. Freedom from bad deeds can only be gotten if those regulations which have been imposed for all varna as life's organization, are observed. For instance, Vishwamitra has said in Balkand (Ramayan) -

यमार्यः क्रियामाणं तु शसन्त्यागवेदिनः ।
स धर्मः यं विगर्हन्ति तमधर्म प्रचक्षेत ।।

The actions when performed by Vedic scholars, they are Dharma and if the act is malacious, it is Adharma.

## ii) Dharma as Justice and Law as well

S. Gopalan[5], a specialist in ancient politics, opines that "when we utilize Dharma making it instrumental for social stability, then the word Law becomes the indicator of this stability. And when we discuss law, then justice gets automatically attached to it. In clear words, Dharma alone is justice and law." 'Dharma in the form of law', has been explained in Kautilya's Arthshastra and Manu's Manav-dharmashastra, at great length. Dutifulness, behaviour, character and ruling the kingdom, have been called the four legs of law. Dharma is based on truth (Satya), behaviour of witness, character on general acceptance and ruling the kingdom rests on righteous intelligence, and regulations prescribed in the scriptures. The eighth chapter of Manusmriti relates to the process of legal justice in conformity to Dharma. In the Shatpath Brahman it is stated, 'Dharma is the gallantry of the warrior class', no other is superior to it. It is that law which enables a weak person to rule over the strong. According to R.P Kangle[6], "the regulations of religious scriptures prove that the king who is lawful is 'the first citizen.' Meaning thereby, it is the duty of the king, as he is the representative of the people, that he be the first one to abide by dutifulness in the form of law and inspire his subjects to be law abiding." In the eighth chapter (14, 15) Manu says, where Dharma is suppressed by Adharma, truth by untruth, there the judicial officers are bound to cease to exist. It is known to all and all proven that one who protects Dharma is protected and the one who flouts it, gets destroyed.

The root of this English word 'Law', is similar to 'Dharma', with the view point of language and science. It

---

[5] S.Gopalan, Hindu social philosophy, 128-129
[6] R.P.Kangle, Kautilya Arthasastra, A study Part III

originates from a Latin letter, 'log' which means binding on all. Dharma's 'Dhri' a letter in Sanskrit, means– adopted by all. The most important factor of Indian thought is that it has treated Dharma as an inspirational force, rather than one binding. English 'law' is indicative of pressure, while Vedic dutifulness is a path to be followed.

### iii) Dharma in its most beautiful form of Shreya

In the ambit of Dharma are included, individuals, society, nation, the caste system arrangement, ruling of the state. Apart from this, one of the highest forms of Dharma is also human welfare. 'यतोऽभ्युदय निःश्रेयससिद्धिः स धर्मः।' (Vaishishki, 1.12) The mantra affirms this feeling only. Dharma proves, 'परोपकाराय सतां विभूतयः', meaning thereby, doing good to others, is an attribute of noble people. A mantra from Rigveda, 'ऊर्ध्वा दधानः शुचिपेशसं धियम्।।' means Dharma in its foremost form, attracts our attention towards sacred and welfare- oriented acts. It opines, the scholars ought to use their illumined intelligence in performing good deeds. It is their duty.

In ancient scriptures, self- knowledge has been specially emphasized. Self-knowledge gives rise to good qualities. Consequently, human beings get involved in activities of social welfare. Rise above narrow outlook, selfishness, one's own profit-loss, and become kind, treating all human beings alike, and expand the feeling of love.

Sarvodaya and the feeling of humanity or humanism are invigorated by Dharma. Attaining this form of dutifulness, not only develops the person individually but he also expands from social and from humanitarian point of view. Describing such an erudite person, it has been said-

मातृवत् परदारेषु परद्रव्येषु लोष्ठवत्।
आत्मवत् सर्वभूतेषु यः पश्यति सः पण्डितः।।

The Gita has expressed the root of Dharma thus, "one who sees, like in himself, the element of the soul in others as well, whatever may happen, considers the state of happiness and sorrow with equanimity, is a true yogi." Shantiparva ( 6.30)

Anushasanparva (11.6.89) of Mahabharat in its comment on peace and discipline, firmly states that, the person who considers all human beings bearing the same soul, one who does not harm anyone ever, and is able to control his anger, he stays happy on this planet and in the other astral level (loka) as well. In Bhagvad Gita (6.29) while describing a superior human being, it is said that,'a person who by practicing yoga is able to feel in his consciousness oneness of the soul, is able to see himself in other human beings and other human beings in himself, he is able to see everywhere evenness.' These mantras teach us, that a person who is able to develop the feeling of soul condition, he attains unison with the supreme soul and overcomes all doubts, lust and anger.

How can the path of humanity and welfare be promoted further has been talked about in Kathopanishad, which teaches, that a human being will have to realize the difference between श्रेय ('superior') and प्रेय ('dear'). Superior action leads to welfare and the action we love to do is dear. A human being ought to perform superior action instead of what is dear to him. This voice of the Upanishads was heard and expressed by poetic scriptures.

In the shlokas of Shantiparv[7], it is brought to light that, kindness towards all and interest in the welfare of all, is dutifulness or Dharma. The ancient essence of Dharma is welfare of all present and friendship among omnipresent. Only that person can know the basic essence of Dharma definitely, who is friendly with all and is by thought, speech and action, working for the good of all human beings.' The ancient scriptures declare the purpose of Dharma to be human welfare. The secret of Dharma is- what appears to be undesirable to one's own self, is not to be done while interacting with other fellow being.

---

[7] Mahabharat by Swami Jagdishwaranand Saraswati, 262, 5.9/109.10

श्रूयताम् धर्म सर्वस्वं श्रुत्वा चैवावधार्यताम् ।
आत्मनः प्रतिकूलानि परेषां न समाचरेत् ।।

In the ancient literature the concept of Dharma that arose, presents the great principles of organized elements in the pattern of life, justice, truth, brotherhood and humanism. From this point of view, Dharma is the manifestation of culture- which makes life worth living. Shri B.G Kokhale writes- Dharma is that means of togetherness and oneness, which permeates fragrance all over the world. If there is one complete word or definition, for the manifestation of Indian culture, it is Dharma. In Buddhist literature many a time a person with values is referred to as 'dhamma matt' or 'dutiful'. To make it more clear, when a person is said to be with values if he follows the set norms, is truthful, intelligent and kind[8]. From this point of view Dharma is the point of inspiration to take us on the right path. This is the central point of our entire life circle. Atharv Veda mantra says-

'स्वधया परिहिता श्रद्धया पर्य्यूढा दीक्षया गुप्ता यज्ञे प्रतिष्ठिता लोको निधनम् ।।

**(12.5.1.3)**

ओजश्च तेजश्च सहश्च बलं च वाक् चेंद्रियं च श्रीश्च धर्मश्च ।।

**(12.5.2.7)**

Swami Dayanand Saraswati in his Rigvedadi Bhashya Bhoomika has translated these mantras thus-

1. 'It is the duty of every human being to adorn themselves with their own substance', adopt nectar like behaviour.
2. 'All human beings must be truthful, as truth is the basis of trust, and when followed in conduct, it proves fruitful. By truthful education scholars are empowered.
3. There be an endeavour to protect living beings, meaning thereby, good be done to all. All these three spiritual exercises are like the Ashvamegh yagna. Without inertness, to get involved in the three spiritual exercises, is to be harbinger of well- being. He further says-

---

[8] B.G.Gokhle, Indian Polical Thought through the ages, p.48

The king, for ruling the kingdom ought to adopt dutiful gallantry. To go beyond happiness-unhappiness, loss-profit, sorrow-joy and remain 'steadfast in truthful duty'. By practicing celibacy, the body be made free of illness. Increase the strength of intelligence and cleverness. Speech be truthful, sweet and likable. Keep the five sense faculties and the five 'active sense organs' away from sinful acts, under one's own control. To have a mighty kingdom adhere to dutifulness, imparting justice as directed by the Vedas.' The kingdom should be for everyone's welfare. This is Dharma. Contrary to it, is Adharma.

The complete concept of Dharma is very profound and extensive. In the ambit, definition and concept of Dharma, all the thoughts that are included, they are all pervading. It has got within itself social groups (Varna Dharma) ethical and spiritual endeavours, four stages of life (Ashram Dharma), obligations towards families (Kul Dharma), regions (Kshetra Dharma), for the country (Rashtra Dharma), ruling the kingdom (Raj Dharma), periods of time (Yug Dharma), humanity ( Manav Dharma), that is why it is so extensive. The basic source of the extensive text of the concept of Dharma is Vedic literature.

From the analysis of different forms of the concept of Dharma, it is discerned that Dharma is the foundation stone for the entire cosmos and it is the linchpin of governing the state. The deep connection of 'Dharma' and 'Politics', be presented before or made available to the material readership, from the argumentative logical viewpoint, conveying the essence, has been the intent of this modest effort by me. What we call 'politics' today, that only was portrayed and arose as royal dutifulness in ancient literature. 'Politics' and 'royal dutifulness' can be explained thus-

**Politics**

In the Sanskrit vocabulary, the word 'raj' means', to shine', and 'niti', derived from root word 'nay', which means 'to lead to appropriate path' meaning thereby, Politics is that which moves ahead, illumined by the righteous path.

**Rajdharma**

That which is adorned by wearing the gem of Dharma, or shines, is royal dutifulness or Raj Dharma!

In both the instances, mentioned above, Dharma is adopted as a policy in administration. Separated from Dharma or impartial rule, it loses its identity. Chanakya has written, treating Dharma as the root of the entire governance thus-

सुखस्य मूलं धर्मः

धर्मस्य मूलं अर्थः

अर्थस्य मूलं वाणिज्यं

वाणिज्यस्य मूलं स्वराज्यं

स्वराज्यस्य मूलं चारित्र्यम् ।।

Dr Sarvapalli Radhakrishnan in 1950, in his report on University Shiksha Aayog, said, "We have to adopt the beautiful values of Dharma, we should never forsake them."

Swami Vivekanand said that Dharma was not communism, in his expositions. From time to time, he said[9] –

1) Dharma is a gem which keeps humanity alive.

2) For the nations good, we must gather spiritual forces and establish national unity.

3) He clarified that he did not belong to any group or sect. Rigid sectarianism will not let the world progress.

Swami Vivekanand's outpour mentioned above, clarifies the difference between Dharma and sectarianism. Secularism is not related or committed to intents unrelated to Dharma or religious intents. Secularism is borrowed from European thought. It is a misleading imagination. Today maintenance of 'indivisibility and unity in India' are burning problem. To maintain unity in India, it is imperative to accept Dharma in its contemporary social form, to protect India's unity. Politics ought to be away from sectarian thoughts, but its segregation

---

[9] Swami Vivekanand, Bhartya Vyakhyan-p.112, 216, 307, 312

from Dharma is not possible. Dharma is all pervasive. The constant order of its principles cannot be flouted by any individual, sect or nation ever. A ruling power segregated from the essence of Dharma, will become self- centred, uncontrollable, corrupt and extremist. By incorporating the values described in the Vedic literature, in the political activities and laws of administration, it is possible to protect Indian pride and prestige. The description of attributes for royal duty and self- government given in verses of Vedic literature, teachings and shlokas is exemplary. Gandhiji said while expressing his views on self-government, "there be many meanings of self- government, for me the truth for all times is there is a single meaning,-Ramrajya. If anyone dislikes the word 'Ramrajya' then I will call it Dharma Rajya." This eternal truth was also declared by Yogiraj-

'यतो धर्मसृततो जयः' – Where there is Dharma there is victory.

## Chapter 3
# Vedic Literature : An Introduction

In the Vedic literature, on the subjects like self-government, dutiful rule (Raj Dharma) or superior ways of ruling the state, there are innumerable teachings, but what do we mean by Vedic literature? The literature that inspired sage Jemini, Shankaracharya, Swami Dayanand Saraswati, Swami Vivekanand, Mahatma Gandhi, Dr. Sarvapalli Radhakrishnan, patriots like them, eminent persons, committed to the country's upliftment, while singing praises of the Vedas, the Upanishads and Smriti scriptures, investigated the texts, wrote treatises and expositions so that knowledgeable Vedic literature could be understood.

The Vedic versification is well entrenched on the gigantic crown of Indian literature. There are only four Vedic compilations but the Vedic literature is extremely vast. Treating the Vedas as the base its purpose is clarified, the appropriation of its mantras and the various scriptures that have been written are also included in the Vedic literature. This way, the Vedic literature can be mainly divided into the following categories-

1. The Four Vedas 2. Brahman Scriptures 3. Aranyakas
4. Upanishads

The most ancient literature of the world 'The Vedas,' is the originating ground of great knowledge, great thought, source of tradition, essence of all subjects of education, religion, justice, truthful conduct and universal welfare. In the introduction of Rigvedic Bhashya Bhoomika, Swami Dayanand Sarswati has explained the root word vid of Veda. He says there are four meaning of `Vid` dhatu-

1. Knowable Knowledge (विद्) ज्ञाने
2. Knowledge of real and unreal (विद्) सत्तायाम्
3. Knowledge of auspicious benefit (विद् लृ) लाभे

4. Knowledge of thought process (विद्) विचारणे

ऐतेभ्यो 'हलश्च' इति सूत्रेण करणाधिकरणकारकपोर्धञ्प्रत्यये कृते वेदशब्दः साध्यते ।

1. When to the instrument of root word 'vid' is affixed 'dhanjy' (धञ्) it mean Veda वेत्ति–जानाति धर्मादिपुरुषार्थं. चतुष्टयोपायान् अनेन इति वेदः।' Meaning thereby, what leads to knowing the means of attaining ascertainment of four purushartha- Dharma, Artha, Kama and Moksha, is the Veda.

2. When to the root word 'vid sattayam' (real or unreal) is affixed emotion of 'dhanjy' then the word 'Veda' presents its pure eternal form. In this reference only Maharshi Vedavyas has said in the Mahabharata-

अनादि निधना नित्या वागुत्सृष्टा स्वयम्भुवा।
आदौ वेदमयी दिव्या यतः सर्वाः प्रवृत्तयः ।।

3. With the root word 'Vid lri' is affixed the instrument 'dhanjy' then it creates the word Veda, meaning,'विद्यन्ते लभन्ते धर्मादिपुरुषार्थान् अनेन इति वेदः' meaning thereby, that through the Vedas not only can you know the obligations of Dharma but by following the directions of the Veda you can adopt the way to fulfil and attain them.

4. With the root word 'Vid viacharane' is affixed the instrument of 'dhanjy' then creates a meaning of 'Veda' which is, 'विचारयति सृष्ट्यादिप्रक्रियाम् अनेन् इति वेदः'–Veda is the process of creation and represents its thought formation and provides solution for the problems arising.

The creation of Veda is thus-

'विद्यन्ते ज्ञायन्ते लभ्यन्ते सर्वे पदार्थाःविद्या व अनेन अस्मिन् वा इति वेदाः ।'

In these four root words instrument and base if 'dhanjy' is affixed, then, from knowledge, knowable substance of the word 'Veda' is derived. The writer of Ashtadhyayi Maharishi Panini has written, treating the meaning of the root word 'vid', as benefit of sovereignty and contained thoughtfulness- 'विद् सत्तायाम् विद्लृ लाभे–विद् विचारणे'- In this thoughtful and extensive meaning of the word 'Veda', it refers to creation from power, life or upbringing through knowledge, profit through acquisition or the culmination of the rhythm. In It, 'profit is included as the obligations of Dharma, earning wealth, fulfilment of desires, and salvation, and all these are the attributes of the creator. In the Vedanta Sutra 1.1.2, it has been explained, in the form of 'जन्माद्यस्त यतः', meaning thereby, that, all creation emanates through it, on the basis of which all remain alive and that in which all are absorbed. Because of this reference of Brahma the Creator found in the Vedant Sutras, the Vedas are in fact the creator. But in the form of a source of knowledge of this world (laukik) and the other world (Parloukik), the name 'Veda' is known everywhere. Thus, practically the word 'Veda' refers to the special scripture only.

Treating the Vedas as an allotrope (apaurusheya) sage Jemini has written, 'तेषामृग यत्रार्थवशेन पादव्यवस्था। गीतिषु साम।' 'शेषे यजुः शब्दः (Jemini Sutra 201.35.37). The way of writing the Vedas is different in each one of them- Rig is an arrangement of verses, Sam is musical to be sung, Yaju is knowledge, Atharva is conspicuous by profound combinations of education.

Basically, there is proof of four compilations of texts of the Vedas available. They have been referred to as compilations, based on the nature of their verses. They cannot be segregated, they have continuity. These four compilations are chronically stated thus-

*Rig Veda, Sam Veda, Yajur Veda and Atharv Veda.*

The Vedas are mainly poetic verses, though they also have a portion of prose. Vedic poetic verses are called 'Rik' or 'Richa', Vedic prose is referred as 'Yanjusha' and the musical verses of the Vedas are called, 'Saam'. A group of 'Richas' and 'Saam' is known as 'Sukt', which means excellent or well worded. The Vedas contain thousands of such 'suktas'. The

Vedas have been attributed by the noun 'Trayi' for having these three types of verses, 'Richa, Yanjunsha and Saam'. Referring to 'Trayi' a mantra from the Atharva Veda states-

'देवस्य पश्य काव्यं न ममार न जीर्यति। (10.8.32)

It means, O human being! See the divine beautiful poetry, that is not erasable or is dimmed ever. In fact, the vedic 'richas' are that superior knowledge which enhances the spiritual power and ability of the soul, for sure, always.

Through the illumination of knowledge of the Vedas, for the purpose of enlightenment of all, Swami Dayanand, wrote, Veda Bhashyas and Satyarth Prakash. In the seventh exhilaration of Satyartha Prakash, he writes, 'Veda is divine knowledge and is derived from the divine.' Its each word and relativity is constant. It contains the seed of all truthful learning. The Vedas do not have the history of a particular person or imagined stories told. They are logical, self-proven, and self- evident. In their broader form, the four Vedas contain 24000 proven verses. Relating to the formation of the Vedas, the Yajurveda and Atharva Veda state-

'तस्माद्यज्ञात्सर्वहुत ऋचः सामानि जज्ञिरे।
छंदान्सि जज्ञिरे तस्माद्यजुस्तास्मादजायत।।

(Yajur.31.7)

यस्मादृचो अपातक्षन्यजुर्यस्मादपाकषन्।
सामानि यस्य लोमान्यथर्वाङ्गिरसो मुखम्
स्कम्भं तं ब्रूहि कतमः स्विदेव सः।।

(Atharv.10.7.20)

The two above mentioned mantras mean- Truth (सत्) that is indestructible, mind (चित्त) that is always a manifestation of knowledge, of happiness, is complete on all grounds, meaning thereby, is omnipresent. For all human beings it is worthy of veneration. It is all powerful. From that Supreme Creator (परम ब्रह्म) alone have emanated these four Vedas, (ऋचः) the Rig Veda, (यजुः) the Yajurveda, (सामानि) the Samaveda and (छंदासि) the Atharva Veda. Thus, it is appropriate for all to follow the way of living prescribed in the Vedas. The meaning of 'जज़िरे'

and 'अजायत', both the words is, 'that which contains many subjects of learning, is only Veda.

The Veda states- The Almighty God, is the birth giver of RigVeda, YajurVeda and Atharva Veda. A simile is used to give the origin of Vedas as- Sam Veda is like thick hair, Yajur Veda is like the heart, and Rig- Veda is like the life force. The Veda holds- that Supreme God, which contains the entire universe, is named, 'Skambh'. That is the activator of the Vedas and is worthy of veneration[10.] From this view point the Vedas are that voice of self- born Brahma, which has no beginning or end. It is perpetual. Our sages have, as a consequence of their penance, experienced coming face to face with the eternal light in its traditionally known form, presented before the world that 'truthful knowledge', the word content of Veda only.

RigVeda is the first canto of science. It is the most ancient book in the world's library. In it, is contained the qualities of substances and descriptions of Dharma. The root word 'rich stutau' (ऋच स्तुतौ) has gone to create 'rik' verses. It means that which narrates the description of auspicious attributes and their possessor is 'rik'. Maxmuller, while commenting on the Veda's says-"In the world's history, the Vedas cover up such an interval of time, which has not been covered by any other literary work of another language.' Maxmuller further says, 'As long as mountains and rivers will remain on the Earth, till then, among the people of the world, the glory of the Rig Veda will be propagated. The libraries, museums provide evidence indicating its ancientness, with the Rig Veda being the first one."[11] Likewise, presided over by famous literary persona-lities of the world, Victor Hugo in 1884 and the French scholar Limpa Delva very enthusiastically said, "It is through

---

[10] Rishi Dayanand Saraswati, Rigvedadi Bhashya Bhumika, Vedotpatti vishaya, p.7-8

[11] Maxmuller, A History of Sanskrit Literature, p. 57-58

the medium of the Rig Veda, that Greece and Rome can strengthen their pathway. There is none other scripture so valuable.

The Rig Veda is the biggest in volume, variety and the mantra count. Rig Veda is counted by two methods. By counting in the first method, it contains, mandal, sukta and mantras, by the other it has eight chapters, varg, anuvak and mantras. It has ten mandals, 1028 sukta, and 10589 mantras. According to the other method of counting it has 64 chapters, 85 verses and 2024 sections. According to the Shatpath Brahman, the Rig Veda contains 4,32,000 words. As far as the numbers of mantras go, there are conflicting opinions among scholars. According to the description given by Shripad Damodar, there are- 10 mandals, number of suktas are 1017+1 ( Balkhilya sukta) total 1028, number of mantras is 10472+80 (Balakhalya mantra), there are a total of 10552 mantras.

The Rig Veda contains knowledge beginning from a straw to all finished products, going beyond the divine itself. What is nature? What is life? What is the purpose of a living being? What are his goals? What are the means to achieve those goals? How should the Swarajya system or self- ruling system be? So on and so forth, the description of all subjects is available in the Rig Veda.

The RigVeda has two Brahmans- Aittarey and Kaushiki. Its sub Veda is Ayurveda. The biggest Sukta in Rig Veda contains 58 Richas and the smallest Sukta has only one Richa. There are 17 mantras of two steps, and 6 mantras of a single step.

According to Taittiriya Aranyak, '**ऋग्म्यो जातां सर्वशो मूर्तिमाहुः सर्वाः गतीः याजुषी चैव सिद्धा।**' Meaning thereby, all tangible elements are made famous by the rik  and all movements are related to the Yajuh. The word Yajuh emanates from the root word Yaj (interpretation 7.20). This is the summation of activity and movement. In the Brahman scriptures it is also called 'Yaj' Yan+juh . It means knowledge, passing, acquiring and redemption have been included, while stressing that all activity be concluded skilfully, are subjects of Yajurveda. In the Rig Veda the attributes full of substances whose creation is talked about, that a human being should duly adopt and make endeavours in that direction, the knowledge for that is given in 'Yaju'. When Yajurveda was presented before the famous French scholar, Voltaire, he expressed his belief that it is the most valuable gift, for which the West will always remain indebted to the East.[12]

Yajurveda refers to work, as life's worship. Another name for worship is 'Adhvar' or 'a sacrifice'. Therefore, it is also called Adhvaryu Veda by us. One entire chapter of Yajurveda, in each of its many mantras has **यज्ञेन कल्पन्ताम्** verses, figuring at the end. Here the meaning of yagna is combination of special learnings or acquiring knowledge. An act of greatness is called 'yagna.' The process of knowledge and science is also yagna. It means without effort received knowledge is not fruitful. The combination of knowledge and right endeavour is necessary in life. The mantra in Yajurveda is, **यज्ञो वै श्रेष्ठतमं कर्म** । To maintain the senses active in the body, the mind, life force energy and air is necessary, likewise, to live it is essential to be active and skilful. For everyone's good, the use of liquid substance and auspicious acts and acts of charity have been taught, for that very reason, it has been named Yajurveda. **सविता प्रार्पयतु श्रेष्ठतमाय कर्मणो** । In the beginning of the mantra, while instructing to perform great acts it has been said, **कुर्वन्नेवेह कर्माणि जिजीविषेच्छतं समाः** । (40.2) Yajurveda has a total of 40 chapters, consisting of 1975 mantras. Yajurveda has a word count of 90,351 words. In the ancient times, Yajurveda had 101 branches. There were two main sections of these branches, one 'Shukla', the other 'Krishna'. Shukla Yajurveda had 15 branches, and Krishna

---

[12] A critical study-Contribution of Arya Samaj through Indian Education, p. 68

Yajurveda had 86 branches. The Brahman of Shukla Yajurveda is Shatpath, and sub Veda is Dhanurveda. Swami Dayanand has written a beautiful and unique treatise on Yajurveda. One of the mantras of his treatise is worth mentioning. This inspires human beings to abstain from laziness and involve themselves in right action for pursuing attainment of goals. Actual redemption and bliss can be achieved by that very person who is well versed in the learning of the Vedas and use of pure speech.

अक्रन् कर्म कर्मकृतः सहवाचा मयोभुवा।
देवेभ्य कर्म कृत्वास्तं प्रेत सचाभुवः। (3.47)

In Vedic literature Samveda is the smallest in volume but from the viewpoint of importance, it is the biggest. While praising Samveda Sri Krishna said, 'वेदानां सामवेदोऽस्मि' (Bhagwadgita 10.20) among the Vedas, I am Samveda. In Chhandogya Upnishad (3.3.1) it is said, 'सामवेद एव पुष्पम्' meaning thereby, Samveda is like a flower, to substantiate on its importance, a flower is small, but its importance is due to its beauty and fragrance. Samveda has a prominent canto on veneration. In it there is a detailed description of spiritual substance of high quality, by virtue of following that, a human being can attain the highest goal of his life, that is moksha or ultimate redemption. From ancient times itself, there has been a close connection of Samveda with human life. To make worship attractive and effective Sam songs were sung. Swami Dayanand has also prescribed, a Sam song after performing every ritual as a matter of rule. For instance-

2 3   1   2   312   3 1   3 1 2
अग्न आ  याहि वीतये गृणानो हव्यदातये।
1   2         312
नि  होता  सत्सि बर्हिष ।।

This mantra from Samveda (Poorvarchik) is a prayer to the Almighty God, seeking concentration of the mind, getting movement in life, good qualities for accomplishment of tasks, and illumine our way to usher on the right path, for His manifestation in our hearts because of performing auspicious actions like veneration and sacrifices.

1  2  3   2   3    2 3   1 2
सं  नः पवस्व  शं  गवे शं  जनाय  शमर्वते
1   2    1 2
शँ   राजन्नोषधीभ्यः ।।

This mantra of Samveda (Uttararchika) is a prayer to the Lord, 'O omnipresent illuminated God' you are a comfort, bestow grace to our milk producing animals, be harbinger of happiness to human beings, horses used for coaches get cared for, cereals and medicines be provided to create happiness and competence.'

The mantra mentioned above, make it clear that Samveda is set to be sung, also that it has two main parts, Poorvarthik and Uttararthik. In between them is Mahanamnyarchik. Poorvarchik has four cantos, containing 640 mantras there are 6 divisions of the book and each division has two sub-divisions. Each sub-division has five 'dashatiyas'. A group of ten 'richas' is known as 'dashati'. But some dashatis contain less or more richas also, like 7, 9, 12, 14........so on. A Mahananyarchik has 10 mantras.

An Uttararchik has 21 chapters or divisions. It has 402 Suktas and 1225 mantras.Thus the total number of mantras in Samveda is 1875. There are eight Brahmans in the form of treatises on Samveda. Ken and Chhandogya are two Upanishads.

Among the Vedas, Samved holds the third position. Sa+Am = Sam  Sa means, dyulok, (antariksh) Rik (attribute), learning (Vidya) and the all- powerful supreme God. 'Am' means the Earth sphere, Sam songs, actions and beings. Thus, in Samveda, there is an assimilation of knowledge and actions. Its relation, with profundities, fasting and seer's views are also discerned. The Brahmans depict a kind of oneness or assimilation, Sam is in fact the name of that element.

Atharvaveda is a beautiful combination of three, knowledge, action and veneration. It is the key to the means of Dharma, Artha, Kama and Moksha. The means to establish peace be in the nation and the world, have been elucidated in it. In the Atharvaveda there are 20 cantos, 111 verses, 731 suktas and 5977 mantras. As far as counting of mantras is concerned the scholars are controversial about it. Atharvaveda is supposed to have 9 branches. Its Brahman is 'Gopath'.

Atharvaveda has other names- Chhandansi (blissful) Atharvangish (Mantra on Knowledge) Brahmadev (Redeemer). While explaining the Atharvan verse in the 'Gopath' it has been said that Atharva verses, due to being conected with the exploration of reality within the substances of the universe, are Atharva. It makes us aware of the underlying reasons for the creation of substances and their importance. For this very reason, in the Vedic literature Atharvaveda has been called knowledge of interaction. It would not be an exaggeration to call it the scientific treasure of human being's movement through life.

For being the source of all knowledge, science and lofty learnings, it is a proven and complete scripture among the four Vedas and the entire Indian literature. By Brahmans arising, through its branches only, was formed the humankind prominently and the Indian culture and civilization developed. In later times, Aryan sages and hermits through musical Brahman scriptures have been singing praises of the Vedas. Ramayan and Mahabharat have also sung their prestigious lore.

That which affirms eternal auspiciousness for mankind, such Vedic literature can never be archaic or stale. The various mantras of the Atharva Veda have sung the importance of the four Vedas. The mantras convey that through the all doer and holder of the universe, the Supreme God, the Rigveda, the Yajurveda, the Sam Veda and the Atharvaveda have emanated-

यस्माद ऋचे अपातक्षन यजुर्यस्मादपाकषन् ।
सामानि यस्य लोमान्यथर्वाङ्गिरसो मुखं स्कम्भं तं
ब्रूहि कतमः स्विदेव सः ।।

(Atharva.10.7.20)

Impressed by Vedic literature, western scholars, like Winternitz,[13] Bloomfield and so on, did commendable work in the field of translation of the Vedas and preparing treatises on it. While introducing the Vedas to the West, Winternitz said in his presentation, "Not only in the Indian literature but also in Indo-European literature, because of being most ancient and important, the Vedas have a prominent place in the history of world literature. From time immemorial, crores of Hindus have been treating the Vedas as 'Divine Knowledge'. They also accept that their thoughts, feelings have been on a parameter, set by the Vedas, for the reason, that the Vedas have been the most ancient, no individual can without a proper understanding of the Vedas, can know Indian spiritual life and culture. Even to understand the Bauddh Dharma, whose birthplace is also India, study of the Vedas is necessary." Representing this very viewpoint, Bloomfield[14] has accepted that the root source of knowledge are the Vedas. According to him the 'meaning of Veda' is knowledge, meaning thereby, religious knowledge. We will have to accept that a human being cannot learn to achieve and attain dharma (dutifulness) Artha (Earning wealth) Kaam (Fulfill desires) Moksha (Final redemption), independently by using his own inherent knowledge. Knowledge is mainly of two types, 1. Natural 2. Causal. All learning is not possible through natural knowledge. The knowledge of the Vedas is possible by causal learning. Rishi Dayanand Saraswati has written in Satyarth Prakash, that 'all learning is illumined by the Vedas'. Thus, it

---

[13] Winternitz, A History of Indian Literature, Vol. 2

[14] Bloomfield, The Religion of the veda, Introduction, p. 17

is clear, that the knowledge of the Vedas is divinely ordained. A human being possessing knowledge of the Vedas prays to the Lord.

यस्मिनृचः साम यजूंषि यस्मिन्प्रतिष्ठिता रथनाभाविवाराः।
यस्मिंश्चितं सर्वमोतं प्रजानां तन्में मनः शिवसंकल्पमस्तु।।

(Yaju.34.5)

Meaning thereby, O Supreme Lord! By your grace like the wheel of the chariot with its middle spoke having got a saw, likewise, in my mind Rig, Yaju and Sam (the three Vedas) and Atharvaveda is well entrenched. In this very mind of mine, all knowing, omnipresent subjects, witness intelligence consciousness is there, such a mind of mine ought to forsake ignorance and become lover of learning.

In Vedic literature, apart from Samhitas the Brahman scriptures also have an important place. The word 'Brahman' is derived from 'Brahma' which has many meanings. For mantras, yagna and the Vedas also the word 'Brahma' is used. The mantra that are expositions on Vedic verses, clarify their meaning, presents their way of invocation, they are only referred to as 'Brahmans.' The study of Brahman scriptures is necessary for understanding Vedic verses. Each Veda has its Brahman Scriptures. Thus, Brahmans are treatises on the Vedas. The truth of this contention is vindicated by Manu's following shloka-

अग्नि वायुरविभ्यस्तु त्रयं ब्रहम सनातनम्।
दुदोह यज्ञसिद्ध्यर्थमृग्यजु सामलक्षणम्।।

According to the mantras, the Supreme soul at the inception of the creation after giving birth to human beings, through Agni and the four Supreme sages, made the four Vedas available to Brahma and from that very Brahma, sage named Agni (Fire), Vayu ( Air), Aditya (Sun) and Angira, took over Rig, Yaju, Sam and Atharva Veda. With the knowledge of these Vedas they illumined other scholars and by their treatises Brahmans came to be. **छंदों ब्रह्मणानि च तद्विषयाणि।**' (Ashta.4.2.65) This is a Paaniniya sutra. This makes it clear that the Vedic Mantras has different parts and Brahmans, which are the exposition part of them. These expositions take up the scripture's veneration process to disclose scientific and spiritual mysteries. In the present times only 18 Brahmana scriptures are available, out of which, Shatpath, Tandeya, Aittireya and Taittreya are considered the main ones.

The last portion of Brahmans is called **Aranyak.** This part is known as Aranyak because it was created by sages residing in ashrams in the jungle. It has symbolic exposition of yagnas. In number they are only 8 today. The important ones among these are, Ettiriya, Shakhyayan, Taittiriya, Brihadaranyak, Jemini and Chhandogya.

In the Vedic literature, next to the Vedas are **Upanishads,** exposing the ardent spiritual feelings and philosophical brilliance of the people of Arya race. Upanishads introduce, deep self- contemplation, along with high standards of sacredness, compulsions and honesty. By means of interactive talks between the teachers and the pupils, teachings have been given to hold relevance for all. Questions on spirituality, philosophy, related to the other world have been raised and the dutiful code of conduct of superior people also has been explained at great lengths. It is mainly in question-answer form, or that is its way of expression. By means of lectures, knowledgeable facts have been discussed and knowledge is imparted, that is why it is apt to be known as Upanishad. Upanishads are also called Vedant as they are the essence of knowledge of the Vedas. Swami Dayanand and other great beings like Shankaracharya have accepted it as proven and authentic. As Dayanand wrote his treatises on the Vedas, likewise, Shankaracharya also gifted the Indian people with price less gift of his treatises written on the Upanishads. Authentic Upanishads are considered 11 in number, with their names as, Ish, Ken, Kath, Prashna, Mundak, Mandukya, Taittreya, Aitareya, Chhandogya, Brihadaranyak and Shwetashwatar. Impressed by the profound teachings of the Upanishads, Mahatma Gandhi expressed his joy by saying, "Whatever has been said in the Vedic literature has its essence in the first mantra of Ishavasyopanishad :

'ईशावास्यमिदं सर्वं यत् किञ्च जगत्यां जगत्।
तेन त्यक्तेन भुंजीथा, मा गृधः कस्यस्विद्धनम् ।।'

Gandhiji contended that, if the entire Indian literature got destroyed, except this one mantra, then also, on the foundation of this very mantra, once again the structure of Vedic culture can be re-established.

Gandhiji's exclamations throw light on the truth, that many streams of the world civilization reached their culmination flowing along with the Vedas, have disappeared in the desert of time. But the source stream of Indian culture was the only one which continued to flow unobstructed. Every Indian ought to be proud of his wealth of Vedic literature. Witnessing a beautiful synthesis of unity in diversity, worldliness and other worldliness, a holistic, equal-ratio development of life, creating feeling of oneness between the Aryans and the non-Aryans through a mode of synthesis, a beautiful adjustment of individuality and society, from the point of view of spiritual way of life, in the Vedic times, all were enjoying the silver age of cultural development. Actual values like, non- violence, sacrifice, oneness in element (तत् त्वम असि) and the concept of the entire Earth being one single family, (वसुधैव कुटुंबकम्) traced their origin to Vedic literature.

## Chapter 4
# Swarajya in Vedic Literature

In the folios written so far, the concept of Dharma, in the Vedic literature, Smriti, Niti and other scriptures has been discussed at micro and macro level and after a graphic view of the Vedic literature, under the political tradition in ancient India, how Dharma was adhered to and how the underlying values were assimilated, characterised, needs to be discussed at great length. More so, if we take into account, the present social scenario, political system and the occurring of events at the international level, it is of great topical value to establish the supremacy of the Vedas.

Dharma bound kingdom, Swarajya or self-government, people's welfare and policy matters like, 'the world being one family' (Vasudhaivkutumbkam) reverberate from the Vedic verses but instead of being just satisfied with their statement, at present the endeavour ought to be for assimilating them in the Indian Constitution, so as to make it richer, error-free and a ruling system, that is harbinger of welfare of all, is auspicious, can be established, its complete knowledge will have to be obtained. This is the very purpose of this book.

**The conscious form of the element of Dharma -**

Dr. Sarvpalli Radhakrishnan, who contemplated profoundly on important subjects like, ancient Indian culture, values in life, Vedic knowledge, education, before expressing his views in words, accepts the fact that "the root of our progress is our ancient civilization. The revered foundation pillars that uphold this civilization have their connection in the main Upanishads. Today, when we are going to commence building a new age for life in our country, we will have to invoke a new life within us to flow, and for that again we will have to revert to the very same Upanishads. The Upanishads have those very basic elements hidden, which have since the beginning of the primal times, structured our history, till date.

The moment questions arise on Dharma in the Vedic literature, we are reminded of the following shloka of 'Brihadaranyak Upanishad, which unveils the curtain over this mystery-

'ओम पूर्णमदः पूर्णमिदं पूर्णात्पूर्णमुदच्यते ।
पूर्णस्य पूर्णमादाय पूर्णमेवावशिष्यते । ।' (5.1.1)

"This Creator is whole and complete, this universe is also complete, from the complete Creator emanates a complete universe. Having got completed from the complete whole, even after the universe is created, the Creator remains a complete whole and intact." Meaning thereby, the Vedic dharma or dutifulness is all pervasive and indivisible. In the mantra mentioned above, the meaning of Brahma is informer of the Vedas. 'ओउम–खं–ब्रह्म'makes it very clear that 'kha' means- Brahma- has emanated from the sky and Veda. It implies in every way a storehouse of knowledge. In a mantra from Kenopnishad, 'तस्यै तपो दमः कर्मेति प्रतिष्ठाः वेदाः सर्वाङ्गणानि सत्यमायतनम् । ।' (4.8) There is a sermon for each human being, that whoever acquires knowledge of the creator, his fame depends on three things—practice of asceticism, regulation of breath and action. On the foundation of these three combined the bulky structure can stand. This bulky structure is the Vedas, its parts and through their combining the truth that emanates. This way thus, 'tap' denotes physical control, 'dam' means mental control and 'karma' means hard work (selfless deeds) will combine to form the foundation of a magnificent structure, that would appear, that will be the truth emanating from the summing up of Vedic knowledge and science.

## Manav Dharma and Dutiful Acts

In the first chapter of the Brihadaranyak Upanishad, this mantra gives a sermon regarding Varna system and Ashram System-

'त्रयो वेदा एत एव वागेवर्गवेदो मनो यजुर्वेदः प्राणः सामवेदः । (1.5.5)

Among the three Vedas, Rigveda be treated as speech, Yajurveda as the mind, Sama Veda as life. Rigveda represents the canto of knowledge, Yajurveda represents the canto of action, and the Sama Veda represents the canto of veneration and prayer. In the seven numbered mantra, these three have been given the simile of mother-father and subjects. The inner meaning of this mantra in a way directs each human being towards his duties, that according to the voice of the Veda, what is appropriate be adopted, with self- cleansing endeavour to abide by a human's dutifulness or Dharma. In the sixth chapter of this Upanishad a very interesting mention of the naming ceremony has been given.

'अथ अस्य नाम करोति वेदोऽसीति तदस्य तद्गुह्यमेव नाम भवति ।।
(6.4.26)

It has been instructed that before giving a newborn a worldly name, the parents must recite, you are a manifestation of the Vedas, a form of knowledge. This mantra denotes that the child ought to adopt the truth and increase his knowledge, and in future to be able to meet each one of his obligations, as one who adopts the truth or Dharma, meaning thereby the Veda, is never distracted from the path of duty. Brihadaranyak Upanishad instructs all-

'दाम्यत–दत्त–दयध्वम्' (5.2.3)

'Suppress your senses, while collecting worldly objects, give them in charity, be merciful for human beings. The entire worldly education is about these three Ds-daman, daan, daya-

'त्रयं शिक्षेत् दमं दानं दयामिति ।' (5.2.3)

According to the instructions mentioned above, it will have to be assimilated that, for effective ruling of the state, making it a duty bound state, work in accordance with Dharma, which is possible by practicing (दम, दान,दया), that is self-control, charity and mercifulness, which the ruler and the subjects ought to act in accordance with, as laid down in the Dharma. They rule while rising in Dharma, which develops continuously. Going opposite to Dharma, is bound to doom. In

Brihadaranyak Upanishad, the first chapter of fourth Brahman mantra 11, the sages warn- One who disregards the tenets of 'Brahma' dharma, has to partake the sin of' Kshatra' dharma.

The said mantra points towards Raj dharma. This mantra conveys, though the king is seated on an uplifted throne but the Dharma is above it. For this reason, the seat of the king is called the seat of Dharma (dutifulness). Meaning thereby, whoever dutifully serves the subjects, maintains his subjects in Varnaashram, Dharma and all along protecting the tenets of Dharma, rules to impart justice, he enjoys kingship.

Brihadaranyak Upanishad, while declaring the mantra, 'धर्म तदेतत् क्षत्रस्य क्षत्रं' (1.4.14) states in detail that, it is for the Raj Dharma to ensure that all the four Varnas are not allowed to get distracted from their duties. There is nothing superior to Dharma. A weakling on following this Dharma is enabled to bring a powerful one under his control. A question has been asked further, What is this Dharma? Clarifying it the sage has said, truth (satya) is dharma. One who talks of dharma, is said to be telling the truth.

In the Vedas and Upanishad, dharma in the form of truth is considered justice. Dharma that was meant to be in the form of justice, law or ordinance, is related to the concept of the constant. The constant is certainly regulatory. In this reference Maxmuller explains, "that which despite having substantial curvature goes through the entire area of nature like a straight line, is known as the concept of Rit or the constant, this is straight, clear and the correct line. It normally means natural law or ethical law. Our life is based on this law and on it we can rely. It is a law that our inner self, resonates with the voice divine, that 'it is constant', 'it is correct,' it is the truth."

'ऋतस्य दृढ़ाहा धरूणानि सन्ति
पुरुणि चंद्रा वपुषे वपूंषि ।।

(Rig. 4.23.9)

According to the said verse of the Veda, the form of dharma is extensive. It makes the soul euphoric. It pushes the human being on the path of justice. It is also clarified in the mantra that a person who does not follow dutiful conduct for attainment of the truth, is deprived of the reward.

With reference to Dharma the concept that the Dharma is supreme and complete, it is the crown of entire universal organization, gains strength. In the Vedas Dharma is told to be beyond time, place and duration. Meaning thereby Dharma is unending, (Anantvaivedah) all pervasive, eternal and is without defect, it is important in itself. For every important act it is the underlying element. In the Brihadaranyak Upanishad it has been very beautifully narrated, that Dharma is loved by the entire world, like honey.

'अयं धर्मः सर्वेषां भूतानां मध्वस्त धर्मस्य सर्वाणि भूतानि मधु (2.5.11)

Thereafter, it is said that Dharma is the truth (satya), meaning thereby, it is the reality. That is the element of the foundation of this world. It gives the entire world a message of humanity and soul condition.

**Republican System**

The head of the Republic has been invoked in the Rig Veda in the following words-

गणानां त्वा गणपतिं हवामहे कविं कवीनामुपमश्रवस्तमम् ।
ज्येष्ठराजं ब्रह्मणां ब्रह्मणरपत आ नः शृण्वन् तिभिः सीद सादनम् ।।

(2.23.1)

The Head of the Republic, we invoke you. Among the valiant you are the most valiant. Your fame is exemplary. You are the biggest king. You are Brahmanaspati. You listen to our invocation, and take your seat in our national house, for protecting us with all your strength and competence. This mantra is evidential of the prevalence of a rich republican system in ancient India.

In the ancient India there has been a tradition of republicanism or democracy. For republic the technical word is 'gan'. What can be a greater proof of the word 'gan' being ancient, than the fact, it has been used 46 times in Rig Veda, 9 times in Brahman scriptures, many a time it has been used at various places. In the eighteenth chapter of Shukla Yajurveda, there are five such mantras (10-14), which have five titles, mentioned appropriate for ruling. In the example given below, it appears that once upon a time different kings were selected for the purpose of administration, each geographical direction that indicates towards divinity in the sphere, for all those directions, different rulers ruled. Rajan is related to the east direction and Vasus **'राज्यस प्राची दिग्वसवस्ते'** (Indra and Vishnu deity, five natural elements and the Sun, Moon and the stars). 'Virat' is related with the southern direction and the Rudras **'विराङसि दक्षिणा दिग्रुदद्रास्ते'** (deity of wind and storm), Swarat is related with the north direction and Marutas **'सम्राडसि प्रतीचि दीगादित्यास्ते'** (sons of storm God Rudra and Prisni), Samrat was related to the west direction and the Adityas **'स्वराडस्युदीचि दिङ् मरुतस्ते'** (12 adityas, son of Aditi and Kashyap) Adhipati related to the upward area and vishwadevas-**अधिपत्यसि बृहती दिग्विश्वे ।**

In the hymns of Shukla Yajurveda the kings of different directions have been described but the areas ruled are not mentioned. In the Etreya Brahmand 8.14 (Huang vol) along with prevalent ruling titles, specific areas have been described while narrating the coronation of Indra. This description helps us reach the conclusion that for each direction and area, before selecting competent persons for handing over the obligation of ruling, their qualities were taken into consideration. Thereafter, they were coronated and a person selected for coronation was made to take a vow- The king of the Eastern direction on being coronated in the kingdom be known as Samrajya, in the southern direction truthful kings were coronated while dining, so were known as 'Bhoj'. In the west all the kings of nichya and upachya were coronated for self- governments, for this reason were known as 'swarajya.' The land of Vishwadevas, that is the upper northern direction meaning thereby the janpadas on the Himalayas, who were coronated for promotion of austerity (Vairajya) came to be known as Viraj. Likewise, in the buffer area, the rulers were known as Sarvochcha, and the dynasties of Kuru Panchal along with those coronated in Ushinar rajyas were known as 'Rajan'.

In the Urdhalok, (Marut and Angiras) titles like Parameshthya, Maharajya and Swavasya adopted by compe-tent and scholarly administrators, were coronated as rulers. Each area was itself small, also from the point of view of the population in it. Therefore, for such areas, it seems 'Ganpatis' were appointed.

The description given above, can be clarified by the following mantra of the Etrey Brahman-

स य इद्देदेवविद् क्षत्रियमयम्। 1. सर्वाजितीर्जयेत 2. अयं सर्वान् लोकान् विन्देत 3. अयं सर्वेषां राज्ञांश्रेष्ठयमतिष्ठां परमतां गच्छेत स्वति साम्राज्यं भौज्यं, स्वाराज्यं, वैराज्यं, पारमेष्ठ्यं, राज्यं, महाराज्यं, आधिपत्यं 4. अयं सामन्तपर्यायी स्रात्, सार्वभौमः, आन्ताद् आ पराधाद्, पृथिव्यै समुद्रपर्यन्ताया एकराद् इति।। (8.15)

The above mentioned, shloka, apart from giving information regarding different types of rulers, also expresses the possibility of the all expansive, whole of Earth, all beings ought to have a long lived master (sarvayush), meaning thereby all beings living on the Earth be independent. In Rig Veda (3.11.3-4) Sarvayush word is used as Shatayush for hundred times capable person. 'Sarvochcha' be their protector, a topmost harbinger of well- being. Thus, peace and happiness will prevail.

Brahman scriptures can be dated back to 1000 BC. During that time, from the prosperity of the republican states it can be conjectured that this system of ruling was prevalent much before that time also. Like the Etrey Brahman, in Taittiriya Brahman the organization of Swaraj was thus-

य एवं विद्वान् वाजपेयेन यजति, गच्छति स्वाराज्यं, अग्रं समानं पर्यति, तिष्ठन्तैऽस्मै ज्येष्ठाय।। (1.3.23)

In the said mantra 'jyeshtha,' connotes the oldest or the 'ganpati' or the President of the republic.

The Shatpath Brahman is divided in 100 chapters, hence it

is called the Shatpath Brahman. In it we get extensive information regarding the contemporary western states in those times, like Gandhar, Kaikaya, Kaushal and Videh and so on, also their rulers and kingdoms. The knowledge of Raja Parikshit and times much later than him in Indian history, is discerned from Brahman scriptures.

In the ancient Indian literature, there are innumerable descriptions which narrate the system of ruling of many kings simultaneously at the same time. V.P Verma opines,[15] that those scholars who have formed a concept of a rule characteristic of uncontrolled, religiosity and despotism, would be surprised to know that in ancient India there were republican institutions. According to Dr Jaiswal,[16] 'The Hindu Republic is a strong example of traditional community self-governance. The description of The Hindu states with various forms of governance, is a great chapter in the constitutional history of humankind. Bandopadhyaya says,[17] the study of these republics is interesting and it is proved by evidence, that in ancient India, from the stand point of divine reigns of ruling held in the hands of one person, pluralistic political discipline developed chronologically. The detailed descriptions of developed forms of these republics are available to us in Buddhist and Jain literature, also in Kautilya's Artha Shastra.

The most important and most logical contention is that the political system, meaning thereby, the republican way of ruling, had its seeds hidden in ancient institutions, as time passed, at many places they developed a strong hold. Initially, the Vedic 'Jan' and 'Kul' were united. Here Kula is not related to gotra. Kula, means the organisation with certain

---

[15] V.P. Verma, Studies in Hindu Political Thought and its Metaphysical Foundations P 31

[16] K.P. Jaiswal, Hindu Polity, p. 21

[17] N.C.Bandopadhyaya, Development of Hindu Polity and Political theorics, p. 239

number of people. Though they were connected on the basis of blood relationship, yet members of communities were independent and local sovereigns. They were consecutively known by words like, 'Gan' 'Vrat' and 'Vishah' and so on. In the republics of the Vedic times, feelings of reverence and love of the nation, also seemed to prevail.

## Chart of Vedic ruling-arrangement (Analysis)

| Circumstance | System | Head | Dakshini | Tantra |
|---|---|---|---|---|
| 1. Pranya | a. No system | No head | No | Sahmati |
| 2. Kabila | b. family (Garhpatya) | Grihi Grihpati, family head | No | Sahmati |
| 3. Gram | Ahvaniya | Gram nipati Adhipati (Village Head) | No | Sahmati |
| 4. Pur-Puri Jila | Sakshidagni | Mahapaur (King) | Dakshna | Both |
| 5. Prant Pradesh | Sabha | Swarat | Dakshina | Both type |
| 6. Rashta-Desh | Sabha-Samiti | Samrat | Dakshina | Both type Tantra |
| 7. Vishwa | Amantran | Brihaspati Vishvavar | Sada Dakshina | Not Elected |

The time from the Rig Veda to Atharva Veda is the time evident of expansion and development of the republican system, which is the glowing history of love for independence, devotion for the nation among the Aryans. As the ' Prithvi Sukta' of the Atharva Veda stands for an unparalleled love for the nation among the Aryans, so is Yajur Veda's mantra, 'वयं राष्ट्रे जागृयाम पुरोहिताः' a loud declaration of self-government. Each one of the state's parameters, has been a fine example of self-government. That was the basic life thread of all the ruling systems of the Aryans.

According to, 'गणा मे तृप्यताम्' only in a republic this feeling can be fully satiated. In the Atharva Veda mantras (kand 8 Sukta 10) are equivocal on the inception and expansion of the republican system, there are special descriptions of constituting organizations like, Gahapatya, Aahvaniya, Dakshinagni, Sabha-Samiti and Amantran and the peak of patriotism.

विराड् वा इदमग्र आसीत् तस्यां जातायाः सर्वमविभेद् इयमेवेदं
भविष्यतीति । ।1 । ।

सा उद्क्रामत् सा गार्हपत्ये न्यक्रामत् । । 2 । ।

सा उद्क्रामत् साक्राहवनीये न्यक्रामत् । । 4 । ।

सा उद्क्रामत् सा दक्षिणाग्नौ न्यक्रामत् । । 6 । ।

सा उद्क्रामत् सा सभायां न्यक्रामत् । । 8 । ।

सा उद्क्रामत् सा समितौ न्यक्रामत् । । 10 । ।

सा उद्क्रामत् सामंत्रणे न्यक्रामत् । । 12 । ।

A state without a ruler (Viraj Avastha)- सागार्हपत्ये न्य क्रामत् (Sagaarhpatye Nyakramat-2)

Before electing leader of the nation, only subjects were there. Life was being spent in a state of uncertainty. In this condition of the state without a ruler, the conjugal relationship of husband and wife led to the creation of family. Husband and wife both, were considered the head of the family. They both had equal rights on their domestic possessions. Husband wife and children cooperated to make domestic arrangements, protection of the house and began to rule in the house. This came to be known as an organization of family headship.

Organization of Gram-Sabha- साहवनीयेन्यक्रामत् (Sahava-niyenyakramat-4) After the organization of family headship, organization through invocation (Ahvaniya) developed. In the word Ahvaniya, there are two sections, aa and ha. On joining aa+ha means to invoke or call. Some intelligent, though fear-stricken people, placed the proposal of forming a village Sabha, before the family heads residing close by and consequently established it. This Gram-Sabha later developed into the Village Assembly. And the Assembly in its expanded peak form came to be known as Council of Ministers. The arrangement related to Gram-Sabha was known as Ahvaneey, and head of the village was known as 'Gramani" (Yaju.15.15) In the form of a leader this 'Gramani' was obliged to protect the village.

Janpad (Jila System) Dakshinagni सादक्षिणाग्नौ न्यक्रामत् (Sadakshinagnau-nyakramat-6)

The chief of the village arrangements had no perks. When many villages together formed a community (puri) or a Zilla, then the organizational work increased and for that reason, the leader or the foremost chief (Agnia) was elected and it was decided to pay him for his portfolio. That is why this arrangement was named Dakshinagni. This very organization also known as Puri, with its chief known as Mahapaur or Raja (the king).

It is mentioned in the terminology (Nirukt)- 'अग्निः अग्रणीः।' 'Agnih, Agranih' meaning thereby, Agnih means Agrani, the leader. Through Yajur Veda we came to know that the organization of Dakshinagni consisted of clever and wise people in each village. With welfare Dakshinagni organization there seems to be an outburst of another system.

Provincial organization -Vidhansabha सा संभायां न्यक्रामत् ( Sa Sabhayam Nyakramat-8)

Due to competition among Janpads (Zilla) or Puris,

disorganization began, then after giving thought and holding consultations the organization that came into being was known as Prant or Sabha. It was ruled by Vidhansabha, the chief was called Ekraat or Swaraat (king).

The rule of the Prant or Pradesh ( the state) was carried on by one advisory Sabha (council) But the ruling system of groups of many states, country or the nation seemed to require two advisory councils. The mantra of Atharva Veda cited is here-

सम्राडसि–असुराणां ककुन्मनुष्याणाम् ।
देवानामर्धभागंसि त्वमेकवृषो भव ।। (6.86.3)

Rashtra Sabha + Samiti System

सा संमितौन्य क्रामत् ( Sa Samitaunyakramat-10)

Under one ruler there were two councils. One was for the town, city or suburb, that took care of the internal organization for the security of its citizens. Its members were known as Sabhya, they arranged for education, medical treatment management and tax collection. For external invasion and war management a committee was formed. It was to work for protecting from the enemy's invasion, suppression and destruction of those who repeatedly invaded or caused encroachment. Thus, it is obvious that for the state organization there was only the Vidhansabha but for the national organization, along with the Vidhansabha, formation of other committees, was considered essential. In the Atharva Veda (7.1.1,2), the king while addressing the Sabha and its members says, 'You educate me, counsel me," be one voice with me, help in management of ruling the state." The description of the Sabha intimates that the formation of the Council was a high-level national organization. The Atharva Veda calls the Sabha or the Council,' narishta', which means nri +ishta or nar + ishta, meaning thereby, it was considered as deity by men or one who is loved by men or subjects, one formed by the subjects wilful consent. This includes, representatives elected by the subjects. In this reference the

Atharva Veda says-

आ त्वा गन्राष्ट्रं सह वर्चसोदिहि
प्राङ् विश्ज्ञांपतिरेकराट् त्वं वि राज। (3.4.1)
त्वांविशो वृणतां राज्याय त्वामिमाःप्रदिशः पञ्च देवीः।
वर्ष्मन्राष्ट्रस्य ककुदि श्रयस्व ततो न उग्रो विभजा वसूनि।। (3.4.2)

साऽमन्त्रेण न्यक्रामत् (Saa Mantren Nyakramat-12)

**Invitation System**

Under the Vedic rule, there is mention of an organization on invitation. The reason behind calling it 'Amantran organization is that its representatives were not permanent. All the states were invited. 'Aa' means state representatives, from all over gathered for counselling in a ruling committee, that was treated as the Amantran Meeting Committee. The representatives of 'Amantran Committee' were not paid any perks. Due to arising of differences and argumentativeness, there were mutual compromises and through medium of conferences, international organizations were formed. This was called in Vedic diction, 'Amantran Organizations.' From the modern eye it can be seen as being fit to be called Nations Organization. According to the Vedas, the Chief of Nations Organization of Amantran was given the name of Vishvavar Brihaspati or Vishwaraat.

स आ नो योनिं सदतु प्रेष्ठो
बृहस्पतिर्विश्ववारो यो अस्ति।
कामो रायः सुवीर्यस्य तं दात्
पर्षन्नो अतिसश्चतो अरिष्टान्।।

(Rig.7.97.4)

All the nations of the world nominate (Vishvavarah) the dearest Vishwaraat Brihaspati, for getting a seat in this international forum, and through the working of the Amantran Committee, save all the nations from enmity with one another, and fulfil their monetary and other aspirations related to gaining power. This Sukta, is about the importance of the Brihaspati and directions for his duty of making arrangement of foodstuff in his friendly nations, as such, referring to him as Shuchi, Shatpatra, Palak or father like nurturer, Anaga, Sukhvarshak (harbinger of happiness) destroyer of enmities, leader of the armed forces and king of the universe. This international organization of nations formulated by the Vedas, expresses a high sentiment of democracy in the world.

In the RigVeda (10-166.4,5,131.3,4) also a similar depiction of the Vedic King and form of the Kingdom is available. At different places through the medium of Vedic verses, Sabha- Samitis have been referred to. Its members have been called, Sabhya and Sabhasad. The Committee (Samiti) has been considered superior to the assembly (Sabha) and therefore, has been declared to be nationally important. When nations unite with the intention of mutual security and protection, to form a United Nations, then the king of this United Nations is provided an institution formed to help by counselling him, which is known as Veda Samiti. With the intention of maintaining a fault free ruling system, ancient political thinkers have been said to have formed and systematized, a Veda Samiti and Rashtra Samiti, governed by the regulations of the Dharma. To make the king knowledgeable about commitment to the prescribed regulations, related to ruling the kingdom and to make a sound timely arrangement, it was imperative for the king to follow the instructions of Sabha and Samiti.

**Elected, Controlled Adhering to Dharma Self-Government**

In the Vedic national organization, there is no mention of kings from the dynastic tradition. In the Vedas there is special stress on the king's election. Along with the mantras giving description of elections, there are mantras which exhibit the fear, the fear of being deposed. If an arrangement for being elected to rule and getting deposed, was in prevalence, it could be taken to be a democracy or a system of people's rule, then we will have to accept that the system prescribed by the Vedas had democratic values fully preserved.

'त्वां विशो वृणतां राज्याय।' (Atharva : 3.4.2) The Veda through this verse states- To rule, the subjects ought to elect you.

There is another mantra of the same sort- 'विशस्त्वा सर्वा वाञ्छन्तु' (Atharva 4.8.4, 3.4.2,6.87.1) meaning thereby, all your subjects should love you. This description makes it evident that, according to the Vedas the right to give consent in electing the king rested with individuals, irrespective of gender, be it a woman or man, wealthy or poor, all had a right to give their consent. Atharva Veda reiterates- 'मा त्वद्राष्ट्र-मधिभ्रशत्।' (6.87.1) O King! May we not be compelled to snatch away your right to rule. There is another mantra reiterating the democratic sentiment-

'स विशोऽनुव्यचलत्।'

'तं सभा च समितिश्च सेना च सुरा चानुव्यचलन्। (15.9.1.2)

The Assembly- Council, defence forces, royal treasury, only cooperate with the king, who works in accordance with the opinion of the subjects.

In the Vedic times, the collective strength of the subjects is known to be 'Vish'. It was 'Vish', that selected the most able person amongst them as 'Vishpati'. Sometimes Vishpati or the king's successors were also appointed leaders of the nation but they were coronated only after seeking the approval of the 'Vish.' In the Yajurveda the approval sought from the subjects is called,'Varana Utsav'. After the 'Varana', the 'Vishpati or the King used to take an oath of protecting the nation and its aggrandisement. On conducting himself contrary to this oath, the king was deposed. There are many mantras related to the coronations of kings in the Atharva Veda. In the minds of Vedic Aryans, was the ennobling sentiment of 'most secretive royal duty' that sounds clear in the Veda mantras. In the instant arrangement, the subjects rights were not restricted to the extent of the king's selection but after nominating him also, the king was made aware of his duties. The mantra named, 'Shatpath's Rajyarohan,'establishes the peak of subject's all pervasive say in matters of importance.

इयं ते राष्ट्र। यंतसि यमनः।
ध्रुवो सिधरुणः। कृव्यैत्व क्षेमायत्वा।
रथयैत्वा पोषयत्वा साधवेत्वा। 1।

This means, the entire nation is being handed over to you, from today you are the ruler and the supreme authority of the nation. You have patience, you are strong. For improving agriculture, advancement of the subjects, their happiness and nurturing and for the wellbeing of all, you are to take care of the nation. After the declaration of coronation, the king would take an oath before the entire community of people present there-

"Members of the Assembly, while accepting the obligetions, imposed on me by you, I am feeling greatly honoured, I take an oath, that if ever I go in contradiction against my subjects, supersede the directives of the Council, then the subjects have a right to deprive me of my life's fruits of noble deeds, progenies and all the comforts I enjoy.' Hereafter, when the ruling rod (Rajdand) was placed in the king's hands, a slight hit with it was also given on the king's back. This ritual was indicative of the reality, that if there would be default in duty, even the king would not be absolved of punishment. In the end, while offering his salutation to the Mother Earth, the king used to seek the Council's support.

In the AtharvaVeda Samhita, there are Mantras expressing this purpose-

सभा च मा समितिश्चावतां प्रजापतेर्दुहितरौ संविदाने।
येना संगच्छा उपमा स शिक्षाच्चारु वदानि पितरः सङ्गतेषु।। ( 7.12.1)

"The Samiti and Sabha be conducive to be inclined towards me. They may counsel me, help me, educate me. O elder ones, I will be soft- spoken, before them."

The Veda mantra accepts the fact that Sabha and Samiti, plays a predominant role in ruling the state. Keeping it in mind the king requests that he should be capable of commanding support from everyone, they should hold the same voice as mine. Sabha and Samiti are like two daughters of Prajapati, I ought never disregard them. After seeking their complete support, I should be like the supreme elevator of the entire nation, be non- deceitful in completing the task.

The prime acts in the Atharva Veda are associated with national glory in this mantra-

ये ग्रामा यदरण्यं याः सभा अधि भूम्याम्।
ये संग्रामाः समितयस्तेषु चाः वदेम ते।। (12.1.56)

It means, the Sabha and Samitis that are there in the village, forest and war, ought to perform important tasks, and their praise be sung on the Earth all over. It can be expressed thus, that the state assembly, Dharma assembly for justice, assembly for religious matters should work in the national interest. This mantra once again reiterates, that the Assemblies and Committees were arrangements to assist. The institution named Sabha (Assembly) performed tasks related to imparting of justice. In this connection the following mantra is mentionable-

विदम् ते सभे नाम नरिष्टा नाम वा असि।
ये ते के च सभादस्ते मे सन्तु सवाचसः।। (7.12.2)

In the above noted mantra of Atharva Veda, Sabha has been addressed as 'Narishta' (revered as divine by men). Its other arrangement has been described by Sayanacharya in these words-Where many gather, opine unanimously, it ought not be contravened by others, as it is non-controversial. For this reason, it is called 'Narisht' or divine for the people. The Sabha getting an adjective of 'Narishta' makes it clear that its decisions possibly, can never face being overrun. In the Rigveda, (10.71.10) an adjective for Sabha is, 'किल्विष स्पृत्' 'Kilvish Sprit', which means reformer of sin or crime. While imparting justice in the Sabha its assembly members may get prone to do injustice or sin, therefore, in the YajurVeda (20.17) there is mention of a prayer for getting absolved of a sin committed while working as a member of the Sabha. In a mantra of the Rig Veda it is said-

'भद्रें गृहं कृणुथ भद्रवाचो वृहद्वो वय उच्यते सभासु।' (6.28.6)

You make your home debonair, your speech be courteous, and you remain in the Sabha, till the end of time.

In the Mandal 2 of the Rig Veda, there is mention of a competent Brahmin-

'उताशिष्टा अनुश्पृण्वन्ति वह्नयः सभेयो विप्रो भरते मतो धना।। (1.24.13)

This mantra informs that the members of the Sabha were called 'Sabhey'. It was a well organised institution. It is evident that in the Rig Vedic times, the Indian states and districts, a high-level advisory institution had already developed, in the form of Sabha.

Like the Sabha (Assembly), the Rig Veda has mention of Samiti (Committee) at many places. Although what exactly was the difference between the two is not clear, but by following the mantras, the scholars of ancient thought have reached the conclusion, that Samiti was a bigger institution in comparison with the Sabha, it represented to the entire 'Vish' or the subjects. Possibly all the village heads from various villages within the nation assembled in it. Few of the prominent personalities of the 'Vish'- Soot, Rathkar and other craft persons used to be present in it. The king also attended the Samiti. The Chairperson of the Samiti was called Ishan. The Sabha was attended by important people other than Samiti members. Sabha only acted as the nation's highest judicial office.

The descriptions of the institutions named Sabha -Samiti, makes the fact clear that, on various subjects, conclusive decision were arrived at by them and arguments were carried out. The members were scholars, eloquent spokesmen and philosophers. After consultations, important decisions were endeavoured to be unanimous. This is the reason that enabled the king to have stable sovereignty, it was considered necessary for the Samiti to adhere to him and it was an accepted fact that if the king tried to be arbitrary, then the Samiti would not adhere to him. This aspect is conveyed in the following mantra of Atharvaveda-

'ध्रुवाय ते समितिः कल्पतामिहं' । (6.88.3)
'नास्मै समितिः कल्पते न मित्रं नयते वशम्' । (5.19.15)

The thoughts directed in the Vedic literature, do not leave any doubt that in the Vedic age kingdoms, institutions named Sabha and Samiti enjoyed sovereignty, which played a very important part in the royal administration. Samiti was an institution of the entire 'विशः' ('Vish'), that selected the king, opined on subjects of royal concern, the people's consent was expressed. The Sabha in addition, dealt with imparting of justice. Kul mukhiyas, the oldest Patriarch also advised King on important subjects. Once on holding the royal position, due to his attributes and qualities, the king was expected to attract the attention of the members of the Sabha on the relevant subjects and fulfil the obligations.

The basic inspirational strength of the kingdom was the inner unity, high grandeur of the Samiti, as evident in the Vedic literature, which makes it clear that the democratic royal organization's ideal was people's welfare and was competent to embody it, in its extensive ambit. The king and the subject both were to be aware of their duties and rights, be unanimous with a single motto in driving the chariot of the nation, consistently to new levels of prosperity and made endeavours in body and spirit, maintaining equal credit, to establish peace and people's welfare. The king would run the administration after seeking advice of his assistants. This sentiment predominated in the country almost till the Gupta Age. The kings who arbitrarily defied people's interest and individual's pervasive freedom, was not only deprived of his kingship of the kingdom, but hard punishments were also inflicted upon him. We come across many such examples in the ancient ruling system. When the king defied the Samiti which was like a daughter to the people, the king got into conflict with his subjects. The wrath of Vish ( subjects) burnt the king and men with knowledge formed new rules-regulations and nominated a dutybound person as the king.

The relationship of the king and the Samiti was one of mutual respect, which made it clear, that the Aryans were deeply experienced as far as the natural degeneration of the royal power went. Afraid of the Samiti's wrath and disharmony, the king requests the members of the Sabha, 'O members of the Sabha, 'I request all of you to immediately, bring back your distracted mind towards me. Let your mind once again trust me, this is what I wish'.

In a mantra of RigVeda-

इन्द्रो राजा जगतश्चर्षणीनामधिक्षमि विषुरूपं यदस्ति। (7.27.3)

Though the Sabhapati had greater rights than his assistants, his consent was of greatest value, but he could not override his assistants and ministers counselling him, as these assistants and counsellors were nominated. They had the right to depose their chief and declare any other competent person their leader. To remain in the royal position the directives to be followed are narrated in the Rig Vedic verses thus-

आ त्वा हार्षमन्तरेधि ध्रुवस्तिष्ठाविः चाचलिः।
विशस्त्वा सर्वा वाञ्छन्तु मा त्वद्राष्ट्रमधिभ्रशत्।
इहैवैधि मा पच्योष्ठाः पर्वत इवांविचाचलिः।
इन्द्रइवेह ध्रुवस्तिष्ठेह राष्ट्रमुधारय।। (10.173.1,2)

In the said mantra there is description of remaining stable (Dhruva) in the position five times, without being deposed. This makes it clear that if during the rule, the nation gets corrupted, degenerates, then the ruler can be changed. This arrangement is known to be a form of democratic system. There should not be an iota of doubt in it.

Atharva Veda expresses a wish—

ध्रुवोऽच्युतेः प्रमृणीहि शत्रूञ्छत्रूयतोऽधरान्पादयस्व।
सर्वादिशः संमनसः सध्रीचीर्ध्रुवाय ते समितिः कल्पतामिह।। (6.88.3)

Our leader should remain stable in his time, be able to depose his enemies. The subjects be happy with him in every way. May he never have a difference of opinion with the Samiti on war. They only keep him permanently. In this mantra of Atharva Veda, the king has been directed to rule according to the tenets of Dharma, at the time of his coronation. The truth of his nomination is also revealed that the king's stability is dependent on remaining in the good books of his subjects. In the Vedas, the attributes and duties of the king have been narrated in more than hundred mantras, out of which the following verses of the Rik are notable –

राजा शमस्य च शृगिणो वज्रबाहुः।
मरान न नेमिः परिता बभूव।।

(Rig.1.32.15)

स घा राजा सत्पतिः यः शासमिन्वति।।

(Rig.1.54.7)

राजा हि कं भुवनानामभि श्रीः।
वैश्वानरो यतते सूर्येण।।

(Rig.1.98.1)

राजा ससाद विद्थानि साधन्।
अग्निर्विश्वानि काव्यानि विद्वान।।

(Rig.3.1.18)

अयं मित्रो नमस्यः सुशेवो राजा सुक्षत्रो अजनिष्ट वेधाः।
तस्य वयं सुमतौ स्याम यज्ञियस्यापि भद्रे सौमनसे स्याम।।

(Rig.3.59.4)

The adjectives used for Varun (God of waters) Indra (God of war and thunderstorms), Agni (God of Fire) Surya (The Sun), Brihaspati (The sage who counsels Gods) and other deities, the duties and rights of the king are identified in the Vedic verses. The verses convey that the success or failure of the king's rule depended on his conduct. 'If the king had good qualities and be committed to his Dharma, then his system of ruling would be for his subject's happiness and their protection. If the king had vices and was egoistic, his ruling system would become corrupt and the suffering of his subjects will increase.

The purpose of the four types of Kings mentioned in the Yajurveda- Swarat, Janrat, Samrat and Sarvarat also of the Rajsooy Yagya (holy ritual) described in the Vedas, was to select the king adhering to the given rules and regulations. The hymns of Rig Veda mentions the procedure of Kings selection (10.72.1). A people's representative elected as king is addressed by the Purohit thus-

"I have brought you from, amongst the subjects. Amidst us live like a king. Rule with stability and be unfaltering. The subjects should continue to love you, guard against losing the suzerainty of the kingdom."

In the Rajsooya Yagya, described in the Yajurveda (10.17), the verse conveys at the time of the king's coronation-

"I coronate you with the Moon's glow, fire's illumination, the Sun's brilliance, Indra's supremacy. You be the leader of the power of the weapons and protect us from the enemy's weapons." The king replies, "I will during my reign carry on the administration, inspired by the ten deities named, Savita (Sun's brightness) Saraswati (deity of education) Twashta (deity for building) Poosha (preserver of animals) Indra (deity of war and thunderstorm) Brihaspati, (Sage counsellor of deities) Varun (deity of waters) Fire, Soma (Moon) Vishnu (God of sustenance)."

सवित्रा प्रसवित्रा सरस्वत्या वाचा त्वष्ट्रा रूपैः पूष्णा पशुभिरिन्द्रेणास्मे
बृहस्पतिना ब्रह्मणा वरुणेनौजसाऽग्निना तेजसा सोमेन राज्ञा
विष्णुना दशम्या देवतया प्रसूतः प्रसर्पामि।। **(10.30)**

Savita is the symbol of produce, inspired by Savita the King's attention is drawn to all kinds of necessary production in his kingdom. Saraswati, is the symbol of voice, admonishing the king that he need never suppress the voice of the nation or the people's voice. Twashta is the symbol of development, the king must fill his nation with construction and beautification, meaning thereby, the brilliance in the nation be enhanced. Poosha is the symbol of protection of animals. It is the duty of the king to take note of agriculture and animal husbandry. Indra is the symbol of valour and wealth. The king must make the nation brave and wealthy. Brihaspati is the symbol of knowledge. Thus, it is the duty of the king to pay special attention to the enhancement of knowledge and science in the nation. Varun is the symbol of the power to punish. The Raj Dharma is all about the dictum that the king ought to use his power to punish for imparting justice and criminals be punished appropriately. Fire is the symbol of brilliance, in this form the king may make all endeavours to make the nation progress steadily. Soma is the symbol of gentleness, hilarity and coolness. It has been called a medicinal drug. It is the king's moral obligation to bring about peace and happiness in the nation and keep the medical department alert for maintaining the nation healthy. Vishnu is the symbol of preservance. As Vishnu has a foot hold in all the three lokas, likewise, the king's influence ought to make him all pervasive in his nation. The Vedas opine that by inculcating the attributes of the ten deities the king must rule and be an inspiration for his subjects.

In the initial mantras of the 20th chapter of the Yajurveda, the king has been described to be taking oath at the time of his coronation-

क्षत्रस्य योनिरसि क्षत्रस्य नाभिरसि ।
मा त्वा हिंसीन्मा मा हिंसीः ।। 1 ।।

Here 'Kshatra' means the nation. The priest while addressing the kingdom says, that, the obligation of creating a fine nation is on you only. You are the navel meaning thereby, the axis of the nation. All your actions and conduct will influence the subjects. The king is admonished to remain far away from inappropriate acts and injustice or else he will have to bear the consequences of the people's wrath. It has been said about the king-

निषसाद धृतव्रतो वरुणः पस्त्यास्वा ।
साम्राज्याय सुक्रतुः । मृत्यो पाहि विद्योत्पाहि ।। 2 ।।

The one who has undertaken Vratas, such as Varun (God of waters) is beaming amidst the subjects, has an excellent kingdom, lofty intent, fine subjects and excellent deeds. Such a king protects us from death and electrocution.

In this mantra the king has been addressed as 'Varun'. The word 'Varun' connotes two things. One is to be elected and the other is finding solutions to problems. The Vedic king was elected by the subjects and he protected the subjects against all kinds of misfortunes. So, from both the view- points, in the Veda, the King was described as named 'Varun.

यत्रोषधीः समग्मत राजानः समितादिव ।
विप्रः स उच्यते भिषग्रक्षोहामीवचातनः ।। (12.80)

In the above mentioned mantra of Yajurveda, it is said that the person who has knowledge of perfect combination of medicines, like the king in the Samiti, that knowledgeable person is called 'Bhishak or the 'Vaidya' (doctor)-

"This Vaidya must be able to kill germs causing diseases, and cure diseases." This way, Samiti will be called a body, wherein the royal group will gather and mutually or unanimously be the assistants, counsellors, fault-rectifiers, protectors of Dharma and lawmakers to the king of their united nation.

How should the king be? The answer to this question has been given in the Yajurveda-

पूषा पञ्चाक्षरेण पञ्च दिशशउद् जयत्ता उज्जेषँ ।
सविता षड्क्षरेण षड् ऋतूनुद जयत्तानुज्जेषँ
मरुतः सप्ताक्षरेण सप्त ग्राम्यान् । (9.32)

The king who fosters all, who's frame permeates in all directions, who is wealthy, efficient in the chores of the Sabha, protector of animals and has knowledge of the Vedas, that person be made the chief by all the people, to progress.

सूर्यत्वचस स्थ राष्ट्रदा राष्ट्रं मे दत्त स्वाहा । (10.4)

The one who like the Sun spreads the light of justice and education, makes everyone happy is competent to hold the royal position.

The Vedas have considered only those administrative officers as competent, who are totally pure, sacred, dutiful, impartial, selfless and are enlightened with knowledge of the truth. The ancient Indian thought, inspired by the Vedas, depicts such practical forms of ruling systems, which make the entire system full of moral values. It presents such a system that is constructive and not destructive.

From the verses of the fourth Veda, it is learnt that in the entire Vedic versification, Raj Dharma was instructed through the medium of prayers to the divine. There is extensive information regarding the election of the king along with the ministers. It is expected of the king to govern the kingdom according to the circumstances present at that given time. He should make such an arrangement that the subject be happy and move in the direction of progress. It is the prime duty of the king to protect his subject's lives. Only that kingdom progresses whose king is discreet, well behaved and is a philanthropic.

On viewing the Vedic context regarding the ruling system, it appears that in the Vedas, the word king was used for the organizer of the system. In the Vedic times the system of polling was strong. The ruling chief was elected for a specific duration of time. A rule that was contrary to Dharma, unjust, of foul conduct, is instructed to be deposed. 'राजा विशामतिथिश्वारुरायवे।' (Rig.2.2.8) Meaning thereby, even though the king is elected for a specific duration of time, his tenure is not permanent. Because, इहैवेधि मापच्योष्ठाः। (Rig.19.13.2, 10.173.2), it indicates that "You be in this position for the entire term of your tenure, such a situation may never arise that you be deposed mid-term." For this, it is the king's obligation to conclude works of people's welfare. The rule conducted in a proper way remains stable and the king is adorned amongst his subjects. The oath taken at the time of coronation shows that the king must adhere to the royal duty and ethical norms. He should abide by the royal duty. He ought to promise that 'I will not be partial or unduly influenced.'

Prompted by action this verse of Yajurveda, tells the king-

अग्निरेकाक्षरेण प्राणमुदजयत्तमुज्जेषमश्विनौ ।
द्वयक्षरेण द्विपदो मनुष्यानुदजयंता तानुज्जेषं ।
विष्णुस्त्रयक्षरेण त्रींल्लोकानुद जयत्तानुज्जेषम् ।। (9.31)

Throwing light on the mutual relationship of the King and his subjects, this verse declares, that the King who in every way acts for the welfare of all his subjects, he only is taken by his subjects automatically towards all round progress. If the King is not for people's welfare, then even the subjects get alienated.

The justice oriented, elected administration depicted in the Vedic verses presents an ideal for the modern system. The Indian system due to following the Western way, is in a state of 'Gud-khal Ekabhav (mixture of wise and unwise)'. From the village panchayat to the Lok Sabha, there is only one polling list for all. For being eligible for this right, there is only one qualification, meaning thereby there is no qualification. In this erroneous system reform is utterly necessary. If power is vested in the hands of undeserving people, it will not lead to the welfare of either the people or the nation. For running the administration of the country, attributes like, true-education, high moral conduct, control over senses, are utterly necessary. The Vedas have stressed the fact of their being mandatory.

Royal men! you must get involved in commendable works related with weapons and scriptures. Meaning thereby, so long as you proceed on the path of duty as human beings, the kingdom progresses and when the conduct becomes evil, then it gets destroyed and corrupt. Great scholars may constitute the Sabha for education, scholars on dutifulness to constitute the Sabha for Dharma (justice), those who deserve appreciation, are of religious inclination ought to be members of the royal Sabha and the one who is possessor of the best attributes, most qualified, be appointed the Sabhapati. By unanimous consensus of the three Sabhas, with lofty political regulations be formed and all the members may conduct themselves within the ambit of the regulations. They be committed to the welfare of all, while performing their own duties.

In the above noted mantra, Sabhapati means officer of the judiciary. How should a chief justice be, it has been said in this reference, that he should be like the Sun, illuminating the truth, meaning thereby, light duty of justice and education. The mantra from the Rig Veda (3.38.6),-'त्रीणि राजाना विदथे पुरूणि परि विश्वानि भूषथः संदासि।' This mantra confirms that ' Vidhyarya Sabha', 'Dharmarya Sabha' and 'Rajarya Sabha', the three collectively adorn the subjects with education, dutifulness and wealth-prosperity.

It directly means, that the king, the chief of the Sabha ought to have the subjects under the King's and Sabha's control and the king and the Sabha be under the subjects and the kingdom. The legal system be for everyone. All must duly abide by it. The second part of this mantra, -'अपश्यमंत्र मनता जगन्वान्न्ते गन्धर्वा अपि वायुकेशान।' 'It means that the nation which has the king and the subjects together, in such nation's Sabhas, there will be prompt workers, intelligent thinkers and committed workers with knowledge of the Vedas.

In the Atharva Veda (19.55.5) also there is this mantra declaring the king to be a member of the Sabha.-'सभ्यः सभां में पाहि ये च सभ्याः सभासदः।'

In the various mantras of the Rig Veda, (mandal 7.sukta 104- mantra-5, 6, 7,8,9) there is detailed description of the judicial system. The central theme of these mantras is that the king along with the members of the Sabha protects the subjects by imparting justice. The Chief of the Sabha and the Commander in Chief of the defence forces, like the Sun must spread illumination of education and like water make the subjects peaceful and content. The judged must never punish innocent subjects. On the other hand, the instructions given by the Chief of the Sabha along with other members must not be flouted by the subjects for protection of Dharma (duty and religion). Almost all the mantras of the Rig Veda, expect all men in royal service to foster the subjects as if they were their sons.

'वरेथे अग्निमातपो वदते वल्गवत्रये।
अन्ति षद्भूतु वामव:।।' (8.73.8)

Addressing the king and Amatyas (ministers), the said mantra conveys, "Both be sweet spoken, comfort and redeem those without mother, father, brother (orphans), children, under privileged suffering from deprivation of food and water, which causes agony like fire burns. This great deed is worth performing for the two of you. Sam Purvarchika (20.4.9) and Atharva (1.15.2) mentions -

'उक्थं च न शस्यमानं नागो रयिरा चिकेत
न गायत्रं गीयमानम्।।'

In the above mantra, while Atharven instructing the king to accept healthy criticism, it is said- A knowledgeable king must understand what succinct speaker says. He should not get discouraged by criticism, but ought to contemplate on it with a calm mind and activate well-meaning subjects.

'ज्योतिष्मतीमदितिं धारयत्क्षितिं स्वर्वतीमा
सचेते दिवेदिवे जागृवांसा दिवेदिवे।
ज्योतिष्मत् क्षत्रमाशाते आदित्या दानुनस्पती।
मित्रस्तयोर्वरुणो यातयज्जनोऽर्यमा यातयज्जन:।।'

(Rig.1.136.3)

In the Vedas very fine thoughts have been evoked regarding the royal administration imparting justice, it is said, as the Sun and Air, through their power of attraction, hold the Earth in the entire heavenly world, likewise, human being making effort with pure intent, great justice, valiant army commander and members of the Sabha can influence the entire subjects in such a way, so as to enable them lead just and high- quality life.

Indicating about the royal duty, it has been instructed, that the king with highly competent members of the Sabha, ought to take the right decision in consultation with the Sabha, treat everyone equally and run the kingdom properly. In the Vedic literature, running the kingdom with political thoroughness is said to be the royal duty.

In the verses of Vedas and Upanishads, at various instants, there are sermons, given for the king who dutifully fosters his subjects well. It says, that for running the kingdom adhering to the tenets of duty, the ministers that the king appoints, be gentlemen, truthful, and must be competent to fulfil rightly, the obligation of the portfolio of ministers. By appointing faulty characters, the royal administration will not generate welfare. That nation will move towards its downfall. Such a state cannot be protected by Dharma even. In the Yajurveda (7.35) while sermonising the king, ministers and the subjects, it is said, the dictates of the justice imparting Sabha of judges, ought never be flouted. The members of the Royal Sabha too should never defy the scholars of the Vedas. One who has high qualities be elected as the chief of the Sabha and the Sabhapati (king) ought to carry on the royal administration following a fine policy.

The Vedic mantras naturally make it very clear that the carrying on of the affairs of the Sabha was obligatory for the Sabhapati (King). While the discussion in the Sabha was on, the members were not to behave contrary to the decorum, was to be specially monitored by the Sabhapati. The Sabhapati or the King himself had to behave in accordance with the Dharma and make the other members follow it. In the Sabha-Samiti those subjects which were of national interest for discussion, on them all the scholars be unanimous in arriving at an appropriate and just decision. In a way the organization of Sabha-Samiti, which has been mentioned in the Vedic verses, seems identical with the present parliament, its members and the speaker and their obligations. The difference is only this, that the present members of parliament are getting alienated from good conduct, speech and competence, are becoming erratic, behaving contrary to Dharma (Duty), their obligations and truth, with a conduct characteristic of non-dutifulness, selfishness, falsehood, and corrupt behaviour, exhibiting in their activities. It is necessary for Indian leaders and the people to do an analysis and by following their ancient tradition ought to build a foundation for a healthy administrative system.

It is expected that the chief of the Sabha and the army chief should be protective of the subjects and their welfare, also spread knowledge. Every auspicious work has been titled 'Yagna'. In all the Vedas and Mantras it has been prayed that the king, members of the Sabha and the subjects ought to endeavour for dutiful progress, meaning thereby, perform good deeds unitedly. The following Rig Veda mantra expresses fully, the above noted sentiment, as it has a special description of the rise of feeling of nationalism-

त्या न्वश्विना हुवे सुदंससा गृभे कृता।
ययोरस्ति प्रणः सख्यं देवेष्वध्याप्यम्।। (8.10.3)

The verse of the Rig Veda, while presenting a ruling system based on the truth, just and appropriate, rich with democratic attributes, says-

स्थिरा वः सन्त्वायुधा पराणुदे वीलू उत प्रतिष्कमे।
युष्माकमस्तु तविषी पनीयसी मा मर्त्यस्य मायिनः।। (1.39.2)

**Internal System of ruling and People's Welfare**

In the Vedic literature, the element of Dharma (Duty) is considered the axis of the King's position and royal administration. Along with it the principles of welfare kingdom have also been presented. Protection of all, helping the poor, providing shelter to the deprived or underprivileged subjects of the state, are included in royal obligations. It is indicative of the two-dimensional intent of the kingdom, the first one being redemption form hunger and paucity and the kings voice creating complete oneness with the subjects. Such a system could be the basis of any highly evolved democratic state's constitution.

The King is described to be brilliant like the Sun and

benevolent in the following verse of the Rig Veda-

अद्या चिन्नू चित् तदपो नदीनां यदाम्यो अरदो गातुमिन्द्र ।
नि पर्वता अद्यसदो न सेदुस्त्वया दृल्हानि सुक्रतो रजांसि ।। (6.30.3)

It means, bearing knowledge of works of importance, O king brilliant like the Sun! The way the Sun through attraction of the Earth receives water from the rivers and returns the double quantity of it in the form of rains, likewise, the money received from the subjects is spent for their welfare, the king fulfils his duty of fostering the subjects, the same way as the Sun brightens the Lokas (regions) in its ambit. Similarly, by protecting the subjects all are to be kept happy.

Atharva Ved describes the Ayakar Parishad (Income Tax Assembly) thus-

यद् राजानो विभजन्त इष्टापूर्तस्य षोडशं यमस्यामी सभासदः ।
अविः तस्मात् प्रमुञ्चति दत्तः शितिपात् स्वधा ।। (3.29.1)

The operative members of the Tax Regulating Assembly have made it a rule that the tax-payer will pay one upon sixteen part of his income, earned through his genuine labour, also accidentally received income for his national welfare. This system saves the tax- payer from the punishment and disgrace of evading tax.

It is the duty of the subjects to pay the nation's share in the form of tax (Bali) liable to be paid, from the income earned within the country or abroad. This would enable them, by an effective use of the system of justice, punish the wrong doers and carry- on welfare activity for the noble ones by granting them comfort and peace. In the Vedic verses there are treatises and stress on dutiful conduct in all spheres of life.

तुभ्यं भरन्ति क्षितयो यविष्ठ
बलिमग्ने अन्तित ओत दूरात् ।
आ भन्दिष्ठस्य सुमतिं चिकिद्धि
बृहत्ते अग्ने महि शर्म भद्रम् ।।

(Rig.5.1.10)

In this mantra along with discussion on taxation, the king

has been directed to strengthen the system of justice for the welfare of the nation and establish peace. The word 'Yavishta' is derived from the elementary word, 'यु मिश्रणामिश्रणयो', which means establishment of justice. So, it is the duty of the king to make gentle people comfortable and bad characters be eliminated. Therefore, the formula of Vedic royal system of ruling is 'a ruling system that enhances the comfort of the subjects and eliminates their suffering, that is a superior ruling system.'

The national head must have a complete knowledge of the composition of the state. He must be aware of where the villages, towns, forests, citadels, ponds, rivers, mountains are located within the nation. What is their condition? Where do people reside? Whether they are comfortably living in content, following the tenets of Dharma (Dutifulness). Proper management of all these issues and protection of the nation has been told to be the prime duty of the king. This is the basic element of the ancient Indian ideology, that the royal rulers ought to treat them like their own sons. Like a father fosters all the subjects alike. In the Atharva Veda(19.37.3) the king has been called the nation's 'Bhritya' or the servant. 'Servant of the nation' is very important from the point of view that, in the Vedic governance of the nation, the reign rested with the subjects. Meaning thereby, in the Vedic system of ruling the nation, description of such a self- government is there, wherein the state belonged to the subjects. In the entire versification of the Vedas, through the medium of verses and mantras on the system of welfare, depicts a ruling system, which is to be followed due to its pricelessness. The importance of this can be traced to the fact, that as after the Vedic age, various sages and other writers wrote in their scriptures well organized write ups on the welfare state of the kingdom, likewise, rulers of various ages during their rule made policies keeping it in mind and gave it a practical form. The acts of people's welfare concluded by the kings have been named yagnas. Atharvaveda (12.5) directs the king-

श्रमेण तपसा सृष्टा ब्रह्मणा वित्तर्तं श्रिता।। 1।।
सत्येनावृता श्रिया प्रावृता यशसा परीवृता।। 2।।

It means it is expected of the king to protect his subjects, redeem them from illness, provide health care, endeavour for their longevity of life, enhancement of joy, keeping the subjects away from bad habits, like holding grudges, for financial management making good land available and all activities related to animal husbandry be concluded.

The initial source of knowledge, the Vedas are such a heritage, which has all types of knowledge and directions and dictates related to management. In the ruling system of the king, for people's welfare, subjects like, medical aid and education have been declared to be of national importance. Atharva Veda (6.68.2,141.1) again directs the King-

चिकित्सतु प्रजापतिर्दीर्घायुत्वाय चक्षसे। रुद्रो भूम्ने चिकित्सतु।

It is the duty of the king to protect his subjects and for the longevity of their life should designate a protector of the people, who should take care of the people's health and arrange for their medical aid.

Further, the Veda says –

तस्मै घृतं सुरां मध्वन्नमन्नं क्षदामहे।
स नः पितेव पुत्रेभ्यः श्रेयः श्रेयश्चिकित्सतु भूयोभूयः
श्वाश्वो देवेभ्यो मणिरेत्य।।

(Ath.10.6.5)

In the protection of Prajapalak (protector of subjects or king) the Rudra (physician) may make appropriate arrangement for increase of population and eradication of diseases. Meaning thereby, for averting infliction of diseases, ghee, pure water, honey and a variety of food stuff be made available to the physician. That medical specialist ought to make such an arrangement in hospitals, that the diseased be looked after the same way, as a father takes care of his child every day and makes efforts to achieve shreya and for providing his food, well-being and healthy, happy life. There is also an indication of employment of women in the medical department as officers and workers, as women are by nature tender, serving the ailing and remedial way treatment comes natural to them. They are well conversant with natural laws and conditions. विवांचिकित्सदृतचिद्ध नारी। (Rig, 4.16.10)

**Education System in the Vedas**

With the intent that human beings may benefit from human scientists and the practical knowledge of medical values, the Vedas come up with a detailed description of a superior ruling system, in which the entire education system is related to the duties of the ruler. The Vedas expect that the citizen be rid of the darkness of ignorance and light the lamp of his rationality, to illuminate the path of his course of action. Expressing this meaning, the  mantra of Sukta 3, in the 18<sup>th</sup> Kand of Atharva Veda states-

इंद्र क्रतु न आ भर पिता पुत्रेभ्यो यथा।
शिक्षां णो अस्मिन् पुरुहूत यामनि जीवा ज्योतिरशीमहि।। 67।।

O Brilliant King! For our progress, make arrangement for education and channelization of intelligence, as a father does for his children. Provide us with such education that may cause illumination of the path of knowledge for us.

In the Vedas education has been accepted as nectar, and referred to as honey-

या वां कशा मधुमत्यश्विना सूनृतावती।
तथा यज्ञं मिमिक्षतम्।।

(Yaju.7.11)

Madhumati kasha means a voice with the attribute of sweetness, describing it the verse states- O teacher and the pupil! Both of you be possessor of the attribute of sweetness, lover of truth and balanced in speech due to rationality, involve yourselves in Yagna or important work.

In various mantras of Atharva Veda (1.34) advocating education it is said-

इयं वीरुन्मधु जाता मधुना त्वा खनामसि।
मधोरधि प्रजातासि सा नो मधुमतस्कृधि।। 1।।

For the curious, knowledge is like the taste of honey, fine and harbinger of happiness, achieved by obtaining education, putting in truthful study, practice, investigation and examination.

जिह्वाया अग्रे मधु मे जिह्वामूले मधूलकम्।

ममेदह क्रतावसो मम चित्तमुपायसि।। 2।।

A student with thirst of knowledge, obtains high education with deep contemplation, and examination. His power of absorption gets enhanced. Self-study opens his eyes of knowle-dge. Properly obtained education is joyful for the mind.

मधुमन्मे निक्रमणं मधुमन्मे परायणम्।

वाचा वदामि मधुमद् भूयासं मधुसदृशः।। 3।।

According to this mantra the life of one with a passion for education is full of attainment of knowledge. Each one of his behavioural facet spreads illuminations of knowledge. His way of living is filled with honey (educative). His movements (going and coming) are filled with honey (permeating sweetness). His way of speaking is full of honey (knowledge). Inland or if abroad, he does good to everyone by his knowledge filled speech. A person, so full with the taste of honey deserves to be addressed as a Mahatman (great soul).

मधोरस्मि मधुतरो मदुधान्मधुमत्तरः।

मामित् किल त्वं वनाः शाखां मधुमतीमिव।। 4।।

The internal meaning of this mantra of the Atharva Veda is that the taste of education is far more juicier and beneficial than the worldly delicious sweets and other interesting things. As a celibate goes on craving for education effortfully, the same way the Goddess of education spells out her affection towards him, meaning thereby, Goddess Saraswati always helps the contemplative students.

For creating a fine society and nation, endeavour to establish the importance of education, is dealt with in the Atharva Veda Bhashabhashyam, in the Sukta of ninth canto,

Sukta 1 known as Madhu Suktam. Following are the quotable mantras of this Sukta-

यथा सोमस्तृतीये सवन ऋभूणां भवति प्रियः।
एव म ऋभवो वर्च आत्मनि घ्रियताम्।। 13।।
मधुं जनिषिय मधु वंशिषीय।
पयंस्वानग्न आगमं तं मासं सृज वर्चसा।। 14।।
स माग्ने वर्चसा सृज सं प्रजया समायुषा।
विद्युर्मे अस्य वा इन्द्रो विद्यात् सह ऋषिभिः।। 15।।
यथा मधु मधुकृतः सं भरन्ति मधावधि।
एवा मे अश्विना वर्च आत्मनि घ्रियताम्।। 16।।
यथा मक्षा इदं मधु न्यञ्जप्ति मधावधि।
एवा मे अश्विना वर्चस्तेजो बलमोजश्च घ्रियताम्।। 17।।

In the Atharva Veda while advocating quality education, it has been said conclusively that a human being should endeavour to get superior knowledge through education, to become brilliant like the Sun. Must have quest for knowledge to continuously raise his level of knowledge and achieve fame. The nectar received by the teachers be utilised to illuminate the soul. On receiving best education, a human being becomes capable of reforming the society and the nation. By performing these welfare deeds, he becomes successful in life and earns respect among the elite. Pointing towards the responsibility of the parents, the verse reiterates, that "as the teachers fill their pupils with honey in the form of knowledge and the way an intelligent student, like the bumble bee extracts from the pollen of the flower, the same way collects knowledge from the teacher, even the parents, ought to in the same manner arrange for high education for children. We should become valiant by receiving education from most knowledgeable and qualified teachers."

अश्विना सारघेण मा मधु नाङ्क्तं शुभस्पती।
यथा वर्चस्वतीं वाचमावदानि जनाँ अनु।। 19।।
यो वै कशायाः सप्त मधूनि वेद मधुमान् भवति।
ब्राह्मणश्च राजा च धेनुश्चानड्वाश्च व्रीहिश्च यवश्च
मधु सप्तमम्।। 22।।

**In these mantras the Veda reiterates-**
O mother, father! performers of auspicious deeds, you illumine with that knowledge which will enable me obtain spiritual power and wealth and a bright future. On obtaining that knowledge I would be able to speak with brilliance among the scholarly people, as only a rational person, is able to extract the attributes and properties from all living beings and all type of things. Such able, analytical viewers, ethical in behaviour, scholars of Vedas are only known as reasonable or knowledgeable..

The following mantra of Atharva Veda (18.3.6) and Rig Veda (10.16.13) relates to proliferation of education-

यं त्वमग्ने समदहस्तमु निर्वापया पुनः।
क्याम्बूरत्र रोहतु शाण्डदूर्वा व्यल्कशा।।

While remaining in disciplined stage of celibacy, it is the prime duty of a pupil, to plant the seed of knowledge, under the able guidance of parents and teacher, so that education proliferates. By the medium of sweetly spoken sermons dispel the darkness of sorrow. Such education be received, so as to lead to physical, spiritual, and social progress. In the mantras of Atharva Veda (18.1) and with slight difference in Rig Veda(10.17.7-9) while invoking Goddess Saraswati sermons have been given—

सरस्वतीं देवयन्तो हवन्ते सरस्वतीमध्वरे तायमाने।
सरस्वतीं सुकृतो हवन्ते सरस्वती दाशुषे वार्यं दात्।। 41।।
सरस्वतीं पितरो हवन्ते दक्षिणा यज्ञमिनक्षमाणाः।
आसद्यास्मिन् बर्हिषि मादयध्वमनमीवा इष आ धेह्मस्तमे।। 42।।
सरस्वति या सरथं यथाथोळ्थैः स्वधाभिर्देविपितृभिर्मदंती।
सहस्रार्धमिडो अत्र भागं रायस्पोषं यजमानाय धेहि।। 43।।

Those worshippers of Saraswati who wish to inculcate grand qualities, remain non-violent, pure in conduct and get educated. Knowledge gathered through sacred conduct, hard work and noble deeds only, proves to be the reason for human welfare. The voice of the Vedas states, that scholars of Vedas without halt propagate education of the Vedas, progress of science and master desirable things. Only a knowledgeable person becomes self -confident, wealthy and famous.

In the Vedic ruling system, subjects well educated, civilized, and committed to national protection, are referred to. Stressing the importance of the education of weapons and scriptures both, the Rig Veda-mantra states-

पुरंदरा शिक्षतं वजहस्तास्माँ
इन्द्राग्नी अवतं भरेषु।

(Rig.1.109.8)

यत्र नार्यपच्यवमुपच्यवं च शिक्षते।

(Rig.1.28.3)

According to the Vedic system the subject of education be monitored by the Chief of the Sabha and army forces, so that there is the same curriculum in the entire state. Everyone in the country must be trained in warfare, to enable them rise to protect their nation, when the occasion arises. Everyone in the nation be lively and illumined enjoying the comforts of life. These teachings will be the same for everyone.

In the field of education women should get precedence as they have a natural eye for it, which helps them discriminate as to what is worth absorbing and what is to be discarded. They know better what is to be consumed and what not. They are capable of discriminating between appropriate and in appropriate. From all points of view in the Vedic verses, minutest details of all fields of concern to human beings have been discussed. For this reason, not only we people but also Westerners, speak freely while planning a system for their national advancement- The Vedas give us the best possible system in the world.

**Planned System of National Prosperity**

The Vedas have addressed human beings as 'born of nectar (Amrit Putra). The Vedas declare that 'all human beings are related in brotherhood'. Accepting this similarity, the Vedas have a superior system based on, 'feeling of equality.' According to the Vedic ruling system no one can be treated as inferior, on the grounds of wealth or position, language or religion. They have equal opportunity to progress and become wealthy.

'अज्येष्ठासो अकनिष्ठास एते सं भ्रातरो वावृधुः सौभगायः।' (Rig 5.60.5) This vast motherland is harbinger of comfort and well-being for all. The Vedamantra of Atharva says-

जनं बि भ्रती बहुधा विवाचसं नानाधर्माणं पृथिवी यथौकसम् ।
सहस्त्रं धारा द्रविणस्य मे दुहां ध्रुवेव धेनुरनपस्फुरन्ती ।। (12.1.45)

Subjects consisting of speakers of various languages, followers of different duties, are accepted the same way in the lap of our mother land, as at home in a family, members different in nature and propensities reside. The same way as a lactating cow, without causing pain to anyone, provides us with thousands of streams of milk, likewise, this land may generate for us prosperity in abundance.

In this mantra while giving stress to equality, it is said, that all are equal, no one is small or big. On account of age, strength, affordability and social position, the king need not discriminate, he ought to constitute such a nation wherein the interests of all are fulfilled, all are nurtured to their satisfaction. Together all may strive for progress and prosperity.

The ancient Indian history that is available, strengthens the path for a human being's all-round development of personality, and the four-fold path of progress of the nation he resides in. It was the belief of the world famous and enriched literary scholars, inspirators of ancient thought, that the establishment of cultured society, peaceful human life and the national development is only possible in a situation, wherein the subjects would be well educated, committed workers and dutiful. It is always said that a particular group of human beings are named a nation. A composition of mind, body and soul is known as a human being. A popular ruling system amongst people aims at balanced development of all three. For this reason, our ancient scripture writers thought it obligatory to propagate and promote amongst the subjects, inculcation of attributes and ethical values.

In Atharva Veda,(17.1.1-6,27) there is a prayer for advancement of self. A human being says- While singing praise of the one praise worthy, famous, most important, most venerable, I wish for the upliftment of myself. By my own spiritual development, देवानां प्रियः भूयासम्– I should be dear to the Gods,प्रजानां प्रियः भूयासम्–I should be dear to the subjects, पशूनां प्रियः भूयासम्– loved by animals, सभानानां प्रियः भूयासम्– I be dear to human beings who are equally able.

Further a human being prays, 'अहं च द्विषते मा रधम्- I should never be swayed by one who is envious, जरदष्टिः कृतवीर्यो विहायाः सहस्त्रायुः सुकृश्चरेयम्–which means, I should be doing multiple tasks for thousands of years, completing my duration of life, performing noble deeds must I conduct myself.

**Panch mahayagya and Shodash sanskar**

The Indian sages, progressed in every direction of life, also beyond human life, continuously for the purpose, a planned system has been gifted. Panch mahayagya, shodash sanskar (sixteen purifications or rituals) and Varnashram are such methods which eradicate negative propensities from within the human being and positivity is generated. It leads to his physical, mental and spiritual progress to be able to participate in the advancement of the nation. In the present competitive and professional age, life being deceitful and disorganised, it would be beneficial for all of us to understand and adopt, the policy of Panch maha yagya daily for advancement. Swami Dayanand Saraswati has reiterated the importance of follo-wing Panch yagyas and Varnashram as propagated in the elucidations related to Vedas in treatises of Rig Veda, for the establishment of self- government in a grand nation. It proves that through these rituals, the body and mind could be cultivated for making it easier to adhere to the stages of Dharma, artha, kaam and moksha. This ritual is not systema-tized. Panch Maha yagyas are as follows –

**1. Brahmayagya-** By practicing yoga, self- contemplation, veneration of God and study of the Vedas, inner cleansing, which leads to learning, education, dutifulness, civil behaveour, enhancement of auspicious attributes.

**2. Devayagya-** By practicing yogic postures and Pranayam (breathing exercises) maintaining the senses healthy and strong, by offering oblation to fire cooperate in purifying the atmosphere. This leads to enhancement of longevity, strength, intelligence and increase development of the ability and affordability to practice well the four stages of life Dharma (duty) Artha ( generation of wealth) Kaam (worldly pleasures) Moksha ( ultimate redemption).

**3. Pitriyagya-** Serving and taking care of alive parents, old family members. This yagya leads to enhancement of humility, civil conduct and gratitude.

**4. Atithiyagya-** Arranging food, clothing, shelter and security for, religious, helpful, truthful sermonizers, sages and hermits. This is a medium to destroy hypocrisy, attainment of true knowledge makes propagation of dharma possible.

**5. Balivaishvadeva yagya-** To properly nurture and care for cow and other animals, the poor, helpless, unsheltered people. This invokes equanimity among human beings, a good heart and the feeling of being helpful to others.

From the above mentioned description it is learnt that the meaning of yagna is not merely lighting the fire and invoking the divine, but each action in human life is like a yagna. For increasing knowledge, education be sought, for cleansing the atmosphere, oblation to fire be done, serving the parents, hospitality for people is learned in Dharma and nurturing each being kindly, are such five great yagnas that bring about welfare of human- beings, society and nation, in every way and redeem them.

Likewise, for four faceted social advancement (organizational art) ancient thinkers have in conformity with the Vedas, considered Varnashram to be necessary. The organization of

Varnashram is such that it provides for all human beings an opportunity to realize their own interest while accomplishing the goal of working for the good of others. For taking a deep view we will have to accept while working for self-development and self, is a pre-condition for national advancement.

To give completeness to human life, its duration has been divided into four parts. For physical strength, increase in intelligence, Brahmacharya ashram is necessary. Grihastha Ashram (family life) is for practical utilization of the power of body mind and soul, meaning thereby, giving birth to a healthy child, establishing means of livelihood, performing social obligations in accordance with tenets of dutifulness. Practicing tapa or austerity is to make strong the collection of weakened powers, and mental and spiritual upliftment, Vaanprastha is recommended. The last stage of life, Sanyas Ashram or asceticism is meant for supreme welfare and the divine's veneration.

To keep the society united, undivided, with the auspicious intent of providing equal opportunity for all, the Aryan sages, based on qualifications and activity (Guru Karma), formulated regulations for a beautiful labour-works-department, mentioned in the Varnashram. It is a fully scientific way of things. As long as a human beings remains in the family life earning his living, till then the caste system is applicable, once a human being enters Vanprastha or Sanyas, then he does not have a caste. Thus, the Varna division relates only to worldly activities. The activities related to the other world involve, proper study of the Vedas, yagnas, charity and duty, chanting of mantras and practicing austerity, are relevant for all equally.

**Wealth of Cow and Formation of the Nation**

In the ancient Indian literature, right from the Vedas to this day, cow has been treated as a great wealth. It is said that 'माता निर्माता भवति' or the one that creates is the mother. From this viewpoint the Vedas do not tire of singing praise of the cow wealth in building the nation. The word 'mother' has been used specially for these three-- one who gives birth, land and cow. In the divine knowledge of the Vedas while addressing the cow as mother, it is said, 'गायो विश्वस्य मातरः'meaning thereby, the cow mother is the protector of all living beings. The mother who gives birth to us inculcates values among us, brings us up right from infancy, but the cow mother with its auspicious attributes, undertakes the great task of building up the nation, on its shoulders.

In the Yajurveda and Rig Veda cow has been described as nectar thus –

माता रुद्राणां दुहिता वसूनां स्वसादित्यानामामृतस्य नाभिः।
प्र नु वोचं चिकितुषे जनाय मा गामानागामदितिं वधिष्ट।।

(Rig 18.101.15)

In this mantra the cow has been called the navel of nectar. Nectar is the creative element, which is never close to death. The cow is its harbinger, that is why it is called Aditi (mother of Aditya, the Sun). The strength of Prajapati is Aditi cow. As a mother always does good to her children, likewise cow has also manifested for the welfare of the universe. It is flaw less. That is why Shruti has called it 'anaga.' The regulatory power of the entire universe is called 'Aditi'.

The fourteenth sukta of third canto of Atharva Veda, is known as 'Goshtha'Sukta. In this sukta cows have been favoured. Cows are the main means of our physical and spiritual progress. The Vedas accept the unparalleled importance of cow. The Sukta on cow, in the Atharva Veda is an extremely beautiful poetic work. In this Sukta while describing well, the aspect of cow as a harbinger of welfare, it has been said that human beings get wealth, strength, food and fame from cow only. Cow is auspicious and manifests valour. With reference to sermonising on paying heed to protection of cows, maintaining them healthy and disease-free, the Goshtha Sukta reiterates-

शिवो वो गोष्ठो भवतु शरिशाकेव पुष्यत ।
इहैवोत प्र जायध्वं भया वः सं सृजामसि ।। (3.14)

It means this cow shed may promote the wellbeing of cows. Living herein, the cows must grow healthy and procreate to increase in number. The owner of these cows must make all the arrangement for cows. In the Mahabharata Sri Krishna has also wished likewise-

गा वै पश्याम्हं नित्यं गावः पश्यन्तु मां सदा ।
गावोऽस्माकं वयं तासां यतो गावस्ततो वयम् ।।

(Anu.parva 78.24)

It means that I should always see them personally and cows may always grace me. Cows are for us, we are for cows. Wherever the cows are, we are there. Because our existence depends on cows. Krishna again wishes-

ममाग्रतो नित्यं गावः पृष्ठत एव च ।
गावो में सर्वत्रश्रेच्व गवां मध्ये वासम्यहम् ।। (80.3)

Cows be in front of me, behind me and on all the four sides. I may live amidst cows. The undercurrent of this great thought of Lord Krishna is a reiteration of the Veda's stating, accepting cows as holder of all the Vedas, thus- 'सर्वे देवाः स्थिता देहे सर्वदेवमयी ही गौः' ।

The word 'gau' is derived from the root word 'gam gatau' dhatu which means speed, acquisitions, knowledge and final redemption. Since it helps in practical realization of all the four meanings, the Vedas call it 'Gau'. In addition, the word 'cow' is used for speech, ray of light, the Earth, a particular person, the senses, so on and so forth. The cow is also considered instrumental in realizing the four purposes of life - dharma, artha, kaam and moksha. Even sages abandoned all worldly possessions but not the cow. Serving the cow was considered a piece of good fortune by them. There is no scripture of ancient Indian literature which does not discuss and praise the 'Cow' as an identity mark of the nation possessing the attributes of the mother creator, such as, sacrifice, personification of affection, service, sweetness, forbearance. The cow is considered the first among the seven powers that protect the prestige of the Earth.

गोभिर्विप्रैश्च वेदैश्च सतीभिः सत्यवादिभिः
अलुब्धैर्दानशीलैश्च सप्तभिर्धायेते मही ।।

The earth is stable on the shoulders of cows, Brahmins, the Vedas, faithful wives, truthful people, the non-greedy and those who sacrifice. The cow named Kamdhenu, was served by the sage Vashishtha, as an extreme permeator of holiness in his religious yagnik actions. The cow is very useful in passing through all the four stages of life, namely celibacy, family life, resigning to the forest and finally asceticism. Because of serving the cow, king Dilip was blessed with a son named Aja. As it is Kamdhenu for fulfilment of wishes, it is also the greatest protector of our health. That is why the Vedic verses address it as, 'Aghaniya' undeserving of death, 'Amrit-nabhi' and 'Piyush-nabhi.' . Its milk purifies internally and serving it has a purifying effect externally. The cow is the main pillar for carrying on yagyas and charity. In the Atharva Veda (4.21.6) and Rig Veda (6.28.6) right from the beginning there are narrations of passing proposals regarding protection of the cow. It is said at an instance-

यूयं गावो गेव्यथा कृशं चिदश्रीरं चित् कृणुथा सुप्रतीकम् ।
भद्रं गृहं कृणुथ भद्रवाचो बृहद्वोत्वय उच्यते सभासु ।।

(Ath.4.21.6)

This means, O cows, with your milk and milk products, you make emaciated human beings healthy and sturdy, make them brilliant and powerful. Not only this, with your auspicious voice, the homes of human beings develop auspiciousness. On account of being immensely useful, in the Sabha-Samiti during the Vedic age, proposals were passed for increasing their number. In the Atharva Veda, there are instructions for conserving such a sacred being.

न तो अर्वा रेणुककाढोअश्नुते न संस्कृतत्रमुप यन्ति ता अभि ।
अरुगायममयं तस्य ता अनु गावो मर्तस्य वि चरन्ति यज्वनः ।

(Ath.4.21.4)

Killer of cows can never have auspiciousness in his life but the cows owned by those performing yagyas, may go to various grazing land and be instrumental in their welfare. In the Rig Veda (6.28.1) and in the Atharva Veda (4.21.1) while praising cow sheds full of cows, it is said-

आ गावो अग्मन्नुत भद्रमक्र न्त्सीदन्तुगोष्ठे रणयन्त्वस्मे ।
प्रजावतीः पुरुरूपा इह स्युरिंद्राय पूर्वीरुषसो दुहानाः ।।

The said mantra iterates that due to the presence of the cows there is contentment. In the cow shed, all coloured cows may have healthy calves and every day in the morning may give milk in abundance for the wealthy ones. In the Atharva Veda, while sermonizing on protection of cows, it has been said—

कोशं दुहन्ति कलशं चतुर्बिलमिडां धेनुं मधुमतीं स्वस्तये ।
ऊर्जं मदंतीमदितिं जनेष्वग्ने मा हिंसीः परमे व्योमन् ।।

(Ath.18.4.30)

In the above noted mantra, it has been said, that the king should make such an arrangement, that the animals that provide milk, ghee, calves and oxen used in agriculture, who protect the subjects, need never be harmed, harassed or killed by human beings. For increasing spiritual power with reference to protection of the wealth of cows, the Vedas say-

वैश्वानरे हरिदं जुहोमि साहस्रं शतधारमुत्समम् ।
स बिभर्ति पितरं पितामहान् प्रपितामहान् बिभर्ति पिन्वमानः ।। 35 ।।

सहस्रधारं शतधारमुत्समक्षितं व्यच्यमानं सलिलस्य पृष्ठे ।
ऊर्जं दुहानमनपस्फुरन्तमुपासते पितरः स्वधाभिः ।। 36 ।।

It means," O human being! get cows and serve them. By rearing cows, we get fine quality oxen for farming, milk, ghee and other fine milk products. All the members of the family become strong and healthy." "Whoever wishes to enhance his physical and spiritual strength, that superior being ought to protect cows and indulge in consumption of milk and ghee."

In the chapter on discipline (Anushasan Parv) of Mahabharat, the writer sage Vyas has considered himself blessed for having described the cow, as a containment of the Vedas. He writes-

गोमि स्तुल्यं न पश्यामि धनं किञ्चिदिहाच्युत।
गावो लक्ष्म्याः सदा मूलं गोषु पाप्मा न विद्यते।।

There is no other wealth like the cows in this world. Cows are the basis of prosperity and wealth. Sin cannot touch them. In this very chapter while Brahma narrates to Indra the importance of the cow, Vyas has written in detail-

यज्ञांगं कथिता गावो यज्ञ एव च वासव
एताभिश्च बिना यज्ञो न वर्तेत कथचन।।
धारयन्ति प्रजाश्चैव प्यसा हविषा तथा
एतासां तन्याश्चापि कृषियोगमुपासते।।
जनयिन्ति च धान्यानि बीजानि विविधानि च
ततो यज्ञाः प्रवर्तन्ते हव्यं कव्यं च सर्वशः।
प्यो दधि धृतं चैव पुण्याश्चैत सुराधिप
वहन्ति विविधान् भारान् क्षुत्तृष्णा परिपीडिताः।
भुर्नीश्च धारयन्तीह प्रजाश्चैवापि कर्मणा
वासवाकूटवाहिन्यः कर्मणा सुकृतेन च। (83.17.21)

It means cows are not only a part of the yagna, but in fact, are a true manifestation of it. Without them Yagnas are not possible. With their milk and ghee, they nurture the subjects. They give birth to oxen to be useful in agriculture. With their help the food crop- that is grown, is used for conclusion of yagnas. The act of oblation in fire, with chanting of poetic verses is also performed. The sacred cows provide milk, curd and ghee. The oxen carry weight even on an empty stomach. These cows provide nourishment to hermits, sages and the king's subjects. Their behaviour is not governed by deceit or illusion. They indulge in activities for welfare. In verses of the Vedas, great personalities of India and sages, have treated collection of sacred thoughts, progenies following the righte-ous path and healthy body, in the class of personal wealth, labelling cows as the best possible wealth, leading to the acquisition of them. Atharva Veda (11.1.34) states- धेनुं सदनं रयीणाम् means the cows are a treasure of wealth. Gold, silver, diamond and all the other gems can lose value in a famine. But a person who possesses even a single lactating cow, can make any piece of land fertile, even in a forest, can begin to fill the stock of food. In the ancient literature due to the cow's extraordinary attributes, it has been called the cow that takes us across the Vaitarni. It means the cow makes, its owner overcome massive tribulations. With reference to this it has been said,

गावो भगो गाव इंद्रो में इच्छाद् गावः सोमस्य प्रथमस्य भक्षः ।

(Rig. 6.28.5)

इमा या गावः स जनास इंद्र इच्छामि ह्रदा मनसाचिदिन्द्रम ।।

(Ath, 4.21.5)

Cows be our primary wealth. The cow fosterer Indra may provide us with cows as this wealth rears the entire universe. It is life for the whole universe.

With reference to the wealth of cows, its knowledge has been forwarded in many ways. The Yajurveda (22.22) iterates- 'दोग्घ्री धेनुर्वोढानड्वान् । This means that the cows that replenish the Earth with milk, carriers of weights, heavily built oxen are our treasure. According to Shri Prakashveer Shastri, in the Sanskrit literature, there is another word connected to the cow, it is Gaveshan. This means something going into depth or seeking the essence, but the birth of this word is a consequence of the multi usefulness of India's wealth of cows. At the twilight in the morning and evening, the dust touches the sacred, hooves and breath of cows while their herds return along with the herd's men and spreads dust in the sky, for this reason the enchanting twilight hour was known as 'Godhulibela' ( hour of the cow's dust). The Vedas do not tire saying this-

गावः सर्वभूतानां गावः सर्वसुखप्रदाम'

Right from the Vedic times cow has been a symbol of religion, culture and civilization. At the sacred stage of spiritualism, during the yagnas the most precious offering to the priest, as a harbinger of his welfare, was considered cow only. Giving cow in charity was considered the greatest act of charity. Among, Indians it is a traditional practice to first spare a bite for the cow before having meals. Vedas salute the cow- 'अध्न्ये। ते रूपाय नमः।[18] O man not to kill cow, we salute you in this form!

According to the Rig Veda, the place where the cow lives comfortably, the mud there also becomes sacred and that place, a pilgrimage. Right from our birth to the time after our death, in all the rituals panchgavya (cow dung, urine, milk, ghee and curd) and panchamrit ( milk, curd, ghee, honey, sugar) are necessarily required. In great yagnas like Chandrayanadi, there is mention of drinking panchgavya.- गोभिःमत्सरं शृणीत। For a guest it was a practice to make a sweet dish out of panchgavya. The urine of cow is considered sacred as the holy waters of the Ganges. It is believed that the cow dung is a pure manifestation of Goddess Laxmi.[19] According to the scriptures, sins settled in our body parts, flesh and marrow, skin and bones, are destroyed on consumption of Panchgavya. Many of the cow's attributes are available in the cow dung, that is why it is known as 'gomaya'. In the Charak Samhita it is said about cow-dung, that it destroys germs. Merely by its odour the minute germs of diseases are destroyed. About cow's urine Charak says-

गव्यं सुमधुरं किंचिद् दोषघ्नं कृमिकुष्ठनुत।
कण्डूघ्नं शमयेत् पीतं सम्यग्दोषोदरे हितम्।।

When stricken by worms, leprosy, itching, jaundice, the use of cow's urine is efficacious as a cure. In the Atharva Veda there is this mantra singing glory of the cow-

एनीर्धाना हरिणीः श्येनीरस्य
कृष्णा धाना रोहिणीर्धनवस्ते

---

[18] Parishishtani, 26, p.784, Shripad Damodar Satwalekar, Rigveda Samhita

[19] Atharva veda Bhasha Bhashyam, 3.14, Discription-qualities of cow in shabdakalpdrum

तिलवत्सा ऊर्जमस्मै दुहाना
विश्वाहा सन्त्वनपस्फुरन्तीः ।। (18.4.34)

The Shruti mantra iterates that, cows of picture description, dull muddy colour, blue coloured, white and black coloured, the golden one and the red coloured cows are competent to bear and rear this loka and have also been called 'Dhana'. Such lactating cows live free and are without any fear. We must take proper care of them. It is our duty to implement policies for their protection, good health and welfare.

This mantra wishes welfare and auspiciousness (Yog-Kshem) for all. It instructs us, to protect and enhance the number of one, who is a harbinger of our good, human welfare, as a matter of duty.

By means of various mantras of Atharva Veda[20] the medicinal potential of cow has been sung, it is said, the cow's milk's white colour contains the effect of Sun's rays. The milk of red, golden and black cow cures diseases and is extremely nourishing. Its milk cures heart disease, anaemia, tuberculosis, asthma and other diseases. One who consumes the milk of these cows, his body remains healthy and disease free and his life is full of auspiciousness. The Atharva Veda sermonizes thus-

सं सिंचामि गवां क्षीरं समाज्येन बलं रसम् ।
संसिक्ता अस्माकं वीरा ध्रुवा गावो मयि गोपतौ ।। (2.26.4)
प्यो धेनुनां रसमोषधीनां जमवर्त्तां कवयो इन्वथ ।। (4.27.3)

Human being should protect the cows and by use of their milk and ghee gain strength and intellect to become valiant, such ace men ought to be holding portfolios as members of the Sabha, appropriately organizing affairs, carrying out ethical policies for the benefit of this world. Recognizing the gloriousness of the wealth of cows, human being say-

To gain power and liquid I consume cow's milk and ghee

---

[20] Atharva veda, 1.22.1, 4.21.6

and nurture the body. It is such a medicine which makes the body healthy and adds to its brilliance. In the main treatise on Ayurveda, namely 'Charak'[21] while commending the cow's milk it is said, **'क्षीर जीवयति'** meaning thereby, this milk is donor of life. It is tasteful, pure and destroyer of disease. Due to the carotene element in the cow's milk it has a yellowish tinge, which protects in it vitamin A,B,C, D, and E. Charak describes the attributes of cow's milk thus-

स्वादु शीतं मृदु स्निग्धं वृंहणं इलक्ष्णपिच्छिलम् ।
गुरु मन्दं प्रसन्नं च गव्यं दशगुणं पयः ।।

Cow's milk has ten attributes. It is tasteful, cool, tender, greasy, thick, pure, pasty, fulfilling, absorbs external effect from a distance and thrills the mind. The Veda mantra sings glory of its life generating attributes thus-

वशां देवा उपजीवंति वशां मनुष्या उत ।
वशेदं सर्वमभवद् यावत् सूर्यो विपश्यति ।।

(Ath.10.10.34)

It is said in this mantra that Indra and other deities get gavyahavya from cows to keep them alive and even human beings live by consuming milk products gotten from the cow. As far as the sun shines to that extent the cow is instrumental in retaining the Universe's creation.

Shruti mantras emphasize that in this world there is no wealth like the cows. These cows are the most precious form of wealth for the humankind. **'गोस्तुमात्र न विद्यते कल्याण'** (Yaju.23-48). It conveys a message to each sensitive human being that they need never kill such a harbinger of wealth. Innocent cow is not to be killed. Killing the cow is an unforgivable crime. The sentiment that 'mother cow is venerable', is thus expressed- 'Like Indra, Varun, Agni, Vayu and other deities, Aditi or the mother cow be venerated and served in accordance with the tenets of duty.

Influenced by the Vedic culture, Dayanand Saraswati in

---

[21] Annapal Prakaran Sutrasthan Ch.27 Shloka 217

his 'Gokarunanidhi' has called the compassionate facet of mother cow, protector of humanity, while praising her greatness and importance at length. For the security of the priceless wealth of the world, protector of the Earth, Swami Dayanand at that time established India's first cowshed in Rewadi and by means of 'Gokrishyadi Rakshini Sabha' and his collection of sermons in 'Updeshmanjari' he represented the Vedic saying of "Ahimsa Paramodharma'.

**Patriotism in the Vedas**
'माता भूमिः पुत्रो अहं पृथिव्याः।।

(Ath. 12.1.12)

The land of my nation is my mother, I am its son. Filled with this noble sentiment, in Canto twelve of Atharva Veda is a Sukta, famous as the Prithvi Sukta. The entire Sukta sings the glory of national patriotism, national prosperity and national prestige. The first mantra is-

सत्यं बृहदृतमुग्रं दीक्षा तपो ब्रह्म यज्ञः पृथिवीं धारयन्ति।
सा नो भूतस्य भव्यस्य पत्न्युरूं लोकं पृथिवी नः कृणोतु।। १।।

It is said that to establish any nation, true knowledge, truthful conduct, initiation, penance, creativity and yagna are essential symptoms. The Atharva Veda makes the king and the subjects both aware to be alert for the security of the nation, thus-

यां रक्षन्त्यस्वप्ना विश्वदानीं देवा भूमिं पृथिवीमप्रमादम्।
सा नो मधु प्रियं दुहामथो उक्षतु वर्चसा।। ७।।

The meaning of this mantra is that if the ruler and the subjects remain alert in protecting the national land, then the cow, in the form of national land begins to harvest honey, sweet and everything in abundance. Brilliance among them enhances, who forsake the reward for protecting the land.

It has been specifically mentioned in the Vedas that a dutiful Sabhapati, soldier or subjects alone are competent to protect the land and supress the enemies. Efficient leadership enhances the power of the nation absolutely-

शिला भूमिरश्मा पांसुः सा भूमिः संघृता घृता।
तस्यै हिरण्यवक्षसे पृथिव्या अकरं नमः।। २६।।

Ordinarily, land means a rock stone or land full of mud. But when governed by efficient leadership, has promising artisans, then that land only begins to gurgle gold, has treasure of many gems in it, illuminates in the form of a well-organized nation, and each one of the dwellers in the nation, bows before it. Venerating the nation as the motherland, this verse of the Veda iterates-

निधिं बिभ्रंती बहुधा गुहा वसु मणिं हिरण्यं पृथिवी ददातु मे।
वसू नो वसुदा रासमाना देवी दधातु सुमनस्यमाना।। 44।।

In its womb containing treasures, the land of the nation may provide us with wealth, jewels and gold. The land that showers boons may foster us. And-

उपस्थास्ते अनमीवा अयक्ष्मा अस्मभ्यं सन्तु पृथिवी प्रसूताः।
दीर्घ न आयुः प्रतिबुध्यमाना वयं तुभ्यं बलिहृतः स्याम।। 62।।

It is the duty of every human being to pay taxes for the protection of land that rears all living beings and be ready to sacrifice himself, if need be. The 59th mantra of the Prithvi Sukta describes beautifully, the national land thus-

शन्तिवा सुरभिः स्योना कीलालोघ्नी पयस्वती।
भूमिरधि ब्रवीतु मे पृथिवी पयसा सह।। 59।।

Peaceful, fragrant, harbinger of happiness, filled with nectar, great promoter, Kamdhenu in the form of national land, fostering us for truth, justice, health and prosperity. This way the Vedic people's rule or democracy presents an ideal system of ruling, wherein there is prosperity, mutual well-being, patriotism, people are unafraid, ethically behaved, have importance of values, welfare of beings, education and health. In the Yajur Veda, while presenting the national anthem the verse iterates-

आ ब्रह्मन् ब्राह्मणो ब्रह्मवर्चसी जायतामाराष्ट्रे राजन्यः शूरऽइषव्योऽतिव्याधी
महारथो जायतां दोग्धी धेनुर्वोढाऽनड्वानाशुः
सप्तिः पुरन्धिर्योषा जिष्णू रथेष्ठाः
समेयो युवास्य यजमानस्य वीरो जायतां निकामेनिकामे नः पर्यन्यो
वर्षतु फलवत्यो नऽओषधयः पच्यन्ताम् योगक्षेमो नः कल्पताम्।। (22.22)

This mantra of the Yajurveda, has been appropriated in

Shatpath at the time of Ashwamedh yagna. Adhvaryu was chanting this mantra in the Ashwamedha yagna, praying for the advancement in the nation of the emperor who had performed the yagna. He says-

O brahmin! in our nation, a brahmin as powerful as the Creator may be born. He is to be valiant and adept in scriptures and the use of armour, destroyer of the enemy, extremely powerful Kshatriya be he. There be lactating cows, fast running horses. Women folk be intelligent. Successful, charioteer, civilized, youthful sons be there. The clouds may irrigate the Earth with ample sweet water, there be a store full of medicines. The branches may bloom with flowers and fruits. The welfare work for all of us be carried out. For invocation of the mantra the 'क्रिया आ जायताम्' has been performed. It is worth knowing the prefix of a consonant 'aa'. The meaning of 'aa' is 'समन्तात्' or in all the four directions. Thus, the implication of 'आ जायताम्' would be Brahmana etcetera must have their influence, not only in one or two directions but in all the four corners of the nation.

There are innumerable mantras in the Vedas expressing high ideals related to the nation. The purpose of national arrangement is, building up the nation, management and maintenance of relations with other nations. To understand the word nation, it can be divided in two parts. 'Raj' and 'Tra', thus, 'Rashtra' or the nation is that whose king is 'trata' or saviour.

**National Security, National Policy**

The ideal of Vedic national system is maintenance of friendly and cordial relations with all nations. But if any nation under the spell of pride initiates aggression and perpetrates cruelty over our subjects, in such a circumstance, it is the duty of a king with good conduct, valiant and brave, follower of the policy of punishment, to subjugate the aggressive king through, the use of his military forces and protect his nation. It is a mantra of the Yajurveda-

दूते दृहँ मा मित्रस्य मा चक्षुषा
सर्वाणि भूतानि समीक्षन्ताम् ।
मित्रस्याहं चक्षुषा सर्वाणि भूतानी समीक्षे ।
मित्रस्य चक्षुषा समीक्षामहे ।। 36.18 ।।

We may look at all nations with a friendly feeling and they
to reciprocate the same friendly feeling, all nations must dwell
in mutual friendship. Atharva Veda states-

यो नो द्वेषत्पृथिवि यः पृतन्याद्योऽभिदासान्मनसा यो वधेन ।
तं नो भूमे रन्धय पूर्वकृत्वरि ।। 12.1.14 ।।

But if any nation nurtures animosity against us or by
armed aggression wishes to subjugate us or desires to destroy
us, then it ought to be eradicated.

वि तिष्ठध्वं मरुतो विक्ष्वीउच्छत गृभायत रक्षसः सं पिनष्टन ।
वयो ये भूत्वा पतयन्ति नक्तभिर्ये वा रिपो दधिरे देवे अध्वरे ।। (8.4.18)

To inspire the brave, the verse iterates, 'O brave! Look for
the wicked ones and take them into custody for punishment.
Those who travel at night in planes to spy on our country like
nocturnal birds and those who obstruct auspicious quality of
yagnas and other ceremonies, they be uprooted.'

In the Vedas, while opposing aggression, along with the
declaration, 'मा हिंसी पुरुषं जगत्' a wish has been expressed for
prevalence of peace. But if someone is bent upon aggression
then for that, the king has been instructed to resort to the use
of power of punishment-

युवं तमिन्द्रापर्वता पुरोयुधा यो नः पृतन्यादप तंतमिद्धतं
वज्रेण तंतमिद्धतम् । दूरे चत्ताय च्छन्त्सद् गहनं यदिनक्षत् ।
अस्माकं शत्रून् परि शूर विश्वतो दर्मा दर्षीष्ट विश्वतः ।।

(Rig. 1.132.6)

The army chiefs who exhibit valour like the Sun and
clouds in the battlefield! The Kingdom that invades our army,
inviting a conflict, such a kingdom be given an equal
response. Using sharp weapons and armours pierce them. On
getting defeated when they run to retreat, rout them
completely.

About accepting women as leaders of the armed forces, it

has been mentioned—

सरस्वति त्वमस्माँ अविड्ढि मरुत्वती घृषती जेषि शत्रून्।
त्यं चिच्छर्धन्तं तविषीयमाणमिन्द्रो हन्ति वृषभंशण्डिकानाम्।। (2.30.8)

As electricity and wind strikes rain clouds, likewise O commendable beautiful ladies, with scientific knowledge and education! Inspiration of magniloquence, warrior leaders like you, in the manner they kill the powerful brave ones in the enemy's armed forces, likewise, subjugate the enemies who are destroyers of our happiness and thereby command our respect.

**Justice Imparting, Self Government or Swarajya**

As the king is well conducted and dutiful in behaviour, so are the subjects and if the king follows the ways of the subjects, then only peace and auspiciousness is maintained and the welfare of all is possible.' The king and the subjects have duty towards each other, on this aspect the verses of the Vedas have thrown light, which is to be comprehended by human beings in the form of inspiration.

'वसवस्त्रयोदशाक्षरेण त्रयोदशं स्तोममुदजयस्तमु ज्जेषँ
रुद्राश्चतुर्दशाक्षरेण चतुर्दश स्तोममुदजयँ स्तमुज्जेषमादित्याः।।'

(Yaju.9.34)

The gist of the said mantra is, that along with the king all must get involved in their duty in an active manner and increase their knowledge. By studying the Vedas ought to strengthen the path of imparting justice. Adhering to their duty in accordance with the Varnashram Dharma, they should administer the nation. At various junctures in the Vedic verses, it is said that a man who is gifted with Sun like qualities and undertakes the obligation of protecting like a father, he alone is qualified to be the king and those who conduct themselves as sons are qualified to be subjects. Practically seen, each mantra in the Veda is a gem itself, on adorning it each person, society and the kingdom would glow, and the entire universe will be illumined by it. See what this mantra in the Rig Veda states-

आ यद् वामीयचक्षसा मित्र वयं च सूरयः।
व्यचिष्ठेबहुपाय्ये यतेमहि स्वराज्ये।।

(Rig.5.66.6)

In this mantra of the Veda special stress is placed on 'swa.' Self-government means a governance in which, the administrative officers work under men who are pure-sacred, dutiful, impartial, with no vested interest. This self-governance is for the good of the subjects, is 'बहुपाय्ये' or is a rule carried out by many. Here the meaning of 'व्यचिष्ठे' is a rule which is vast, all pervasive and must have motility. Each person adhering to dutifulness is in an endeavour to live happily and this way of ruling is impartial. 'ईयचक्षसा'. It means omniscient, friendly in behaviour and making efforts for everyone's welfare, only have a right to rule. In this mantra the use of 'सूरयः' has been to mean, scholars illumined with truthful knowledge alone are qualified to rule.

The above noted mantra of the Rig Veda, is such an example of Vedic imagination, which is found hither-thither in the Vedas, following it in the Vedic kingdoms, yam-niyama (rules-regularity were adhered to, the education of ideals like, non-violence, truthfulness, non-stealing, celibacy, non-possessiveness is imparted right from the beginning to students in Brahmacharya ashram. In the Guru's (teacher's) house students learnt yam-niyama (rules-regularity) and were treated as eligible to rule. Today there is neither the education of yam-niyama in schools, colleges and universities nor is attention paid to self- control. Consequently, everywhere there is flow of imprudence, excessive desires, catering to the call of senses, materialistic demonization and extreme selfishness. In today's self-government, only getting the right to rule is the goal for everyone, for which only attainment of a certain age is the criterion for eligibility, but no retirement age is mentioned. Gentleman or evil, scholar or an ignorant one, are all eligible for self- rule. For this reason, it can be said, following the Vedic tenets of dutifulness, Ram-Rajya came into being, on forsaking them Ram is lost in the past, only rajya (rule) is retained.

**Veda and Humanism**

It is a well- known truth that only elevated human beings lead to the building of an elevated human society and only an elevated society makes it possible for the individuals to develop personality. Both make each other complete, and the individual comes first. He is a unit of the society without it the society cannot be formed. For this reason, the Veda has given the first thread to society—'मनुर्भव ।' O human being! become human, be contemplative. This contemplation should be filled with a feeling of well-being for all. That is why Vedic sage says in Yajurveda (34.1.6), 'मे मनः शिव संकल्पमस्तु'My mind should have commitment of Shiva, with only feelings of wellbeing and auspiciousness in it. These commitments must convert into actions and help in the development of the community. In the society there should be a maternal feeling, friendliness among all, and feeling for the community be extended, for which the following mantra of the Yajurveda is quotable-

'मित्रस्याहं चक्षुषा सर्वाणि भूतानि समीक्षे ।
मित्रस्य चक्षुषा समीक्षामहे ।। (36.18)

I should look up to everyone with a friendly eye, we should look at each other with mutual friendship. This is what is Vedic humanism and this humanism is man's duty. It was the effect of this noble concept of the Veda, which forced the world famous scholar Maxmuller to say, " if it is asked which literature should be an inspiration for clearing the inner foulness of our life, falling back upon it, we could move on the path of progress, make our lives worldly- wise, be revered truly, then my finger will point towards India, as an inexhaustible treasure of the most important, most valuable and knowledgeable ingredients of human history is available in India, only in India, is collected in India only".

In the West humanism began in 19th and 20th century as an ideology. Its thread came into hand as a consequence of the reawakening of Greek and Roman philosophy in the 14th and 16th century. The main aim of this movement was reestablishment of the glory of human beings. The ideology that reaffirmed human values and glory, came to be called humanism. This word is derived from a Latin word 'humnus'. Humanism and humanitarianism, both are related to human qualities of dutifulness, serving others, self-sacrifice, mutual affection and compassion. This is humanitarianism also. Humanitarianism elevates a human being higher and superior to an animal, The Webster Twentieth Century Dictionary (Page 888), holds[22]'humanism' to be an ideological system- "humanism is the name of a system of those thoughts and actions which are interested in human welfare and ideals." Rolf Bortone Parry has written while expressing his views on the said definition,"Humanism is those wishes, activities and accomplishment which make an ordinary person acquire high quality nature." Humanistic ideals are neither for an ordinary human being nor a divine personality. Briefly it be said that it is the other state of an ordinary human being and the possibilities of experiencing it.

Western thinkers consider ethics to be the root feeling of humanism. But these ethics are restricted to terrestrial life, materialism and worldly pleasures. Opposed to this were, Indian thinker Swami Dayanand Saraswati who lived by the tenets of Vedic culture, Ravindra Nath Tagore, Yogiraj Aurobindo and Dr. Radhakrishnan have all connected humanism with worldly and other worldly life. According to all of them, humanism is that life philosophy, that discriminates for the feeling of people's welfare, without preconceptions, opinionated views and pre-positions, and conveys the great message of sacrifice, for a human being for this life and other, undergoes a purification to acquire qualities

---

[22] Welster Twentieth Centure Dictionary, p.888

for a worthy human being, moves forward for a wholistic development.

In a human being's existence, there are both worldly and other worldly elements. But he becomes grand only on acquiring truthfulness, goodness and beauty, manifesting in the great activities they carry on. In the Vedic verses great tasks have been referred to as Yagna. Each action in life is Yagna. This thought has gained supremacy. This is what is reiterated in the Rig Veda," (Purush Sukta (10-90) each human being must get involved in activities like conducting a Yagya. Truly speaking, Yagya is that grand commitment, which requires entire strength and great intelligence for inspiring to do it. In the universe a Yagya is going on all the time. The meaning of Yagya is not just lighting a fire and offer fire- wood or ingredients of Homam as oblation in it. The main attribute of Yagya is good of others and sacrifice. Knowledge, action, veneration, yoga, philosophy, science and all, are the inherent parts of this Yagya.

The mantras of Rig Veda and the Yajurveda (25.22,35.22) are not only a philosophy. It has life's practicality and the sentiment of all welfare. The Vedas truly illumine the path of accomplishing life sojourn of human beings. Mathematics, Astrology, Ayurveda, knowledge of seafaring and flying aeroplane, various arts, commerce and so on, various subjects are included in the Vedas. Swami Dayanand in his writing, Satyarth Prakash, has segregated these subjects in four portions—Science, Action, Veneration and knowledge of the Vedas. The Vedas for human welfare provide the rules of ethics which are relevant for all countries and all times. The meaning of Veda is knowledge of the soul of the universe and the aim of education of Vedas is to explain the creation of human life and life of the universe, 'विदन्ति जानन्ति... सर्वे मनुष्याः सर्वाः सत्यविद्या यैर्येषुवा' तथा 'विद्वांसश्च भवन्ति'. According to this mantra, this human life and universal life is for welfare of people. The welfare of the people is possible by practicing humanism. The ladder to the destination of humanism is eternal. Eternal means permanent truth. It can be contended with certainty, that humanism is the permanent truth of human life. Till we do not wow to it, we cannot attain in life truthfulness, goodness and beauty. The element of eternity cannot be bound to the boundaries of a country or time. The Dharma is great, that makes the human being aware of the element of self. Veda itself iterates that for a self- realized person the entire universe is like one family. 'यत्र विश्वं भवत्येक नीडम् ।'The flow of the tri- stream of knowledge, action, veneration, that is equally useful for all the sons of the Earth.

Thus, the Vedic sages on the ground of invincible faith in the element of eternity and truthful commitment, began to solve the mystery of the puzzle of human welfare, but they did not move on with blind faith. They were very well aware of the fact that due to multi manifestations of the Creator, untruthful products are treated as the truth. It is clearly said in the Yajurveda (Ch.40.17.2) and in Eshavasyopnishad, verse 15, that many a time the truth is covered with glittering golden pot.

'हिरण्मयेन पात्रेण सत्यस्यापिहितं मुखम् ।'

After this mantra there is a prayer to the Lord that vanquish the glitter of untruthful and make us see the truth. 'तत्वं पूषन्नपावृणु सत्यधर्माय दृष्टये ।' (Yajur Kavyashaka 40.15) this mantra is also overflowing with the same sentiment, that God may enable us see, what the truth is. In the Vedas, there is prayer to God for granting such intelligence, that we may want to see the truth, in Suktas related to Megha and Saraswati. The aim of these Suktas is to adorn the human being with humanitarian attributes. With pure knowledge and questioning intelligence, a human being is able to discriminate between appropriate and the inappropriate and move on the right path. A human being without knowledge is influenced by selfishness and knowledgeable one is inspired by action for other's welfare, a selfish human being is one who is oblivious of the self and is immersed in the ocean of interests other than the self. Contrary to it a self-realized person sees all beings in his self and sees his own self in all beings- 'आत्मवत् सर्वभूतेषु यः पश्यति सः पण्डितः।'One who feels the happiness and sorrow of all beings, does not hate anyone, is venerable-

'यस्मिन्तत्सर्वाणि भूतान्यात्मैवा भूद्विजानतः।
तत्र को मोहः कः शोकऽएकत्वमनुपश्यतः ।।

(Yaju.40.7)

In Indian philosophy, the element of self is the inspirational element for all pervasive humanity. Veda expose the all- pervasive humanity before us and through the inspiration of the element of self, human beings illumine the path of happiness and prosperity. 'आत्मवत् सर्वभूतेषु' is the mantra for practicing during lifetime, conveying the message of truthful speech, truthful commitment and truthful deeds.

The mantras of Atharva Veda and Rig Veda, while expanding humanism convey the message of 'अहिंसा परमो धर्मः' This has been called 'महाव्रत' by sage Patanjali. Following the Vedic dictum of kindness towards all beings Smriti and scriptures of Dharmashastra also strongly condemn violence and non-vegetarianism. Even in yam-Niyama, non-violence is the most prominent. The mantra of Atharva Veda is 'अनागोहत्या वै भीमा' (10.1.29) which means killing the innocent is a heinous crime. In the Rig Veda there is this commitment, 'ननिर्देयो मिनीमसि'meaning thereby, 'we will not kill anyone.'The Vedas touch the very tender spot of humanity that human beings ought to eat food sharing with others. Keep in mind that all beings get food to eat. Those suffering from ailments, destitute and under refuge, must get food to satiate their hunger. According to the Rig Veda (10.117.6), 'केवलाघो भवति केवलादि' which means, one who enjoys eating alone, packs sin for himself.

The other unique features of the Vedic mantras are the wish for amiable feelings, wish to bid farewell and wish for world peace. While praying to God for wishing amiability the devotee says- each action of mine must be inspired by welfare.

I should do selfless service. My life must be self-regulated, even in adversity I need never be deviated from the path of my duty. There is a Rig Vedic mantra-

'भद्रं कर्णेभिः शृणुयाम देवा भद्रं पश्येमाक्षभिर्यजत्राः।
स्थिरैरङ्गैस्तुष्टुवांसस्तनूभिर्व्यशेमहि देवहितं यदायुः।।'

(Rig.1.89.8)

In this mantra, praying to all the natural divine powers the devotee says, 'O deities! our ears should hear only good. O reverend ones, our eyes may see only good. Our body parts be stable. We ought to remain in prayer always. Our body may remain in good health till the Lord grants life.Wishing for auspiciousness the Rig Vedic mantra states- land, water, air and the wealth of animals be harbinger of happiness and source of life force for all beings. The same way the mantra (36.8) of Yajurveda is,'शन्नोऽस्तु द्विपदे शं चतुष्पदे।' It means, 'Lord our actions be for the welfare and comfort of two legged and four legged animals. The Atharva Veda (17.1.7) wishes well-being for all being- 'यांश्च पश्यामि यांश्च न तेषु मा सुमतिं कृधि।'

Each one of the words of Vedic verses is filled with humanitarian aspects of life. It has been clearly said in the Rig Veda (5.51.15) 'पुनर्ददताघ्नता जानता संगमेमहि।'. We should mingle with charitable, non-violent and scholarly people. The central idea is, that large-heartedness, non-violence and pure knowledge are symptoms of humanity. We should adopt them and conduct ourselves accordingly. The message of humanism is that our heart be without foulness, the mind be one not split, speech be tender and full of wellness, the mind be healthy, we may view things with equanimity. The Sabha and Samiti may have noble thoughts. Together we may move on the path of welfare and move the nation on the path of progress.

In the inexhaustible source of humanitarian knowledge, the Vedas are available humanitarian values constituting the Suktas. If we could adopt them in our lives then we will be rid of the debt of sages of India, who devoted their entire lives and power of knowledge, in making all human beings realize the knowledge of self. If we could benefit a little from this basic heritage, then today many problems will find their solution on this Earth. The world is looking forward to it.

**From Upliftment of the Self to National Uplift**

In the eighth Canto of Atharva Veda, about rendering a message of self- upliftment it is said, 'O human being! Auspicious deeds are only duty. Earning food and wealth by indulging in auspicious deeds, one could be free of deprivation. Treading the path recommended by scholars and teachers and protecting it is everyone's duty. In each life there be a combination of deeds for other's good and sacrifice. In all the Suktas soul elevation is treated at a higher pedestal, rather than materialistic progress. the mantra of 24th Sukta of the 3rd Canto says thus-

शत हस्त समाहर सहस्र हस्त संकिर।
कृतस्य कार्यस्य चेह स्फातिं समावह।। (3.24.5)

The mantra inspires the human being to become skilful in a thousand ways and through thousand skilful acts earn wealth and prosperity, to spend in good deeds to move towards progress. Give directions for people's welfare, in the Canto 18, Sukta no.2, mantra 18 of Atharva Veda, it has been sermonizes-

'याँ ते धेनुं निपृणामि यमु ते क्षीर ओदनम्।
तेना जनस्यासो भर्ता योऽत्रासदजीवनः।।' 30।।

The gist of this is that give milk and food to weak and helpless, indulge in actions meant to bring about well-being, which leads to a life without hurdles. The verses of Atharva Veda like the Rig Veda show direction for working towards veneration, society and national welfare. For the king and his subjects both, the message of dutiful behaviour and its completion is given. Likewise, there is a prayer in the Yajurveda–

'अग्ने नय सुपथाराये अस्मान् विश्वानि देव वयुनानि विद्वान
युयोध्यस्मज्जुहुराणमेनो भूयिष्ठां ते नमऽ उक्तिं विधेम'।। (40.16)

The meaning of this mantra is, 'O brilliant Lord! From a noble path take us close to wealth, as you know, all kinds of acts, make us fight against the evil, sin within us, (help get rid of it) we salute you.

By this mantra we learn such a superior way of ruling, that instructs the king to move on a pure path, get wealth from its subjects and the subjects in this flawless system are able to get prosperous. Vedic verses preach that a human being must earn wealth through truthful deeds, use its own products, never to try control over other's possessions and spend the money earned through hard work for the welfare of others. The first mantra of Ishopanishad expresses this sentiment. The mantra says-

'ईशावास्यमिदं सर्वं यत्किञ्चजगत्याम् जगत्।
तेन् त्यक्तेन भुंञ्जीथा मा गृधः कस्य स्विद्धनम्।।' 1।।

Our ancient tradition is that the use of wealth be for propagation of education, serving the poor and unhappy, improvement of economic system and deeds for people's welfare, this tradition has been followed continuously. Specially in the Atharva Veda, we find the mention of those important things in the seed form, which present before us a ruling system for welfare- "The king taking care of the subjects, their security, enhancement of animal husbandry, sound economic and agricultural system, and along with it, disease-less health, longevity of life, is also been told to be the medium of welfare. Under the scriptures of Ayurvedic medical system, in the Atharva Veda, description of the regulations in the medical field, systems, and the duty of a doctor have been given at length. The policies of each rule have been praised with the viewpoint of service to beings. It has been treated as an object of faith.

In the Vedic literature there have been prayers at various stages for a well formed, duty bound and dutiful welfare royal system of ruling the kingdom and the nation. It is also told that so long as the rules of Dharma were followed by rulers, till then Dharma in its full form was alive, but the rulers who deviated from the path prescribed by the Vedas, could not fulfil the tenets of duty and became liable for the downfall of the nation. All the present so called democratic ruling systems of the world, cannot face the Vedic self- government from any viewpoint. We will have to accept this reality, that if India has to establish its identity once again on the international stage, then in conducting the state administration, it will have to adopt and assimilate the example of dutiful self-government as described in the Vedic verses.

In the Atharva Veda, it has been told that the result of Dharma is, increase of brilliance and vitality, fearlessness and patience. It is necessary for it to practice celibacy and keep a check on speech. Control the mind and senses. On adhering to the prescribed duty, a human being can be adorned with a mighty kingdom. In the Atharva Veda in a mantra it is said-

श्रमेण तपसा सृष्टा ब्रह्मण वित्तर्तं श्रिता।
सत्येनावृता श्रिया प्रावृता यशसा परींवृता।। (12.5 1.2)

It means for acquiring a kingdom hard work is necessary. Hard work is a part of duty, as laziness is the biggest hurdle in duty. It is also said.'आलस्यो हि मनुष्याणां शरीरस्यो महान् रिपु: ।'

As the nation must be empowered with the strength of weapons for self-defence, likewise, for spiritual empowerment the strength of the Spirit is essential. Without the strength of the Spirit, the strength of weapons is handicapped. On seeing the strength of the weapons bereft of the strength of the Spirit, sage Vishwamitra said, shame on the power of the weapons.

धिग् बलं क्षत्रियबलं ब्रह्म तेजो बलं बलम्।।

In the Yajur Veda it is said that the nation where these two powers are present in mutual amalgamation, that nation reaps the benefit of nobility and is considered fortunate.

'यत्र ब्रह्म च क्षत्रं च सम्यञ्चौ चरत: सह।
तं लोकं पुण्यं प्रज्ञेषं यत्र देवा: सहाग्निना।। (20.25)

The clear meaning of this mantra is that the power of the

weapons protects the power of the Spirit and the power of the Spirit protects the power of the weapons. The power of the Spirit is the symbol of flow of education, progress of knowledge and science, development of spiritualism, all pervasive duty, truthfulness, justice, in the nation. For the progress of the nation both powers must develop. For this reason, in ancient times sacred sages were advisors to the king and helped in making the nation rich ethically.

Giving a sermon on dutifulness the mantra of Atharva Veda (12.5) -

'ब्रह्म च क्षत्रं च राष्ट्रं च विशश्च त्विषिश्च यशश्च वर्चश्च द्रविणं च।। 8 ।।

It is said that the duty of a Brahmin is to acquire high knowledge and propagate it. Kshatriya Varna's duty is gallantry, courage, form a force full of brave people, punish the evil, and protecting the subjects.

The duty of the Vaishyas is to increase wealth through noble means. It is the duty of all human beings that through genuine efforts they should get possessions, and duty protect them, also increase their quantity to put in proper use. Along with it, in the ninth and tenth mantra there is mention of means of longevity of age, enhancement of education, fame, power and strength. Stress has been given on inculcating good values for the upliftment of the subjects and increase of animal husbandry.

1. आयुश्च रूपं च नाम च कीर्तिश्च प्राणश्चापानश्च चक्षुश्च श्रोत्रं च। 9 ।।

2. पयश्च रसश्चान्नं चान्नाद्यं च ऋतं च सत्यं चेष्टं च पूर्तं च प्रजा च पशवश्च। 10 ।।

These mantras make it evident that the progress of human society is the progress of Dharma, and Dharma is that attribute through its medium, physical, mental and spiritual progress is possible. There are three types of hurdles in the spiritual and national progress, 1) shortcoming of lack of knowledge 2) shortcoming of non-strength 3) not having the strength of good deeds. Overcoming these shortcomings and replacing them with the wholeness of good attributes, is possible through charity. From this point of view the duty of charity is an easy path for the redemption of a nation.

Charity be indulged in for educating the ignorant, to make the weak strong, to enhance the power of good deeds among those lacking in them. By eradicating these three types of shortcomings, an effort be made for national progress, this is what the Vedas sermonise. This could be called a great path for national advancement. The Vedic literature basically is the source for the entire world's (beings) welfare. Nations simmering internally with Jealousy and malevolence, struggle and doubt, anger and passion, can be pacified by the medium of Vedic literature.

Through the medium of Vedas, Vidhi- Nishedhas it has been explained with clarity. Whatever is dutiful act that is Vidhi (worship), and what is against duty it is Nishedh (Ban). In Poorvameemansa and Vaisheshik it has been said, that in the Vedas what has been ascertained for a human being is Dharma (dutifulness), and what has not been recommended to do is non-dharma. Later the rulers by accepting these elements of Dharma, became harbingers of welfare, epitome of sacrifice, and charity. Consequently, they were popular among people and came to be known as Dharmaraj.

**Concept of Oneness of the Soul**

The philosophy of equanimity and oneness is described in the Rig Veda. In the tenth Madal of the Rig Veda's last Sukta, one ninty one (2,3,4) and in sixth Canto of Atharva Veda, sukta sixty four (1,2,3) is related to a human being's pure conduct, pure thoughts, pure commitment and sermons of equanimity. Through the medium of these mantras the Veda, wish human beings well. Wishing well is a form of duty, as duty is not only the internal intention leading to all great deeds in this world but is also its main observer. Maharshi Dayanand has presented it in the form of Sangathan Sukta-

1. संङ्गच्छध्वं संवदध्वं सं वो मनांसि जानताम्।

**2. समानो मंत्रः समितिः समानी, समानं मनःसह चित्तमेषाम् ।**
**3. समानी व आकूतिः समाना हृदयानि वः**
**4. समानमस्तु वो मनो, यथा वः सुसहासति ।।**

All the above noted three mantras, establishing duty related values, sermonises, all human beings must live together, should have a feeling of amicability. Without being partial be filled with the sentiment of justice, truthful concepts, people ought to do their duty. Do not act against Dharma, do not say anything opposed to dharma, and do the assigned tasks. The knowledge of dharma be gotten in four ways- through, teachings of sacred souls and scholars, self- purification, wish for truthful effort, and through the learning of the Vedas gotten from the divine. This is what makes one understand the truth and falsehood, which is not possible, otherwise. All human beings have this competence to be able to differentiate between truth and falsehood and illumine their mind and intellect. The Veda mantras direct us to conduct ourselves without trickery and deceit, with anyone. Together we should share the products available. It is also an instruction of the Veda, that the products be distributed and consumed in accordance with the need of the individual uniformly. This only makes imparting of just Dharma possible.

The voice of the Rig Veda expresses that the thoughts that promote everyone's welfare, they ought to be accepted. Limits must be adhered to in behaviour. While remaining in the stage of acquiring knowledge, practice of educational study, celibacy and so on, practice Dharma. With the concurrence of fine members of the Sabha, the duties of the king and other officials be fixed. Intellectual, physical power and valour be promoted for the purpose of administration and protection of the state. There be purity of conduct, good attributes be imbibed, and foul ones discarded. The king's instructions must be for promoting truthfulness and Dharma. To give and take any product the transaction be mutually dutiful. Dharma only helps a truthful person. The mantra of Yajurveda puts forward this thought-

दृष्ट्वा रूपे व्याकरोत्सत्यानृते प्रजापतिः ।
अश्रद्धामनृतेऽदधाच्छ्रद्धासत्ये प्रजापतिः ।। (19.77)

In this mantra Prajapati gives a sermon to human beings on Dharma, that only truth be adopted, not falsehood. Truth alone is Dharma (duty), falsehood is Adharma (Non -duty). They have visible and invisible symptoms. The symptoms of duty and non- duty, that are related to the external effort, are visible, and the symptom related to the soul is invisible. This mantra places importance on a human being's soul and external façade, both being pure. Contemplation, meditation and actions be inspired by truthful duty. All pervasive Dharma is based on this truth alone. Veda reiterates 'सत्येनोत्तमिता भूमिः', meaning thereby, this Earth is stable on the foundation of truth. Mainly in the Upanishad the feeling of, 'तत् त्वम् असि' exists, which represents the principle of oneness. According to Dr. sarvapalli Radhakrishnan, 'Tat Twam Asi' is an active ethical service. He has mentioned the thought of Duesan, who has written that Bible has presented a very high ethical principle'- Love your neighbour as your own self.' The question arises, why should I do so, when by nature I experience happiness and sorrow both myself, not in my neighbour. The Bible does not have an answer to this question of Dusan, but Vedas have it. 'Tat Twam Asi' is the gist of three elemental dictums, "You ought to love your neighbour, because you are also a neighbour."

In the Upanishad, the concept of equality is not only elemental, but it also shows the path of ethics. This truth has been clarified in the story of King Janashruti and chariot driver Suyugva Rakva, in Chhandogya Upanishad (4.1.2, 4.4). It is said that, it all belongs to Brahma (The Creator). In this Upanishad through the story of Satyakam Jabali, it is said that for ascertaining the attributes of a person his birth or conditioning is not held as responsible. That is why the feeling of 'Tat Twam Asi' is a feeling of complete equality.

In the various Suktas of Vedic Cantos, we learn that the king who is instructed to carry on smoothly the Varna Ashram arrangement, he instructs everyone to remain in Dharma. In the verses of the Shruti, right from the beginning, there is no mention of it. Here and there the exposition of Varnashram Dharma and the importance of its protection, that has been mentioned, which binds the persons related to it in regulations. A king upset with Dharma and its regulations is also instructed to be liable for punishment. For the national system of imparting justice and mutual social behaviour, it is necessary that work be done in accordance with the instructions of Dharma. This Dharma, by no means can be discriminatory, but in work specifications may form oneness. With the aim of lawful conduct of the administration, Plato has in his book 'Republic,' while expressing his thoughts on the principle of justice, mentioned, that the establishment of justice is only possible in a kingdom, if the sections of society, the king, soldiers, and economic section follow the principle of work specialisation and do not interfere in the work of one another. One who flouts the rule of work specialisation and non-interference is liable for punishment by the king. In Shruti, Upanishads and so on, many centuries ago, there was talk of the society, nation and the universe being united in oneness, on the ground of work specialisation. In this unification there was assimilation of ethical values like, sameness, justice, assigned effort, amicable feeling, good behaviour, and good conduct. These values make it evident that in ancient political structure the concept of Dharma was meaningful. These are the values to understand which, not only the scholars of Indian politics but also western thinkers also, are bound to study deeply, laid down in the Vedic literature.

Western thinkers like Duning and Maxmuller, have created this fallacy that India is only restricted to Dharma and the element Meemansa or philosophy has no contribution in political science, as political science developed in the West, but it has been shattered now. Their singular viewpoint is at fault, as they have taken the Dharma propagated in Vedic literature as religion. To understand the Vedic selfgovernment applying the concept of Dharma's micro vision, wisdom, intelligence, an eye for knowledge is required. In the ancient India the prevalent successful popular rule was expounded by Shruti and that is why it came to be known as Dharma Shastra. In life at all levels, be it personal work, or social obligation or a royal duty or a Shruti on universal welfare, Upanishad, or the Puranas, it has been instructed to be carried out in accordance with the tenets of Dharma. As the Dharma is flaw less, likewise, the entire life filled universe be flawless. The entire Earth be ruled by one single Vedic authority. With this reference in the Aittiriya Brahman the sage says, 'सार्वभौमः सर्वायुधः अन्ताद् आ पराधात् प्रथिव्यै समुद्रपर्यन्ताया एकराड्इति।'

It means beyond the ocean till the point the Earth extends, that entire land must have one single Arya King, The Earth be one Arya kingdom and the entire Earth be one Arya family. 'आर्य परिवार–वसुधैव कुटुंबकम्' expresses this high ideal. It means that among human beings there should never be ill feelings. Today the human being caught up in lowly thoughts and desires and greed, is making his life foul, and is partaking in the downfall of the human community, it is necessary that he should revert to his prosperous, priceless, ancient, but relevant for all ages, all pervasive values of the Vedic literature, for imbibing. To fulfil Artha and Kaama, which is essential for life, make Dharma and Truth the basis, then only attainment of human goal moksha will be possible. That is why probably, Dharma, Artha, Kaama and Moksha are called Purushartha. Working selflessly, a human being may attain it. Thus, the entire thought of society and kingdom in its all- pervasive form, on both levels, social and political, rests on the principles of Dharma. In the ambit of the principles of Dharma the primary principles of kingship, manifested in their worldly form as royal protector, and developed further later.

In every way Dharma is knowledge and science as well. It is an art of living. It is the directive element of politics and society. All the historical proofs make it evident that many years before Plato and Arastu's 'The Prince' and 'The Politics' were written, Kautilya's Artha Shastra was there. Vedic literature existed much before that. The words like 'lok ranjan' (People's welfare) Prajaranjan' (Welfare of the Subjects) 'Janahit' ( Good of people) 'Jan kalyan' ( Welfare of people) and Raj Dharma ( Royal Duty) are used repeatedly in Vedic verses, Brahman scriptures, Aranyaks and Upanishads. These are part of the priceless sermons given by sages. This proves that our ancient literature existed, much before the West was conversant with democratic values. 'Swarajya' is a vindicating example, which is also called 'Dharma rajya'. The election in the kingdom, of the king and its ministers, oath taking, judicial system, economic prosperity, the King and his subject's respective duties are described in Vedic literature and present a high levelled base for democratic organization of Dharma. Dharma has been declared to be the basis of the entire human behaviour. The entire organization rested on the truth in the form of Dharma. This is the reason why countries of the world try to get out of the snare of materialism and seeking solace for the soul are looking for ancient rays of light. Rig Veda says- 'कृण्वन्तो विश्वमार्यम्' declares that the entire Earth be ruled by Vedic system.

*Chapter 5*
# The Rajdharma in Manav Dharmashastra

The form of Dharma propounded by Vedic literature has been assimilated in the Smritis. The political system of a large country like India, has been minutely thought over by the Smritis. The ancient rule was so prosperous and at the peak of its progress, is learnt by the fact, that in the present times, the form of prevelent democratic system has its foundation in the way of ancient administration. Secret advise is available to us in Smritis and other texts of Dharmashastra.

The composition of these Smritis or Dharmashastra was done later than the Sutra scriptures. Dharmashastra are those scriptures which are expositions of the Raj dharma and that of its subjects, the process of justice, system of punishment, social conduct and thought, caste system and duties, ethics, good conduct and scripture's related regulations, described herein. Along with it the protection of the welfare of human beings, policies for his welfare and the law for his freedom for advancement, its underlying thought, is also narrated extensively. The great foundational systems and an outline of high regulations on duty, prepared by Smriti Scriptures for the traditional political system of ancient India, is not anywhere else in the world history.

Deret in his book 'Religion Law and State in India', writes, "the Dharmashastra literature, that has more than two thousand scriptures are available today, is the greatest source of a Dharma bereft of pre- conceptions and partiality." In the present times, Manu Smriti and Yagyavalkya Smriti are two such Smritis before us, which are equally recognized in every corner of India. It is an amazing fact, how these two scriptures have minutely thought over the issues of social system, royal duty, administration related regulations, in ancient times. Regarding the time of the composition of both these scriptures, there is controversy.

## Composition of Manusmriti, Composer and Time of Composition

According to Dr. Jaiswal, 2nd Century BC was the time of Manusmriti. Yagyavalkya is ordinarily considered to be between 150-200 BC. Those who treat Smriti scriptures as relatively new, will accept the fact that the main spokesman (Swayambhu) is Manu. The followers of western thought and ideology, modern thinkers, while contemplating on Manu look for his mention and introduction to his life in the Vedas. It is their contention that in the RigVeda the word 'Manu' appears many a time with reference to a person.[23] At times he is referred to as father or the beginner of the Yagya, or sometimes, he is described as the igniter of fire. Manu who has treated the Vedas as derived from the Divine himself or superhuman, it would be unjust for that very 'Manu' to be traced in the Vedas while tracing his history and it is also time wise untenable, as the duration of the composition of the Vedas is much before Manu. In the Vedas, the word 'Manu' is used referring to God, not to any human being. Manu says that the divine is called by various names, one of them is also 'Prajapati Manu'.

एतगेके ववन्त्याग्निं गनुगन्ये प्रजापतिग् ।
इन्द्रमेकेपरे प्राणमपरे ब्रह्म शाश्वतम् ।। (12.123)

Manu Smriti (Laws of Manu) is ancient and its spokesman is Swayambhu Manu (self manifested archetypal first man). It is seen right from the Vaittareey Samhita Brahman Scriptures, to later Indian literature, only Swayambhu (Self manifested) is famous as Dharmashastrakar (compiler of tenets of duty) or Smritikar (Law maker). Vishwaroop (790-850) has in his commentary in Yagnavalka Smriti and comments on Yajur Veda, produced almost 200 shlokas of Manusmriti. Later, another writer Gyaneshwar, (1040-1100) also included many

---

[23] Rigveda 1.8.16, 2.33.13, 1.124.2, 8.30.1, 10.63

shlokas of Manu smriti in his commentary.[24] Shankaracharya has in his Vedanta Sutra commentary, presented shlokas of Manu Smriti, to vindicate his own thoughts, in some of them the name 'Manu' is mentioned clearly. Scholar P.V.Kane, in his writing 'Dharmashastra ka Itihaas' mentions that Manu's contentions feature in the commentary of Shabarswami known as Jamini Sutra and in the great Bauddhist poet Ashwaghosha's creation Brajkapanishad. On reading Yagya-valkya Smriti it appears as if Manu Smriti is kept in front, has been abridged and rendered in one's own words. Professor Surendra Kumar writes- Research shows that presently available Manu Smriti in its versified form, was in fact written in the form of sermons originally. Later the pupils of Manu compiled them and gave it the form of a text or scripture. According to Buhler, Donigar and Smith (translated Manu Smriti), 'Manu Smriti has a total of 12 chapters and 2685 shlokas.' It has been translated in various languages. Buhler George writes in his book, 'Sacred Books of East' (1886), 'Manu was the legendary first man, the Adam of the Hindus.' J.M. Deret in 'Manusastra Vivarana' has rated Manu Smriti as the most important contribution of India, in the field of system of justice.'According to U.N. Ghoshal, 'Manu Smriti is not only amazing but is formally written scripture on ancient political system.'

In the 18th century Manu Smriti was attributed a lot of importance by the founder of Arya Samaj, Rishi Dayanand. In his most popular book Satyarth Prakash, he has declared Manu Smriti to be highest quality, ministerial scripture on duty and said that he is the first sermonizer on human being's and human society's honour and systems The contentions of Manu were made the basis of Satyarth Prakash. By representing almost 514 shlokas or parts thereof from the Smriti in their authentic form.

---

[24] Yagya Valkaya Smriti Shlokas, 2.7, 1.15, 1.35, are brief essence of Manusmriti shlokas-2.12, 2.69, 1.41, 44, 8.40

Indian literature mentions Smriti spoken by Manu, by various names like, Manu Smriti', 'Manu Samhita', 'Manavdharma Shastra, 'Manav Shastra' and so on. Among Smritis or Manav Shastra, Manu Smriti is the most proven, authentic, highest quality scripture. Contemporary to Manu Smriti, many other Smritis came into light, but could not withstand the brilliance of Manu Samhita and could not create an impact, although Manusmriti's domination is maintained even today, like the olden days. The pride of being the most ancient among all the Dharmashastras and belonging to the time of inception of the Creation, shielded by Manu Smriti. Even in Shatpath, Taitireeya Sumhita (2.2, 10.2, 3.1.9.2) and other Brahmana Scriptures there is mention of Manu, as 'मनुर्वै यस्किञ्चावदत् तद भैषजम्' meaning thereby, 'whatever Manu said is efficacious like a medicinal drug, and brings about welfare,' such sayings being there are a proof that Manu Smriti is most ancient, meant for all times scripture of duty (dharma shastra).

The systems propounded by Manu are relevant for all times and are all pervasive and in that form being the truth and practical for the purposes, it is rooted in the Vedas. For this quality of Manu Smriti, it is the most revered scripture. It is Manu's strong contention- 'वेदोऽखिलो धर्ममूलम् । (2.6) It means Vedas are the foundation of the roots of Dharma. Manu in his curiosity for dharma considered the Vedas most authentic –

'धर्मजिज्ञासमानानां प्रमाणे परमं श्रुतिः ।' (2.13)

It means, for one who is curious to know the Dharma, the Vedas are the most authentic. 'Adhering to them, decide what is right or wrong.' In Brihaspati Smriti and Mahabharata there is mention that, by foul arguments, one who defies Smriti deserves defamation. One important cause, out of the reasons that attribute pride to Manu Smriti, is also the fact that, Manu was a famous 'tatva' philosopher, a propagator of Dharma, a sage and in his times he adhered to Dharma, he was just, popular among subjects and was rich with power of knowledge. Manu has treated the sayings and conduct of only those people as authentic proof of Dharma, who practiced celibacy and were scholars of the Vedas.

From all viewpoints Manu Smriti has been the power of panacea for the human community in the past and at present and will remain so in future as well. It is the only text of law and regulations. In it on one hand, there is the form of Varnashram system related dharma, dictating deeds for the welfare of the individual and society, ethical duties, honourable limitations, descriptions of code of conduct, it also affixes for high quality social systems, rules and regulations, along with formation of spiritual sermons, instrumental in getting human being's ultimate redemption. On one hand, Manu Smriti is a unique combination of materialistic and spiritual teachings, for the individual and society, it is a scripture of duty and code of conduct, on the other hand, it is also the 'constitution' formed to run the ruling system smoothly. Manu Smriti is treated as the main foundation of 'Hindu Code Bill'. In Judicial courts among books related to the process of justice, the mention of Manu Smriti is compulsory. Not only in India but also in foreign countries Manu Smriti has its influence. According to Prof. Surendra Kumar, "In Phillipine island in front of The House of People's premises, there are the statues of four persons, who contributed in the building of the foundation of their tradition. One of them is that of Sage Manu. The law in Bali and Java, is quite like Manu Smriti. 'Dhamyathat' in Burma seems to be inspired by this memory. Even the rules- regulations and conduct in Nepal also follow the Smriti.

**'Dharma' Beginning, Middle and End of the Universe**

According to K. Motwani,[25] in the unknown past of history, the sermons Manu gave to his progenies (human beings, pupils) that can be known in one word, 'Dharma'. Manu has called 'Dharma' the beginning, the middle and end

---

[25] K.Motwani Manudharma Sastra, p.6, 24 and 25

of the universe and this is what pervades in the entire universe. Making this concept of Dharma clear he said, "Dharma is not restricted to only social give and take or action and reaction. It is regulatory of each happening, be it natural, organic, mental, social and spiritual. In its ambit the entire universe is covered. This keeps assembled, all the components of the universe, moving or immovable minerals, vegetation, living beings, human beings and deities and so on. Likewise, it keeps amalgamated the development of various states of human beings, physical, mental and spiritual, different levels of a human being's consciousness, various groups of society and the values of people residing in various countries of the world, under different circumstances. Dharma is the process of presenting one thing at a time and place, in many forms and uniting many in a single form.

Many a time doubt arises, that if Dharma, which has the power to bring together all, was not explained clearly, then the Hindu kingdom would be dependent on the personal whims of an individual, and he will interpret Dharma according to his own fancies. But if ancient scriptures are studied minutely, it would be known that this doubt is baseless. As it is clear, that the literal meaning of Dharma is to keep everyone together. On a macro level, on a humanitarian level, it makes each one well entrenched in his specific duty and on a social platform, it makes social behaviour amenable to reasoning.

The macro concept of Dharma has been treated by Manu as inspirational power behind the state's work group, when it lacks, the kingdom and individual too loses its identity. Besides, by a deep analysis of Dharma, it is learnt that the concept of dutifulness is inbred in all the body parts of a being. The king though placed at the highest position of Dharma, yet is considered secondary to Dharma. A king immersed in Dharma is worthy of being called a king, who is instructed, by Raj Dharma in Manu Smriti. It provides for an essentially required substance for study, that is, the ancient

Indian political tradition in the right perspective. Manu's Dharmashastra, which we can call text on social relations, directives, instructions or sermons, has been widely read among Indians and has been the main source of Indian social behaviour. It is not only for Indian people but is relevant for the entire human race. For more than one thousand five hundred years the Dharmashastra principles instructed by Manu have been the form of life of Indian social and political existence. The Rajdharma indicated by Manu holds relevance in today's politics from all viewpoints. The seventh, eighth and a few other chapters of Manu Smriti describe Dharma and Raj Dharma in detail. For extensively explaining the position of dutifulness and its importance in political systems and administration related policies, Manu Smriti is the foundation of these chapters. In the Manavdharmashastra, Dharma has been accepted in its all pervading form, which can be physically and secondarily, classified in the following manner-
**1.** The primary meaning finds it related to spiritualistic goal. Development of honour and the spirit, attainment of the state of no sorrow, meaning there by, the state of redemption, and the conduct that is conducive to it, is known as duty. This Dharma is all pervasive, relevant for all times and for all people. What is not to be given up and is worthy of adoption, is the propagation of such a dharma, which is the primary goal of the Dharmashastras. Manu has described this Dharma in the following shloka---

वेदाभ्यास तपः ज्ञानम्, इन्द्रियाणां च संयमः।
अहिंसा, गुरुसेवा च निःश्रेयस्करं परम्॥ (12.83)

The study of the Vedas, the practice of fasting, learning truth related education, control of senses, conducting Yagyas, and meditation, are the six great deeds instrumental in attainment of moksha (redemption). By adhering to this Dharma, a human being concludes his life sojourn in an auspicious manner.

एतद्धोऽभिहितं सर्वं निःश्रेयसकरं परम्।
अस्मादप्रच्युते विप्रः प्राप्नोति परमां गतिम्॥ (12.116)

**2.** secondary meaning pertains to it as a means public behaviour. Perfect behaviour helpful in achieving three types of spiritual, mental, and physical progress, performance of duty, law, is related to worldly duty, wherein changes occur at times due to difference in countries and times. For example-

तं देशकालौ शक्तिं च विद्यां चावेक्ष्य तत्त्वतः।
यथार्हतः संप्रणयेन्नरेष्वन्यायवर्तिषु।। ( 7. 16)

The Dharma has to be in tune with the country, time and prevailing situation, power, education, meaning thereby, knowledge of appropriate punishment in accordance to the committed crime and after amply contemplating on these issues, a cruel and bad character must get appropriate punishment. When, the question of the king and the role of Raj Dharma arises in protecting Dharma and adhering to it, then the Manavdharmashastra becomes a guide to political science. The practical test of Manu's political system is Dharma only. Manu interpreted Dharma as duty or its mental orientation and propensities, which make it relevant as sociological text. The one who has sovereignty, also has obligations to perform. To fulfil his duties and obligations, the king observes fasts or takes a vow. To protect the subjects from a state of anarchy or a state of lawlessness, is the first and foremost duty or obligation of a king. There was no physical authority above the king, empowered to control him. If the king had any guide, it was the 'Dharma.'

**Systems Based on Vedic Knowledge**

Manu who had invincible faith on Vedic authenticity, has declared, that only that nation runs well, which adheres to Vedic knowledge as its foundation. The king must endeavour to create such a nation. Manu says-

'पितृदेव मनुष्याणां वेदश्चक्षुः सनातनम्।' (12.94)

The Vedas are the floodgates of knowledge for the protectors named as fathers, who foster and are also mentors for the people. The Vedas are guidelines to be followed by scholars and other men also. Meaning hereby, that treating it as the foundation, the scholars of the Vedas are to sermonise on the 'Dharma'. The scriptures opposed to the Vedas only misguide human beings.

या वेदबाह्माः स्मृतयो याश्च काश्च कुदृष्टयः
सर्वास्ता निष्फलाः प्रेत्य तमोनिष्ठा हि ताः स्मृताः ।। (12.95)

It means scriptures opposed to Vedas are fruitless and against the truth. They are not competent to provide relief from afflictions or clarify doubts.

चातुर्वर्ण्यं त्रयो लोकाश्चत्वाश्चाश्रमाः पृथक् ।
भूतं भव्यं भविष्यं च सर्वं वेदात्प्रसिध्यति ।। (12.97)

In the Vedas instructions have been given regarding the various regulations for Brahmins, Kshatriyas, Vaishya and Shudras, the four varnas and their system, the Earth, the Sky and all the other astral levels, around the Earth, planets, knowledge of present, past and future, etcetera, celibacy (brahmacharya), family life (Grihastha) proceeding to the woods (Vanaprastha) and asceticism (sanyas), the four prescribed ashrams of life. It means the knowledge of the systems of the entire living universe is made available to us by the Vedas.

Manu says that the knowledge of the five elements and the micro powers is also in the Vedas-

शब्दः स्पर्शश्च रूपं च रसो गन्धश्च पञ्चमः ।
वेदादेव प्रसूयन्ते प्रसूतिगुणकर्मतः ।। (12.98)

Word, touch, form, liquid and smell and so on, the powers of the elements, the knowledge of their creation, their attributes, their utility and that of entire unconscious and conscious world, is available in the Vedas.

Truly, due to possessing unique qualities, utility and being a complete storehouse of knowledge and science, the Vedas are destroyer of faulty deeds and harbinger of happiness. The basic idea is that follower of the path of the Vedas, conducts himself according to the Dharma and attains that spiritual happiness which is highest bliss.

**Directions, Instructions for an ideal kingdom**

Manu in the eighth chapter gives instructions for protection of the subjects and fostering them vide the following shloka-

धर्म एव हतो हन्ति धर्मो रक्षति रक्षितः।
तस्माद्धर्मो न हन्तव्यो मा नो धर्मो हतोऽवधीत्।। (8.15)

It means whosoever, destroys the dharma, dharma destroys him. And the one who protects dharma, is in turn protected by dharma itself. The king must always remain alert, that the forsaking of dharma may not become the cause of his and the kingdom's downfall and while protecting the subjects he need never deviate from dharma. For protecting the subjects only, he is entitled to one sixth part of the food produce. According to Manu, a king who extracts taxes without protecting the subjects is a sinner.

योरक्षान्बलिमादत्ते करं शुल्कं च पार्थिवः।
प्रयतिभागं च दण्डे च स सद्यो नरकं व्रजेत्।। (8.307)

A king who imposes Bali (tax) or the one sixth part of food produce, without protecting his subjects, soon becomes miserable as the subjects do not cooperate with him, on account of his being negligent of them. These thoughts of Manu give information about the pact between the king and the subjects. This also reveals the principle of double transference of the subject's deeds. According to that 50% of the benefit of people's religious acts or losses born by them was shared by the king, in the same proportion as he was able to fulfil his obligation or failed to do so.

Manu Samhita is specially focused on Raj Dharma. That is why it is famous as 'text of royal duty'. For the protection of the subjects and their welfare, Manu has at various junctures thrown light on the King's attributes and qualities by writing-

सोऽग्निर्भवति वायुश्च सोऽर्कः सोमः स धर्मराट्।
स कुबेरः स वरुणः स महेंद्रः प्रभावतः।। (7. 7)

The king must inculcate in himself the powers of Fire, Air, the Sun, the Moon, Dharma, Kuber, Varun and Indra, to establish peace and happiness in the Kingdom. His kingdom be wealthy and prosperous, possessing the wealth of minerals and be highly prestigious. He ought to be able to curb crime and criminals, keep crime under control. As the Sun absorbs water from its rays, likewise the King may get tax from his subjects. Taxes be collected in a manner, without causing inconvenience to the subjects. He may exercise the power to inflict punishment in a just manner and protect his subjects.

इंद्रायाणां जये योगं समातिष्ठेद्दिवानिशम् ।
जितेंद्रिया हि शक्नोति वशेस्थापयितुं प्रजाः ।। (7. 44)

The Chief of the Sabha and members of the Sabha can only carry on the ruling system smoothly, if they were free of the vices of indulgence in carnal and material enjoyments and greed, meaning thereby, they must have control over their senses. The subjects remain under the control of those rulers who have their senses in their control.

कामजेषु प्रसक्तो हि व्यसनेषु महीपतिः ।
वियुज्यतेऽर्थधर्माभ्यां क्रोधजेष्वात्मनैव तु ।। (7. 46)

The above mentioned, shlokas draw attention to the effect of human weaknesses on the system of ruling and warns that the king who is on the path of adharma and is indulgent in (10) vices emanating from lust and (8) vices emanating from anger, causes the downfall of his own self along with that of the kingdom. Kings under the spell of lust and anger, misappropriate funds and use punishment inappropriately, lose all grace, meaning thereby, get deprived of wealth prosperity and their kingdom.

मृगयाऽक्षो दिवास्वप्नः परिवादः स्त्रियो मदः ।
तौर्यत्रिकं वृथाट्या च कामजो दशको गणः ।। (7.47)
पैशुन्यं साहसं द्रोह ईर्ष्यासूयार्थदूषणम् ।
वाग्दंडजं च पारुष्यं क्रोधजोऽपि गणोऽष्टकः ।। (7. 48)

While intimating about the information regarding the demerits of lust and anger Manu has said—Lust gives rise to 10 vices- gambling, indecent talk, carelessness, lust, laziness, bad company, use of intoxicants, indulgence in luxury, inflicting criticism on others, wondering around in vain and there are 8 vices emanating from anger- back biting, bad conduct, to rebel, jealousy, unnecessary blaming, splurging money in unholy deeds, speaking harsh, and hard words and punishing the innocent.

Manu said to alert the king along with all the others that these vices lead to one's downfall. It is better to die, rather than get involved in them.

In the shlokas of the seventh chapter, on the subject of Raj Dharma, Manu has said, while describing the qualities of a superior, competent disciplined king, that only a king who has conquered his senses, can keep his subjects under control. Control of one's senses is the main quality required for keeping the kingdom in one's spell. Practicing dutifulness, yoga, attainment of knowledge and conquering the senses, makes the King 'Jitendriya'. Without exercising control over the mind, breath and body, the king can never be popular among his subjects. Lust, anger, greed and pride are hurdles in fulfilling his duties, prove instrumental in sending any ruler to hell. A king caught up in the ten demerits of lust and the eight demerits of anger, deviates from the path of Dharma, loses his wealth and his body gets destroyed. Greed is the root of all vices. It is in the interest of the king and his subjects to stay away from the effect of vices and carelessness, be dutiful, involve in auspicious deeds by proving quality, in his acts and nature.

क्षत्रियस्य परो धर्मः प्रजानामेव पालनम्<br>निर्दिष्टफल भोक्ता हि राजा धर्मेण युज्यते ।। (7.144)

The first duty of a Kshatriya (Community of warriors) is taking care of the subjects. This is the gist of this shloka. By concluding the tasks assigned, a king is able to protect himself, meaning thereby, moves on to the path of his own Dharma or Adharma ? This difference be kept in mind while the king gets involved in acts of people's welfare. Royal men need never get caught up by greed or lust. The sermons of duty are given only to those who make use of them intelligently and are conscious beings.

In ancient India a lot of importance was given to the training of princes and for the purpose, most erudite teachers were appointed. The inspirator and teacher of this tradition, Manu has in shloka 7, 37, 38, 39 instructed the king to remain within the boundaries of honour as laid down by learned teachers of the Vedas.

ब्रह्मणान्पर्युपासीत प्रातरूत्थाय पार्थिवः ।
त्रैविद्यवृद्धान्विदुषस्तिष्ठेत्तेषां च शासने ।। (7.37)
वृद्धांश्च नित्यं सेवेत विप्रान्वेदविदः शुचीन् ।
वृद्धसेवी हि सततं रक्षोभिरपि पूज्यते ।। (7.38)
तेभ्योऽधिगच्छेद्विनयं तिनीतात्मपि नित्यशः ।
विनीतात्मा हि नृपतिर्न विनश्यति कर्हिचित् ।। (7.39)

Through the said shlokas, Manu says, only that King is great who is educated, disciplined and honourable. So, it is in the interest of the king to respect and welcome scholarly teachers. Under their supervision imbibe knowledge of Rig, Sam and Yajur, tri- Vedic education. It means by remaining in the company of scholars, intelligence be developed consistently and continuously.

त्रैविद्येभ्यस्त्रयीं विद्यां दण्डनीतिं च शाश्वतीम् ।
आन्वीक्षिकीं चात्मविद्यां वार्तारम्भांश्च लोकतः ।। (7.43)

Only those people are qualified to be the King and members of Rajsabha, who have tri-Vedic education permanent law of punishment, education regarding imparting justice, education of spiritualism (the divine attributes). In this shloka, it is Manu's contention, that the king's pure conduct is the actual foundation of his rule. The royal men must learn the Vedas, politics, spiritualism and knowledge of philosophy, from scholars of Vedas and learn business and the subject of industry from those, adept in worldly wisdom. This way a king fulfilling the required qualifications, will not only be inspired by his own conduct of Dharma, but he will perform all his duties with efficiency and excellence.

Upholding of Dharma, Artha, Kaam.

सत्याहुः संप्रणेतारं राजानं सत्यवादिनम् ।
समीक्ष्यकारिणं प्राज्ञं धर्मकामार्थकोविदम् ।। (7.26)

The rule competent to inflict punishment is the one, which uses punishment for the sake of Dharma, is truthful, is adept in these three sections, Dharma, Kaama, and Artha. He writes again-

तं राजा प्रणयन्सम्यक् त्रिवर्गेणाभिवर्धते ।
कामात्मा विषमः क्षुद्रो दण्डेनैव निहन्यते ।। (7.27)

The king who is competent to protect Dharma (Dutifulness) wealth (Artha) family life (Kaam), is entitled to inflict punishments.

This way Manu fixed these regulations for a king who inflicted punishments, should be a promotor of Dharma, Artha, and Kaam. He has been named 'trivarga' (three sections). This trivarga can be understood in the following way-

**1. Dharma-** 'यतो अभ्युदय निःश्रेयससिद्धिः स धर्मः ।'

( Vaisheshiki-1.1.2)

One whose conduct is conducive to spiritual, mental, physical, progress in three sections and attainment of moksha, is abiding by dharma or duty. Similarly, **'चोदनालक्षणो धर्म'** (Poorv Mimansa2.7.2) or duties of human being, mentioned in the Vedas are Dharma.

**2. Artha-** Acquiring wealth and enhancing it by just means.

**3. Kaam-**Enjoying worldly pleasures, and desires, in accordance with Dharma.

**4. Moksha-** With Trivarga when Moksha is also attached, then it is named as Purushartha'. In Manu Smriti chapter four, shlok 238.239..., these beliefs have been clarified and it is said, that after breaking the cycle of life and death, to remain in a state of freedom (Mukti) is Moksha.

In the shloka no. 132 of the first chapter and 176th shloka

of the fourth chapter Manu has tried to teach that the-

'अर्थकामेष्वसक्तानां धर्मज्ञानं विधीयतै ।' (1.132)

'परित्यजेदर्थकामौ यौ स्यातां धर्मवर्जितौ ।' (4.176)

In the shlokas Manu wishes to say that the purpose of attainment of Moksha will only be meaningful or possible if it is achieved by means of Dharma. Wealth earned and pleasures enjoyed through Adharmic means are not permissible. One involved in earning wealth and desirous of Kaam, can only attains knowledge of dharma and proficiency in it. Earnings through pure means is necessary in life according to Manu. A man should remain satisfied and assist other beings to get rid of their pain, be helpful. One who is proficient in dharma and has knowledge of necessary regulations and rules and conducts himself, in their accordance, is known as, 'Dharmakamarthakovid'. To achieve it is a human being's goal of life and having a proficiency in it is the success of human life, and a symbol of happiness.

**Work Based Varna System**

Accepting the Varn System propagated by the Vedic culture, Manu has treated it as the main foundation of the social system. According to the Vedas an individual is a part of the society, and as such, is supposed to employ his full strength, for the progress of the society and that is the prime duty of all. For the fulfilment of this intent, the sages have divided human life in four Ashrams and human society in four Varnas, while assigning the work tasks. Dr. B.R Ambedkar, considered the Varna system division in four, as against the variety of the contemporary Indian society, though more rooted in the Vedas, also questioned the identification of Shudras by asking, 'Who were the Shudras?', instead of four, only three castes (Varna) have been recognized, Brahmins, Khshatriyas and Vaishyas. Thus, those who have been mentioned as Shudras, have been assimilated by Dr Ambedkar among Vaishyas.

Manu has declared while entrusting the king to establish

the Varnashram system-

स्वे स्वे धर्मे निविष्टानां सर्वेषामनुपूर्वशः।
वर्णनामाश्रमाणां च राजा सृष्टोऽभिरक्षिता।। (7.35)

It means, involved in each one's respective dharma, all Varnas and ashramas have been entrusted to the king for protection. That means, the king is the protector of the Varna system and the four Ashram system of life. It is the duty of the person posted on the seat of the king, to enable those who are adhering to the caste and four stage system, to remain in its ambit. The king and kingdom is created to build the society adhering to the tenets of Dharma, which means, in accordance with the system of regulations. Manu has attributed importance to the duty of each one and says a dutiful person is dear to all-

स्वानि कर्माणि कुर्वाणा दूरे संतोऽपि मानवाः।
प्रिया भवन्ति लोकस्य स्वे स्वे कर्मण्यवस्थिताः।। (8.42)

He again says, that while doing one's respective duty and remaining in the ambit of one's assigned work as duty, a human being gains popularity. By referring to each one, it is discerned that a duty-bound kingdom is that, wherein, all the residents are involved in fulfilling their respective duties or are not careless. A king who loves Dharma ensures, that each human being has purity of conduct, while adhering to his duty, ends up generating auspiciousness. In the scripture of Manavdharma, the recognition of the following four varnas has been clearly declared-Brahmin, Kshatriya, Vaishya and Shudra.

In the mantras of Yajurveda (31.10.11) and Shatpat Brahman (5.5.4.9), these four Varnas have been mentioned.

'चत्वारो वर्णाः। ब्राह्मणा, राजन्यो वैश्यः शूद्रः।।'

Accepting the mantras of Shatpat Brahman and the Yajurveda, as they are, Manu says with reference to the caste system-

'लोकानां तु विवृद्ध्यर्थं मुखबाहूरूपादतः।
ब्राह्मणं क्षत्रियं वैश्यं शूद्रं च निरवर्तयत्।।' (1.31)

For special development of the society, its prosperity, progress, and peace, Brahman, Kshatriya, Vaishya and Shudra were created in similarity with body parts in the sequence of face, arms, torso and feet of the society, being similar in their attributes, came into light. Meaning thereby, the four castes system came into being.

सर्वस्यास्य तु सर्गस्य गुप्त्यर्थं स महाद्युतिः ।
मुखबाहूरूपज्जानां पृथक्कर्माण्यकल्पयत् ।। (1.87)

In the 87th shloka of the first chapter, Manu describes briefly the advent of four castes system, and writes- For the protection and prosperity of the entire world, the super illuminous God ascertained four varnas and their respective work. In shloka no. 88, 89, 90 and 91, there is discussion on the obligations of the four varnas-

अध्यापनमध्ययनं यजनं याजनं तथा ।
दानं प्रतिग्रहं चैव ब्राह्मणानामकल्पयत् ।। (1.88)

Brahman: Learning and teaching, performing Yagnas, are the main tasks performed by Brahmins. For Brahmins this instruction is also given, that he can accept alms but as far as possible must get his income for livelihood by performing yagyas. Brahmins have full freedom to develop their ideals of intelligence and spread them. The one who has attributes of education is known as Brahmin. Manu in the shloka 168 and 193 of chapter two has warned- A Brahmin against performing the task of Yagya is considered to be in the category of a Shudra.

प्रजानां रक्षणं दानमिज्याध्ययनमेव च ।
विषयेष्वप्रसक्तिश्च क्षत्रियस्य समासतः ।। (1.89)

Kshatriya: क्षत्रियः 'क्षदति रक्षति जनान् क्षत्र' : One who performs the task of protecting the subjects is a Kshatriya (Warrior). Kshatriya is a manifestation of the weapon. Fostering and protecting the subjects is the task assigned to Kshatriyas. Maintaining internal peace, and administration protecting the country from external aggression, to see that those in royal service are rendering their job properly and completely, are in the ambit of a warrior's duty. This description makes it clear that ruling the kingdom was like a working institution, it was expected of it that it takes care of the people's interest. It was this section of warriors, and the king was included in it. It must be mentioned that Brahmins played the role of advisors in the administration. Their words carried weight. It was dharma regulation for a Kshatriya, that he should get yagnas conducted, study the Vedas and promote the society and nation through charity.

पशूनां रक्षणं दानमिज्याध्ययनमेव च ।
वणिक्पथं कुसीदं च वैश्यस्य कृषिमेव च । । (1.90)

Vaishya: The said shloka is indicative of such a rule and social system in which rearing of animals, promoting the increase of their numbers, agriculture, business, were the main tasks performed by Vaishyas, for earning wealth. By the medium of production and distribution, making the human society progress, was the duty assigned to Vaishyas. Kings saw to it that this section should maintain an ethical level, using it as an instrument of service to the people. Manu has prescribed that Vaishyas may devote time to learning about yagnas and the Vedas and for enhancement of education, intelligence and duty, must spend a part of their income on it.

एकमेव तु शूद्रस्य प्रभुः कर्म समादिशत् ।
एतेषामेव वर्णानां शुश्रूषामनसूयया । । (1.91)

Shudra: Those who are ignorant, uneducated and for this reason are incapable of doing important tasks, those who cannot afford royal management and without knowledge of agriculture and commerce are not capable, can exhibit their efficiency in serving others to earn their living and adhere to the dharma.

The allocation of responsibilities, work or duty for various varnas by Manu, are mainly with the intent of creating a compact work- based society, wherein human beings could cooperate and contribute for the development of the nation, in accordance with their competence and capacity. Every human being is an important part of the nation. The kingdom is like a body and Varnas are its important parts. From this viewpoint, expressing this doubt is inappropriate, that it is so since inception. In a decorative way deed is explained. It appears that a human being is not by birth but by his work, meaning thereby, on account of his mental intelligence, competence, capacity and behaviour makes a place for himselfin the varna . In the Manu Smriti at many instances, it is clearly and indicatively explained, proving that Manu affixed the varna system on the basis of work, not birth. The word 'varna' itself affixes this system proving it to be work-based. Below the origin of the word varna is given- 'वर्णो वृणोते:' (nirukta 2,1.4) It means, that which is adopted in accordance with work done, is varna. Throwing light on it, Rishi Dayanand in Rigvedadi Bhushya Bhoomika writes-

वर्णो वृणोतेरिति निरुक्तप्रामाण्याद् वरणीया वरीतुमहीः।
गुणकर्माणि च दृष्ट्वा यथायोग्यं व्रियन्ते ये ते वर्णाः।।

It means, "keeping in view the attributes and deeds, when one gets duly deserved right, it is called 'cast'." It must be noted carefully that Manu has kept the rule of Yagya and study of Vedas, for all varnas. From this viewpoint Manu has considered spiritual development, the primary Dharma of all human beings. Internal purity and conscientious way of thinking makes human beings capable of uplifting themselves, society and the nation. It is the duty of the king to ensure spiritual upliftment of his subjects in the nation, by appropriately discharging his duties and inflict punishment.

Manu, in the shlokas of the seventh chapter advises to remain alert, by writing, that 'Brahmins beware of offered respect, as if it were poison.' Meaning thereby, in the euphoria of pride on getting reverence, he may guard against deviating from his duty assigned by the Vedas. While giving the right to inflict punishment to the king, it has been said -

The Kshatriya king who deviates from truthfulness, is destroyed by the power to inflict punishment, with it being binding on him too. Likewise, there are instructions for Vaishyas, that 'दद्याच्च सर्वभूतानामन्नमेव प्रयत्नत' (9.333), the Vaishya can go on taking but should also continue to give. It clearly means that a Vaishyas do not have a right to receive only. Out of the receipts from the society, one part he must spend for people's welfare. The principle of trusteeship by Gandhiji resonates with Manu's thought, Gandhiji repeatedly, while drawing a sketch of future India, held capitalists as the trustees of people's money. This example points towards the practical facet of the Manavdharma scripture.

Likewise, Manu while giving instructions of spiritual upliftment, says that the Shudra may not remain stuck in his lower state, instead he should develop his spiritual element, for which Manu iterates-

शुचिरुत्कृष्ट शुश्रुषूर्मृदुवागन हंकृतः।
ब्राह्मणाद्याश्रयो नित्यमुत्कृष्टां जातिमश्नुत्ते।। (9.335)

It means a Shudra who is physically and mentally pure and sacred, has been committed to serving the Varnas higher to him, Brahmins and the other two, is sweet in speech, without pride, can get promoted to a higher Varna. Such a description is also given in the $10^{th}$ chapter-

शूद्रो ब्राह्मणातामेति ब्राह्मणश्चैति शूद्रताम्।
क्षत्रियाज्जातमेवं तु विद्याद्वैश्यात्तथैव च।। (10.65)

In these shlokas Manu has expressed the concept of Shudras, not lacking in any way. He has addressed them with adjectives like, clean, sacred, superior and a good listener and so on. One who serves can never be impure. That is why there is this provision that by indulging in good deeds he has the right to be exalted to higher Varnas.

Manu has prescribed five duties for remaining within the ambit of Varna.

अहिंसा सत्यमस्तेयं शौचमिन्द्रियनिग्रहः।
एतं सामासिकं धर्मं चातुर्वर्ण्येऽब्रवीन्मनुः।। (10.63)

'For all the four Varnas, it is beneficial not to indulge in violence, speak the truth, not snatch other's wealth by unfair means, maintaining sacredness and remain in control of the senses. One who duly adheres to these respectable attributes in letter and spirit, can only discharge his duties actively.

A good example of Varna based in accordance with work assigned, is given in shloka number 63 of the eighth chapter-

आप्ताः सर्वेषु वर्णेषु कार्याः कार्येषु साक्षिणः ।
सर्वधर्मविदोऽलुब्धा विपरीतांस्तु वर्जयेत् ।। (8.63).

Manu has supported the participation of all the Varnas in the Council of Justice. His contention was that those who were scholars of dharma in all the Varnas, possessed full knowledge of dharma, are flawless, are not cunning and are truthful, they ought to be made to give evidence in the judicial procedure, the ones who conduct themselves contrary to it, should never be allowed to give evidence.

The above mentioned contention, is sufficient to prove the point, that each Varna is important in the view of the assigned work it performs. Together the composite work output makes the society appear like one unit. While studying Manu Smriti many shlokas seem to be mutually opposed or contrary to each other. Therefore, it is necessary to add here that many shlokas were added later when the society had begun to get distorted. Not only related to the Varna system, but a king possessing divine attributes, follower of Grihastha Ashram system and many other subjects which are completely contrary to the instructions and sermons given by Manu. In accordance with the Shruti and Upanishad, if we analyse this system propagated in Manu Smriti, we will reach the conclusion that the shlokas that are in contradiction are interpolated and thus not tenable. My study is based on those very shlokas, which are completely in consonance, without contradictions and are relevant for all times.

**Ashram Dharma**

ब्रह्मचारगृहस्थश्च वानप्रस्थो यतिस्तथा (6.87)

As the Varna system is the basis of human beings performing their duty in the form of their work, the Ashram system of four stages of life, is the chapter which enables human beings pass the test to attain happiness and ultimate redemption. The Ashram system is divided in four ashrams. They are, 1. Brahmacharya 2. Grihastha,3. Vaanprastha 4. Sanyas, the four stages in life, a human being goes through, for fulfilling of duty or practicing Dharma. In a nation where, while adhering to Yam-Niyam, people move from one stage to another, that nation can never deviate from Dharma. It is obligatory on the four ashrams to hold on to the thread of Dharma steadfastly and assigned duties be performed, as per the age criterion prescribed. The duty of various stages as described by Manu is narrated here under-

## I. Stage of Brahmacharya (Celibacy)

In the Brahmacharya ashram one practices whatever is taught and devote time to it. Through celibacy and 'tapa' or austerity the nation is protected. Till the age of 24 having lived at a Gurukul or residential school, the child was to imbibe education. In keeping with the Vedic culture, Manu has prescribed the attributes of this ashram, that a celibate must enhance his knowledge through self-learning constantly-

'यःस्वाध्यायमधीतेऽब्दं विधिना नियतः शुचिः ।
तस्य नित्यं क्षरत्येष पयो दधि घृतं मधु ।।' (2.107)

It means, as by consuming milk, curd, ghee and honey, the body gets satiated, becomes sturdy and healthy, likewise, by self- learning a human being's life becomes peaceful, full of good qualities, gains knowledge and possesses virtues. These are instrumental in attainment of Dharma, Artha, Kaam and Moksha.

इंद्रियाणां विचरतां विषयेष्वपहारिषु ।
संयमे यत्नमातिष्ठेद्विद्वान्यन्तेव वाजिनाम् ।। (2.88)

While instructing regarding control over senses, Manu Samhita iterates, that a Brahmachari keeps his senses in control in the same way as an efficient rider of a horse keeps it under his control. Uncontrolled senses make a human being deviate from the path of Dharma. So, it is the prime duty of a self- learner that he should practice celibacy and perform his duty.

Control of senses for enabling completion of tasks, has been highlighted by Manu Smriti thus—

श्रोत्रं त्वक्चक्षुषी जिह्वा नासिका चैव पञ्चमी।
पायूपस्थं हस्तपादं वाक्चैव दशमी स्मृता।। (2.90)
एकादशं मनोज्ञेयं स्वगुणेनोभयात्मकम्।
यस्मिञ्जिते जितावेतौ भवतः पञ्चकौ गणौ। (2.92)
इंद्रियाणां प्रसङ्गेन शेषमृच्छत्यसंशयम्।
संनियम्य तु तान्येव ततः सिद्धिं नियच्छति।। (2.93)

Eyes, ears, nose, tongue and the skin, speech, mind and so on, the eleven senses, whose dictates, if a human being can overcome, his spiritual power increases. He becomes flawless. Such a self-controlled person is competent to achieve his ideals.

With the purpose of making life regulated and under self-control, in the second chapter of Manu Smriti, for a Brahmachari it has been prescribed that he, while maintaining control over his senses, must invoke fire, and many other rules to be followed without being lazy. The rule of Brahmacharya prescribed by the Vedas has enamoured many Western scholars. Dr. E. Periyar writes- "The saviour of the youth's body, character and intelligence is only Brahmacharya."

Today, the way students are misled and are becoming unruly, leading a life without any values due to indulgence in vices leading to their physical downfall, taking place so speedily, is a cause of worry.' The downfall of the youth is the nation's downfall." In view of the present dismal state of education it is necessary that the arrangement of 'Gurukul System be brought about. The regulated and controlled daily itinerary, practicing of celibacy can only maintain security of the country. The way the aggressiveness and propensity of migration among the youth, is increasing speedily, to curb it the administration, will have to bring about extensive changes on war footing, in the education policy.

In the age of instrumentation and competition, as a change

is taking place continuously, the youth is incompetent to withstand its tornado, a child is taught to compete in the primary classes, the soul is not permitted an opportunity to blossom at all. Today the teachers and guardians will have to learn from this mantra of Yajurveda-

हे बालक!

मनस्तऽ आप्यायतां वाक् तऽआप्ययतां

प्राणस्तऽ आप्यायतां चक्षुस्तऽ आप्यायतां

श्रोत्रं त ऽ आप्यायतां। यत्ते क्रूरं यदास्थितं

त्ततऽ आप्यायतां निष्टय्यायतां तत्ते शुध्यतु

शमहोभ्यः। ओषधे त्रायस्व स्वधिते मैनँ हिँसीः।। **6.15**।।

O boy!

Your heart may blossom like a flower,

Your speech be sweet.

Your pran (life force) be strong, your eyes may have brilliance.

Sinful thoughts may never touch you.

Become sacred.

All life, have peace of mind.

Our complete Vedic literature, Smritis and Nitis were far sighted. For this reason, maintaining the rules of Ashram system, they propagated Brahmacharya as the first step of the nation's protection.

## (II) Stage of Grihashtha Ashram (Worldly Pleasures)

Manu has written about the importance of the Grihastha Ashram of family life and worldly pleasures –

यथा वायु समाश्रत्य वर्तन्ते सर्वजन्तवः।

तथा गृहस्थमाश्रित्य वर्तन्ते सर्व आश्रमाः।। **(3.77)**

It means, the way all living beings, owe their lives to the air element, likewise, the other three stages are dependent on the Grihastha ashram (the stage for fulfilment of worldly desires). The Grihastha ashram only sustains the remaining three ashrams, as it is Grihastha ashram that nurtures the other three ashrams regularly by lending knowledge and food as alms. Thus, Grihastha is the elder and most important ashram.

Treating the Grihastha Ashram like the ocean, Manu has written an important shloka-

यथा नदीनदाः सर्वे सागरे यान्ति संस्थितिम् ।
तथैवाश्रमिणः सर्वे गृहस्थे यान्ति संस्थितिम् ।। (6.90)

The way huge rivers go to meet the ocean, likewise, all ashrams have to abide by the Grihastha for being proven worthy. It is evident from Manu's assertions that Grihastha Ashram is not meant for only luxurious living. Sacrifice, austerity, hard work and charity are included in it. The one who adheres to Grihastha Ashram truly is bound to be prosperous. If Grihastha Ashram be called a laboratory and a source of inspiration for Vanprastha and Sanyas, it would not be an exaggeration.

## (III) Vaanprastha Ashram (Renunciation)

Having concluded duties of a grihastha, a life which is regulated, full of activities leading to welfare, self- learning may be pursued. This does not mean running away from one's obligations. The obligations limited towards 'family' finds its expansion. A human being not only belongs to his family but is for the entire society. Vaanprastha is characteristic of non-attachment, sacrifice and non-possessiveness. Those belonging to Vanpratha, only live in jungles to establish Gurukuls. These Gurukuls are the main centres of education. In Yajurveda, chapter 20 mantra 24, it has been told to be appropriate for one, in Vanaprastha, that he should hold 'satsang', practice yoga, nurture good thoughts and attain knowledge, sacredness. On these lines Manu teaches-

स्वाध्याये नित्ययुक्तः स्याद्दान्तो मैत्रः समाहितः ।
दाता नित्यमनादाता सर्वभूतानुकम्पकः ।। (6.8)

It means, always be involved in self learning, be spiritual, friendly with all, curbing ones senses and imparting education as a matter of charity, be merciful and not take anything from anybody, these are the qualities for one in Vanprastha.

For the king also it is an instruction, that he should enter the Vanprastha, it must be mentioned here, that after attaining a certain age he was to abdicate from the throne on his own.

Unlike present times, they did not hold on to the throne. In the ancient ruling system, there was provision for retirement of royal administrative officials, but in the present times the holders of power do not observe any age of retirement. Consequently, those who had to play the role of path finder are themselves deviated from the path, seem to have all sense of direction of ruling the state. It appears that the scientific and practical systems of the Vedas and Upanishds have been accepted by Manu. Such a system, which is useful and exemplary for all times. It will have to be understood and accepted and it will only be possible if ancient literature is made a subject to be widely studied and taught and assimilated in the present regulations.

## (IV) Sanyas Ashram (Asceticism)

In the fourth stage of age there is the law of renunciation (Sanyas Ashram). Manu has given a sermon in the sixth chapter, high lighting the importance of the sanyas Ashram-

इंद्रियाणां निरोधेन रागद्वेषक्षयेण च।
अहिंसया च भूतानाममृतत्वाय कल्पते।। (6.60)
अध्यात्मरतिरासीनो निरपेक्षो निरामिषः।
आत्मनैवः सहायेन सुखार्थी विचरेदिह।। (6.49)

For the purity of self and its upliftment, Manu has prohibited consumption of liquor and meat. According to him, it is the prime duty of a Sanyasi to impart knowledge by delivering sermons. He gets beyond attachment and malevolence and behaves without animosity with all, to attain Moksha.

In this way we get detailed description of the dharma of a sanyasi, in various mantras of Manusmriti (6.46.48,53,66) a sanyasi must elevate himself to the state of a pure soul and make others so. Speak the truth and impart education as charity. Overcome anger and deliver sermons for every one's welfare. Internally and in external behaviour must be pure for being eligible for moksha. A great ascetic is not only a citizen of his own country but tends to belong to the entire world.

## Common Duties to Regulate Varna Ashram System

For the institution of Varna system, Manu has instructed ten attribute related duties to be performed regularly by the members of all the four varnas, which are as follows-

धृतिः क्षमा दमोऽस्तेयं शौचमिन्द्रिय निग्रहः ।
धीर्विद्या सत्यमक्रोधो दशकं धर्मलक्षणम् ।। (6.92)

1. In the said shloka, the attributes given, are to be understood with their deep meaning, well before being inculcated. The first is Dhriti or maintaining of courage. 2. The second one is Kshama or forgiveness- Beyond insults and praise, meaning thereby, without being too sad or happy, maintaining a stable mental state, be forgiving. 3. Dam- Keep the breath-mind focused on duty and control oneself from drifting to the path, prohibited or opposed to dutifulness. 4. Asteya- Non-Stealing-Do not feel drawn to someone else's belonging, give up stealing others money. 5. Shauch or Cleanliness- Along with internal purity, external cleanliness and sacredness in behaviour. 6. Indriyanigrah means control over Senses- Maintain a control over ones five senses without indulging in luxurious living. 7.Dhih or Sense of Justice- Give up lethargy and bad company, be in the company of great people and scholars, practice yoga and attain knowledge to enhance intelligence and conscience. 8. Vidya or Education means, acquiring knowledge, being truthful, involve in auspicious deeds and speech, leading to well-being, is education and whatever is opposed to it is non- education (avidyya), which is not to be adopted. 9. Satya or Truth- To accept a commodity as it is, is the truth. By giving a foul argument the truth never be distorted. 10. Krodh or Anger- Stay away from anger, think with a calm mind. Anger destroys the conscience and a person without a conscience defiles the atmosphere around him, thus a human being must remain calm. Swami Dayanand in the Sanskar Vidhi, has given the first place among these ten attributes, to Non-violence (Ahimsa), meaning thereby, not to think badly of any other person.

For all Dharmas Manu has analysed at length the said ten attributes. He says-

चतुर्भिरपि चैवैतैर्नित्यमाश्रमिभिर्द्विजैः
दशलक्षणको धर्मः सेवितव्यः प्रयत्नतः ।। (6.91)

People in all the four stages- Celibacy, Family Life, Vanpraastha or practicing renunciation, ought to necessarily adhere to these ten attributes in their lives. There is a shloka of Gita-

समशत्रौ च मित्रेय तथा मानऽवमानयोः
शीतोष्ण सुख दुःखेषु समसंग विवर्जितः ।।

In this shloka it is conveyed that, a person who is beyond enmity and friendship, reverence and insults, cold and heat, happiness and sorrow and maintains equanimity in all situations, does not get distracted, is in all respects a knower of dharma or dutifulness.

By inculcating all these attributes in one's character and adhering to the four ashrams of Brahmacharya, Grihastha, Vanprastha aand Sanyas, a creator of a beautiful society comes to be. The infrastructure of ashram system, its formation was created by ascetics and sages, in a way that after reaching from one ashram to the other human beings could forsake selfishness, become pure and selfless, illumined internally and in external conduct thus get enlightened to cause illumination for all others.

Mahatma Gandhi, has described the tenets of duty in the form of eleven vows-

'अहिंसा सत्यं अस्तेयो ब्रह्मचर्य परिग्रह
शरीरश्रम अस्वादो सर्वत्र भजवर्जयेत्
सर्वधर्म समानत्वे स्वदेशी स्पर्श भावना
ही एकादश सेवानि सम्रत्वे कृति निश्चयेत् ।।'

Influenced by the Vedas, Upanishads and all the other ancient Indian thought, Gandhiji had a firm conviction that by adhering to these eleven tenets, self-government can be attained. He wished that the future of India must be on a stable foundation and each citizen must be a part of this foundation.

Veda, Upanishad and thereafter, Manu Smritri also have delivered these sermons for each human being of the nation. According to the time, age and circumstances, these have been presented in a different way, and some new interpretations have been added-

**(1) Ahimsa or Non-Violence-** Regarding non-violence Gandhiji has stressed and said, that each citizen of India may never allow his motherland to get bruised due to violence. India should through non-violent means must attain the goal of self- government and be known as ambassador of peace. This non- violence ought to be on all the three levels- in thought, speech and action.

**(2) Truth (Satya)-** In 'My Experiments with Truth,' Gandhiji writes, 'There is no divinity, other than the truth, and to attain truth is the only means to non-violence.' It was his contention that falsehood is the perpetrator of evil and weaknesses. Truth makes a human being courageous.

**(3) Non-Stealing (Asteya)-** Stay away from greed and theft. Even thinking about someone else's possession is a big crime.

**(4) Celibacy (Brahmacharya)-** Explaining the meaning of Brahmacharya, Gandhiji said, "Controlling the senses, is proceeding towards the goal of the Creator's realm and attainment of truth." A celibate ought to remain involved in self learning and endeavour to uplift himself. Vices, lead to a human being's downfall.

**(5) Non-Possessiveness (Aparigraha)-** A human being should not collect things beyond his needs. Nature provides us with a chance to fulfil our daily needs, which should be used properly by us. Indulgence makes a human being powerless. Greed for more creates a situation of paucity for others. In Young India (05.02.25) Gandhi ji wrote establishing India's identity, "India basically is a Karmabhumi (land of action) not a Bhogbhumi (Land of Indulgence)"[26]

---

[26] M.K.Gandhi young India 5-2-25

**(6) Physical Work (Shram)-** Each one must complete the task assigned. It is the duty of every section of society to fulfil their duties.

**(7) Removal of Untouchability from Society (Asprishyata)** - With the goal of removal of untouchability from society, Gandhiji said, 'No work is inferior or superior. Whoever works is a worker'. This is what Gita sermonizes –'योगः कर्मसु कौशलम्' meaning thereby, efficient and pure deeds are yoga or commendable.

**(8) Savourless food (Aswad)-** It means instead of spicy and pungent tasting food, opt for plain, limited and nourishing food for consumption. In 'Young India' related to this, a food list has been given.[27] Meticulously following this food chart, the body is maintained heathy, without disease.

**(9) Fearlessness (Nirbhayata)-** Gandhiji says that one who is not erroneous, has a clear heart and is non-violent, is fearless. If the goal is selfless, a noble cause, then fearlessly be active. A timid person can neither uplift himself nor the nation.

**(10) Tolerance (Sahishnuta)-** By the advent of 19th century, orthodox values got divided into branches and sub-branches, the society had many spiritual lineages established in it. Gandhiji himself accepted that dharma was for him, the truth, non-violence, sacrifice and only dharma-based politics is acceptable. We must get rid of lineages, not dharma. A human being must be tolerant of one another's feelings. From this point of view the meaning of religious tolerance means to adopt tolerant attitude for various religions. Gandhiji himself said that the divine does not reside in the idol, but in faith and good deeds, it means only pure and welfare activities must be a person's dharma or duty.

**(11) Swadeshi-** It was Gandhiji's contention that the economy of the country can only be strong, if we use only

---

[27] M.K.Gandhi young India 1187-1928

swadeshi (indigenous products) goods. For the purpose, handicraft and village industry will have to be given a boost. Swadeshi does not only refer to products, but also language, culture, education, love for human beings, are all included in it. The independence of the nation is only possible, when we adopt our language, our culture, national education and have good feelings and love for all human beings.[28]

To mention Gandhiji's eleven tenets in this scripture is necessary for the reason, that it establishes the values of Vedic culture, which is still intact and relevant. Through the medium of great personalities their importance has been highlighted. Gandhiji repeatedly mentioned in his sayings "I do not wish to establish any ism. I am only reiterating what is derived from Vedas, Upanishad and Gita."[29] Veda and thereafter what Manu has sermonized in his shlokas and then what Buddha and Gandhiji said, proves that, ancient literature was relevant for all times and was a path breaker. Manavdharmashastra is such a key, which finds a solution for all types of problems.

**Action Non-Action Analysis**

In the ancient Indian Thought the analysis of action and non-action draws attention to a human being's purity of conduct and the glow of his character, which only has a steak left in the present democratic system. Through the medium of Manu and Yagnavalkya Smritis, information regarding deeds worthy of performance and the ones to be forsaken can be made available to modern human beings, which is helpful in deciding whether it is appropriate or inappropriate and that way can prove useful. Manu has given the most useful sermon for human beings, then only that action be performed, which is approved by one's own conscience.

यत्कर्म कुर्वतोऽस्य स्यात्परितोषोऽन्तरात्मनः ।
तत्प्रयत्नेन कुर्वीत विपरीतं तु वर्जयेत् ।। (4.161 )

---

[28] Dr.M.S.Rajlingam p.37
[29] Harijan p.36, 28.3.1919

It means the performance of acts that satisfy the inner soul and create happiness, be done effortfully. Do not perform acts opposed to the inner soul. Acts opposed to the soul means, those actions that cause fear, doubt and one feels ashamed of. The form of action be pure. 'सत्त्वस्य लक्षणां धर्मः (12.38) Manu explains the root of duty, while clarifying it, he says, Vedas are the root of dharma, thereafter, Smritis created by scholars, those ones possessing fine attributes and containing great thoughts are the second root of human duty. The third root of duty is virtuous conduct. 'Satisfaction of the spirit' has been told to be the fourth root source of duty by Manu, he says that a conduct in consonance with the Vedas, is only dear to the soul. An inappropriate action, detrimental to the interest of the other, can never be loved by the soul.

**Trividh Karma**

In the twelfth chapter of Manusmriti there is mention of the three types of actions and their consequences.

शुभाशुभफलं कर्म मनोवाग्देहसंभवम् ।
कर्मजा गतयो नृणामुत्तमाधममध्यमाः ।। (12.3)

Actions undertaken for the dictates of the mind, speech and body bring about auspicious or inauspicious consequences and according to those actions a human beings gets a top quality, medium, or low state of life after birth. The shloka number 5,6, and 7 three types of bad deeds are narrated.

Manasik (Mental)

परद्रव्येष्वभिध्यानं मनसानिष्टचिन्तनम् ।
वितथाभिनिवेशश्च त्रिविधे कर्म मानसम् ।। (12.5)

Vachik (Speech)

पारुष्यमनृतं चैव पैशुन्यं चापि सर्वशः ।
असंबद्धप्रलापश्च वाङ्मयं स्यच्चतुर्विधम् ।। (12.6)

Sharirik (Physical)

अदत्तानामुपादानं हिंसा चैवाविधानतः ।
परदारोपसेवा च शारीरं त्रिविधं स्मृतम् ।। (12.7)

Snatching away another's money or theft, thinking ill of others, being spiteful, being jealous, are all included in the category of bad deeds at mental level. Non-duty through speech is- harsh speech, false praise, ingenuine flight. Violence, adultery are in the category of physical bad deeds.

In shloka number 9, narrating the ill consequences of bad deeds it has been written-

शरीरजैः कर्मदोषैर्याति स्थावरतां नरः।
वाचिकैः पक्षिमृगतां मानसैरन्त्यजातिताम्।।

Due to bad physical deeds, a human being is reborn as a tree, bad deeds through speech lead a human being to born as a bird or deer and due to mental ill deeds, he is born in the family of out-castes.

नाधर्मश्चरितो लोके सद्यः फलति गौरिव
शनैरावर्तमानस्तु कर्त्तर्मूलानि कृन्तति।। (4.172)
यदि नात्मनि पुत्रेषु न चेत्पुत्रेषु नप्तृषु।
न त्वेव कृतोऽधर्मः कुर्तुर्भवति निष्फलः।। (4.173)

Manu in the said shlokas opines that, bad deeds committed in this astral level do not show results immediately, the Earth and the cow do not produce fruits then and there. It spreads slowly and de- route the perpetrator of non-duty.

Manu warns that Adharmic indulgence invariably has consequences, even if the body is killed immediately, the consequences are borne by the descending family, If not by the son, then the grand son has to bear the consequences, grandson inherit the property of father or grandfather, likewise, they also have to bear the fruit or ill fruit of their good and bad deeds. This principle is not opposed to the Vedas.

To attain a good state Manu sermonizes to do good deeds, in the 11, 12, 14 and 15 number shloka of chapter 4 he writes-

न लोकवृत्तं वर्तेत वृत्तिहेतोः कथञ्चन।
अजिह्मामशठां शुद्धां जीवेद्ब्राह्मणजीविकाम्।। (4.11)
सन्तोषं परमास्थाय सुखार्थी संयतो भवेत्।
सन्तोषमूलं हि सुखं दुःख मूलं विपर्ययः।। (4.12)

वेदोदितं स्वकं कर्म नित्यं कुर्यादतन्द्रितः।
तद्धि कुर्वन् यथाशक्ति प्राप्नोति परमां गतिम्।। (4.14)
नेहेतार्थान्प्रसङ्गेन न विरुद्धेन कर्मणा।
न विद्यमानेष्वर्येषु नात्यामपि यतस्ततः।। (4.15)

Manu has presented a system of ethical upliftment for all times, by propagating the Vedic concept of Work based life for human beings in his sermons. Wealth acquired through inappropriate means, pollutes the national character. On this basis only Manu has instructed the King, royal officials and the subjects, not to follow a way of life opposed to the scriptures.

It means stay away from cunningness, while doing duty. Happiness is possible only through contentment, 'सन्तोषमूलं हि सुखं'meaning thereby, not craving for too much wealth and possessions, is for good. Because, 'दुःखमूलं विपर्ययः' greed for wealth becomes a cause of misery. Manu says, a human being ought to give up laziness and pursue an activity recommended by the Vedas and concludes that, get products conducive to it and lead a life of contentment. Life may become as hard as it could, but never earn money through dishonest means. Being too indulgent in material things, leads to Adharma.

### Sermon on Non-Violence

Manu has forbidden non-violent behaviour and denounced non-vegetarianism. Inspiring to be non-violent, Manu has written at many instances-

वर्जयेन्मधु मांसं च प्राणिनां चैव हिंसनम्।। ( 2.177)

Liquor, meat, and violence towards human beings is forbidden, give it up.

अहिंस्रो दमदानाभ्यां जयेत् स्वर्ग तथाव्रतः।। (4.246)

One should stay away from non-violent, cruel, crooked people, be dutiful and able to conquer the mind to be happy through charity of education.

अहिंसया च भूतानां अमृतत्वाय कल्पते।। (6.60)

Maintain a feeling of love towards every being, develop more competence for the final redemption. All these evidences, prove that Manu did forbid all types of violence. In the third chapter, Manu has clearly instructed, that in the performances of Yagnas, pure food stuff be used. Manu has used the Vedas as evidence for his sermons. Yajurveda is supposed to be the Veda of practical work, in its first mantra only there is a plea for protection of animals.

'यजमानस्य पशून् पाहि।' (1.1)

It means the animals of a Yagna performer be protected. Likewise, according to a mantra of the Rig Veda, only those who are vegetarian, have a right to perform Yagnas.

'ऊर्जाद उत यज्ञियासः पञ्चजना मम होत्रं जुषध्वम्।।' (10.53.4)

This means only those who have cereals for food, and those men with a propensity to do Yagna among the five types (Brahmins, Kshatriya, Vaishya, Shudra and Nishad) may conduct Yagnas.

The valuable education of deeds for welfare, harbinger of goodness, speech for everyone's good, enhancement of spiritual power, has been through-out imparted by Manav-dharmashastra.

मंगलाचारयुक्तानां नित्यं च प्रयतात्मनाम्
जपतां जुह्वतां चैव विनिपातो न विद्यते।। (4.146)
नात्मानमवमन्येत पूर्वाभिरसमृद्धिभिः।
आमृत्योः श्रियमन्विच्छेन्नैनां मन्येत दुर्लभाम्।। (4.137)
सत्यं ब्रूयात्प्रियं ब्रूयन्न ब्रूयात्सत्यमप्रियम्।
प्रियं च नानृतम् ब्रूयादेष धर्मः सनातनः।। (4.138)

While describing good deed, Manu clarifies that those who are involved in welfare activities and make endeavours for spiritual upliftment constantly, their life does not face degradation ever. A human being should accept the little money earned through fair means happily. Ought not to consider himself poor and be possessed by a feeling of lacking. Money is not unattainable. A hardworking person has the capacity to earn enough money.

So, Manu says, duty must be performed truthfully. A human being must analyse the nature of his deeds himself and decide what is for good? Sermonising about self- analysis, Manu says, a person ought to be in solitude and indulge in self investigation for proceeding on the path of welfare. The one who acts according to the Vedas, only is able to attain happiness.

**King's Characteristics**

While placing acts for the welfare of the entire community and not for it in the category of duty or non-duty, Manu has given special instructions regarding acts befitting a King, which are indispensable in ruling the kingdom. Firstly, Manu says, 'for being competent to be a king' one must possess eight special qualities. The king's conduct and nature be in consonance with the divine great powers, and their workings.

The King has eight facets-

इंद्रस्याक्र स्य वायोश्च यमस्य वरुणस्य च ।
चंद्रस्याग्नेः पृथिव्याश्च तेजोवृत्तं नृप्श्चरेत् ।। (9.303)

In the shloka number 304 to 312 Manu has himself explained these attributes, which are as follows-

**1. Indra :** As creator of rains, Indra (Rain God) gives abundant rain to quench the universe, likewise, the king must, provide for its subject's happiness and comforts, fulfil their needs and keep them satisfied.

**2. Vayu :** As air enters all living beings and places and circulates, likewise, the king ought to go everywhere through his spies and be informed of all places, enemies and subjects related to the people of his kingdom.

**3. Yam :** The divine power to kill and control, as it is according to dharma or justly punishes at the time of deeds bearing their fruits or consequences, similarly, the king, without discriminating between friend and foe, ought to punish his subjects imparting justice. Manu has used the word, 'Dharmaraat'. Dharma means rule of justice and one imparting that is 'Dharmaraat'.

**4. Ark :** As the Sun receives water heated by its rays, likewise, the King can also without harassing or making his subjects bear a loss, collect taxes from them.

**5. Agni :** Like the destroyer of impurities, the purifier fire, the King must destroy sinful deeds of evil people.

**6. Varun :** As water in its current of a whirl- pool, sucks up living beings, likewise, the King ought to take criminals and enemies into bondage, and put them in the jail.

**7. Chandr :** Lends coolness to all, consequently, as on viewing the full Moon our heart swells with happiness, likewise, the king be harbinger of peace and happiness to his subjects. His subjects must feel thrilled at his sight.

**8. Kuber :** It means possessor of abundant wealth. In the Manavdharmashastra it has been called 'Kuber'(7.7) and 'Dhara' and 'Prithvi' (9.311) have been referred to as its synonyms. As the 'Dharti' or the Lord, possessor of wealth fosters all beings equally, likewise the King ought to impartially, treat all the subjects equally, as a father takes care of the sons.

**Yog Kshem**

According to Manu the king who inculcates these great qualities is an effective ruler. Through his brilliance he succeeds and influences his subjects. The King must be aware of the difference between Dharma and Adharma, justice and injustice, appropriate and inappropriate. To be dutiful, he must have knowledge of regulations and laws and accordingly he ought to carry on the ruling system at that time. Dharma is worth performing, regulations and laws worthy of following have been treated as a system. Manu has sermonized and instructed the King regarding the behavioural conduct within the ambit of different aspects of ruling system and said that each one of the king's activities, be inspired by people's welfare, keeping it in view he should regulate punishment, justice, law, the taxation system and international relations.

The entire seventh chapter is in context of royal duty. In

the 99th shloka of this chapter Manu sermonizes-

अलब्धं चैव लिप्सेत लब्धं रक्षेत्प्रयत्नतः ।
रक्षितं वर्धयेच्चैव वृद्धं पात्रेषु निःक्षिपेत् ।। (7.99)

Meaning thereby, it is the duty of the king, 1. Make endeavours to achieve, what has not been achieved. 2. What has been achieved, protect that. 3 What is secure, enhance that. 4 And distribute it among deserving people.

एतच्चतुर्विधं विद्यात्पुरुषार्थप्रयोजनम् ।
अस्य नित्यमनुष्ठानं सम्यक् कुर्यादतन्द्रितः ।। 7.100)
अलब्धमिच्छद्देण्डेन लब्धं रक्षेदवेक्षया ।
रक्षितं वर्धयेद् वृद्धया वृद्धं पात्रेषु निःक्षिपेत् ।। (7.101)

Manu has termed these four, the kingdom's inherent values to be pursued and has instructed the king to be involved in an endeavour to achieve these without being lazy, and the money earned through dutiful deeds be spent in performing good deeds. Manu expects from the king to propagate\ through the medium of wisely picked up persons, true education, truthful duty and by his good conduct, be effortful for the progress of the kingdom and the subjects. In Yagnnavalakya Smriti (1.100), Mitakshar has described welfare thus-

'अलब्धलाभो योगःलब्ध परिपालनम् क्षेमः 'The meaning of yoga is to achieve that, which is unattainable, and 'kshem' means what is achieved, protect that. If both are understood together, then it will mean what is already there, protect that. Thus yoga-kshem is a king's duty.

धर्म्याणि कार्याणि सम्यक्कुर्वन्महीपतिः ।
देशानलब्धांल्लिप्सेत लब्धांश्च परिपालयेत् ।। (9.251)

Manu opines a king while concluding dutiful tasks, ought to have a wish to capture areas, not conquered yet and be eager to undertake the obligation of maintaining the areas already captured well.

If Yogakshema was to be deeply analysed, it will appear that it is the complete gist of royal duty. As duty, truth, justice, obligations, society's formation, (Varna Ashram Dharma) administrative system, people's welfare and other valuable subjects and their achievement, protection, and enhancement are included in the two words 'Yoga-kshema.'. In the present democratic system, this very valuable concept could be adopted, to balance the imbalanced system and uncontrolled people and people's officials be brought under control. The administrative officials ought to realize its topicality, for adoption by them and assimilate it in social schemes and policies.

**Judicial System-Kantak Shodhan**

For welfare of the people, it is necessary that the ruling system works smoothly without hurdles. With reference to it Manu says-

रक्षादार्यवृत्तानां कंटकानां च शोधनात्।
नरेंद्रस्त्रिदिवं यान्ति प्रजापालनतत्पराः।। (9.253)

It means by protecting well conducted people and punishing those causing pain, evil doers and taking due care of the subjects, a king enjoys the ruling of an extensive kingdom. In this shloka a saying is incorporated, 'त्रिदिवं यान्ति' or 'त्रिदिवं प्राप्नुवन्ति' -which means the king is able to acquire rule of all the three lokas (astral levels). Meaning thereby, the Kingdom of such a king expands day by day. This saying is in vogue even today. In the ninth chapter of Manu Smriti, from the 251 to 324 shlokas, much stress has been laid on removal of obstruction in people's welfare. Obstruction in people's welfare means, those anti- social elements who spread disorder in the society, destroy happiness and peace, by flouting the law, cause distress to others, are against the society. The basic meaning of 'Lok-kantak' is also this-piercing like a thorn to cause pain. To be rid of these Manu says-

कण्टकोद्धरणे नित्यमातिष्ठेद्यत्नमुत्तमम् (9.252)
निर्भयं तुभवेद्यस्य राष्ट्रं बाहुबलाश्रितम्
तस्य तद्वर्धते नित्यं सिच्यमान इव द्रुमः (9.255)

The king whose valour, meaning thereby, whose power to punish makes the subjects in the kingdom, fearless, anti -social elements in fear of punishment forsake crime, that king like a well irrigated tree, keeps on growing.

Manu advises the king ought to punish smugglers and thieves and protect his subjects. If he is unsuccessful in protecting the people, in that circumstance the subjects in disillusionment, may rebel. Manu says, a king who does not undertake the responsibility of protecting the subjects, he gets deprived of the privilege of royal enjoyments. The king is entitled to extract taxes from his subjects only in case, in his kingdom the subjects feel protected and are fearless. Such a kingdom like a well irrigated tree goes on growing continuously. The topicality of Manu's saying is proved by the fact that in present times, people frustrated with the long time - consuming legal procedure in India, in many small and big states, they took the law in their hands and killed many corrupt rulers, publicly. People are losing faith in the system of justice and legal system. Anti-social elements are gaining power. It is a state of chaos. The present legal specialists must gather information regarding the judicial-administrative system, as it was described in the Manusmriti scripture.

Those imposters as sages and ascetics who created fear to extract money, who assume respectable exterior, actual thugs, resort to palm reading, to loot money, extract money, royal workers, charging money against a false promise of concluding a task or evil ones, who use a symbol to roam around clandestinely, have been called, 'lok kantak' by Manu. It is the duty of the King to that he should duly punish the evil doers, in accordance to their fault or crime. In inflicting punishment never be care-less or slow. For keeping evil persons under control, they had to be identified for punishment and at public places the king had to post groups of soldiers and spies.

एवं चरन् सदा युक्तो राजधर्मेषु पार्थिवः।
हितेषु चैव लोकस्य सर्वान्भृत्यान्नि योजयेत्।। (9.324)

In the said shloka Manu says, the king aspiring to free his

kingdom of evil people, himself may remain involved in royal duty and appoint officers to discharge theirs on subjects of welfare.

## Law of Punishment

For carrying on timely administration of the kingdom, Manu has delivered sermons on law of punishment-

दण्डःशास्ति प्रजाः सर्वा दण्ड एवाभिरक्षति ।
दण्डः सुप्तेष जगर्तिः दण्डं धर्म विदुर्बुधाः ।। (7.18)

The law of punishment only rules the subjects, punishment only protects the subjects from all directions. Wakes up the subjects drawn in a slumber, meaning thereby, that crime committed due to carelessness or in solitude, due to fear of punishment, do not thrive. The fear of punishment is such a fear which bothers, even while asleep. That is why intelligent people consider the law of punishment, the main duty of the king. In the 16 th shloka, Manu instructs the king that, punishment be inflicted keeping conformity with the norms of the country, time, power and education, which means in accordance with the crime committed, punishment be inflicted. For unjust use of punishment is the destroyer of the king.

दण्डो हि सुमहत्तेजो दुर्धरश्चाकृतात्मभिः ।
धर्मादद्विचलितं हन्ति नृपमेव सबान्धवम् ।। (7.28)

Manu holds, infliction of punishment is brilliant. In the shloka no.14 it has been considered as brilliant as Brahma, meaning thereby, it is educative. It cannot be undertaken to inflict punishment or judgement by an ordinary, unscholarly person or incompetent person, Adharmic punishment destroys the King. Further it is written-

यावानवध्यस्य वधे तावान्वध्यस्य मोक्षणे ।
अधर्मो नृपतेर्द्रष्टो धर्मस्तु विनियच्छतः ।। (9.249)

Inflicting punishment on the innocent is as much Adharma for the king, as is sparing one deserving punishment. It is only appropriate for the king to that he may inflict punishment imparting justice, and it is duty.

Further writes-

शुचिना सत्यसन्धेन यथाशास्त्रानुसारिणा।
प्रणेतुं शक्यते दण्डः सुसहायेन धीमता।। (7.31)

Only possessors of good conduct, gentlemen and having knowledge of Niti Shastra (scriptures on ethics), intelligent persons, can afford to use justice in the form of punishment. Thus, with the assistance of dutiful men, the king should undertake to impart justice. Inflicting punishment for imparting justice, enhances the king's fame.

समीक्ष्य स धृतः सम्यक्सर्वा रञ्जयतिप्रजाः।
असमीक्ष्य प्रणीतस्तु विनाशयति सर्वतः।। (7.19)

The punishment that is inflicted after thinking over the matter fully, that makes the subjects happy in every way. Inflicting inappropriate punishment without duly thinking over the matter, leads to the downfall of the king.The form of punishment that destroys sins, has been described by Manu thus-

यत्र श्यामो लोहिताक्षो दण्डश्चरति पापहा।
प्रजास्तत्र न मुह्यन्ति नेता चेत्साधु पश्यति।। (7.25)

Punishment is like, dark complexion, blood red eyed horrendous man but that form of punishment is only for the welfare of the subjects. Presenting an impartial law of punishment, Manu says-

पिता आचार्यः सुहृत् माता भार्या पुत्रः पुरोहितः।
नादण्ड्यो नाम राज्ञोऽस्ति यः स्वधर्मे न तिष्ठति।। (8.335)

गुरुं वा बालवृद्धौ वा ब्राह्मणं वा बहुश्रुतम्।
आततायिनमायान्तं हन्यादेवाविचारयन्।। (8.350)

Mother, father, teacher, knowledge holders of Shrutis and so on, are punishable by the king. A criminal maybe one's own relation or even a scholar, royal duty dictates that a king sitting on the seat of judgement must be impartial, means, must read out the verdict without being partial. The King who does not adhere to his duty, is liable for punishment.

कार्षापणं भवेद्दण्ड्यो यत्रान्यः प्राकृतो जनः।
तत्र राजा भवेद्दण्ड्यः सहस्रमिति धारणा। (8.336)

Keeping the King also in the ambit of punishment Manu

Samhita iterates, that rule is just, wherein, on the king being proved guilty, he be punished. According to the scriptures, as compared to a common man, for the king a thousand times more punishment be fixed.

Likewise, the ratio of punishment related to class and ordinary section has been referred to by Manavdharmashastra thus-

अष्टपाद्यं तु शूद्रस्य स्तेये भवति किल्विषम्।
षौडशैव तु वैश्यस्य द्वात्रिंशत्क्षत्रियस्य च।। (8.337)
ब्राह्मणस्य चतुःषष्टिः पूर्णं वापि शतं भवेत्।
द्विगुणा वा चतुःषष्टिस्तर्दोषगुणविद्धिः सः।। (8.338)

People belonging to high class, who are rational, on being proved guilty are liable for more punishment. If involvement in crime is proved evidentially, in that circumstance, a Vaishya is punished more than a Shudra, Kshatriya is liable for more punishment than the Vaishya and Brahmins get much more than the Kshatriyas. It means the more knowledgeable and prestigious one is, he will get as much more punishment for his crime. On the basis of knowledge Manu has treated Brahmins with most reverence, but for a Brahmin indulging in unfair and unscrupulous activities is not absolved of punishment, for him maximum punishment has been fixed.

वृषो हि भगवान्धर्मस्तस्य यः कुरुते ह्यलम्।
वृषलं तं विदुर्देवास्तस्माद्धर्मं न लोपयेत्।। (8.16)

Manu says about one who conducts himself contrary to Dharma-

The person flouting the tenets of Dharma may be an important person in the society, even then he will be known as lowly. The dharma, that is harbinger of happiness, wealth, prosperity, protection, to it adhering is everyone's prime duty.

यस्य स्तेनः पुरे नास्ति नान्यस्त्रीगो न दुष्टवाक्।
न साहसिकदण्डघ्नौ स राजा शक्र लोकभाक्।। (8.386)

Manu only says, that very royal administration is superior, wherein all are disciplined. Only that King is great, whose kingdom does not have thieves, philanderers, speakers of evil talk, deceitful dacoits and where the king's order is not overlooked, and people observe good conduct.

## Assembling of Brahma Sabha

Dharmashastra sermonizes the king that he ought to assemble a council for justice for protecting the Dharma. The Council of justice has been called the Brahma Sabha.

यस्मिन्देशे निषीदन्ति विप्रा वेदविदस्त्रयः ।
राज्ञश्चाधिकृतो विद्वान्ब्रह्मणस्तां सभां विदुः ।। (8.11)

In a country or place where three Vedic scholars are seated, and one Vedic scholar, specialist of a particular subject, appointed by the King, that council is called the Brahma Sabha or the Nyaya Sabha ( Council of Justice.). Brahma Sabha stands for a council of erudite Vedic scholarly judges. The shloka number 8.9 mentions-

यदा स्वयं न कुर्यात्तु नृपतिः कार्यदर्शनम् ।
तदा नियुञ्ज्याद्विद्वांसं ब्राह्मणं कार्यदर्शने ।। (8.9)

The said shloka mentions that in the absence of a king, for taking formal decisions Brahamans be appointed. In this shloka the use of the word 'Brahamin' is not for one belonging to the brahamin Varna, but for one scholar who would be appropriate for appointment as the chief justice.

तत्रासीनः स्थितो वाऽपि पाणिमुद्यम्य दक्षिणम् ।
विनीतवेषाभरणः पश्येत्कार्याणि कार्यिणाम् ।। (8.2)
प्रत्यहं देशदृष्टैश्च शास्त्रदृष्टैश्च हेतुभिः ।
अष्टादशसु मार्गेषु निबद्धानि पृथक्पृथक् ।। (8.3)

Manu has at length discussed the aspects of conduct, truthful speech, evidence, regarding eighteen types of cases heard in the Sabha and so on, in the entire process of Brahma Sabha. His contention is, first of all the King seated on the throne of Dharma must give up a harsh outlook, adopt a lenient approach while taking decisions in judicial cases. The purpose behind it is that in the presence of a mild frame of mind of the king, the evidence could be carried out smoothly, and the culprit may feel fearless in putting forward his viewpoint. Manu has upheld Sanatan Dharma as the basis for the working of Council of Justice, in deciding against incidents involved in eighteen types of law cases, regarding Land property, borrowing, possessions, business, salary, breaking-commitment, Sale-purchase, ownership of animals, theft, corruption, gambling, partition of heritage, harsh speech, insidiousness, crossing over or encroachment beyond boundaries, cases involving duties of men and women, rape and other unscrupulous activities.

The scholars composing the Council of Justice, are all members in conformity and for dispensing of justice, Manusmriti gives a message of Dharma (dutifulness)-

आचारः परमो धर्मः श्रुत्युक्त स्मृति एव च।
तस्मादस्मिन्सदा युक्तो नित्ये स्यादात्मवान्द्विजः।। (1.108)

What has been said in the Vedas and Smritis, is most important and is worthy of being followed in conduct. For spiritual upliftment it is necessary that the king ought to adhere to Dharma by complying to Vedas and Smriti.

Manusmriti declares with reference to justice-

वेदोऽखिलो धर्ममूलं स्मृतिशीले च तद्विदाम्।
आचारश्चैव साधू नामात्मनस्तुष्टिरेव च।। (2.6)

All the Vedic literature, the four Vedas and Smriti are the source of Dharma abiding conduct, upheld by scholars. The four Vedas are not human creation. Being a storehouse of truthful learnings, they are the first evidence of dutiful decision. Triple (Triguni) form of learning, the four Vedas, Rig, Yaju, Sam and Atharva have been called 'Akhil Veda' (Complete Veda). Those who have studied the Vedas thoroughly or those scholars who are able to explain the Vedas well, they alone are the true inspiration of Dharmashastra and are competent to impart justice in compliance of the Vedas.

The qualities of Dharma have been mentioned by Manu thus-

वेदः स्मृतिः सदाचारः स्वस्य च प्रियमात्मनः।
एतच्चतुर्विधं प्राहुः साक्षाद्धर्मस्य लक्षणम्।। (2.12)

Shruti Veda, in accordance with Veda and above-mentioned scriptures, gentlemen's way of conduct which is keeping in with Vedas delivered by the Supreme Divine instructing good deeds and is dear to one's own spirit, are the four paths of dutiful qualities. These help in discriminating between Dharma and Adharma.

Giving inspiration to protect this very dharma, Manu says-

धर्मो विद्वास्त्वधर्मेण सभां यत्रोपतिष्ठते।
शल्यं चास्य न कृन्तन्ति विद्वास्तत्र सभासदः।। (8.12)
यत्र धर्मो ह्यधर्मेण सत्यं यत्रानृतेन च।
हन्यते प्रेक्षमाणानां हतास्तत्र सभासदः।। (8.14)
पादोऽधर्मस्य कर्तारं पादः साक्षिणमृच्छति
पादः सभासदः सर्वान्पादो राजानमृच्छति।। (8.18)

It means, in a Sabha where in Dharma is present, yet after being injured by Adharma and Adharmi is not punished, in that Sabha the members get stabbed by Dharma itself. In a Sabha where Adharma prevails over Dharma, falsehood shadows the truth, in the presence of the Sabha members, meaning thereby, the Dharma is superseded in the presence of scholars, in that Sabha all are like dead bodies. In a Council of Justice wherein, through partiality injustice is perpetrated, there Adharma gets divided into four parts or the four persons share the liability of non-dutiful deed, the doer, evidence, member of the Council, and the chief of the Council (the King). These four deserve to be infamous. The subjects criticise them.

Manu says, other than this, in a Brahmasabha, wherein the King conducts himself appropriately, the evidence is truthful, impartial decisions are taken on the basis of arguments, there the Dharma is upheld-

राजा भवत्यनेनास्तु मुच्यन्ते च सभासदः।
एनो गच्छति कर्तारं निन्दाऽर्हो यत्र निन्द्यते।। (8.19)

In a Sabha one deserving heaping of insults is insulted, one deserving veneration is venerated, one punishable is punished, one to be revered is offered reverence, there the king or

Emperor gets rid of sin and gets purified.

Evidence must be very well investigated and the truthfulness of his statement, both play the main role in the decision on the case. Instead of taking a hurried decision, it should be done after investigating all facets of the case. On this important aspect, Manu has sermonized-

सत्येन पूयते साक्षी धर्मः सत्येन वर्धते।
तस्मात्सत्यं हि वक्तव्यं सर्ववर्णेषु साक्षिभिः।। (8.83)

By speaking the truth, the person giving evidence is purified, truthful statement enhances the state of Dharma. Meaning thereby, people belonging to all Varnas, while giving evidence must speak the truth. On presentation of the case, the criminal would be punished and innocent will be protected. The person who does not speak the truth while giving evidence must be punished, (89,59). Manu says-

आत्मनः साक्षी आत्मा, आत्मनः गतं आत्मा।। (8.84)

'The soul itself is the witness of a soul.' The destination of the soul is the soul itself. Thus, it is the duty of the witness, not to dishonour his soul and not to give evidence against its soul. According to Manu, Brahmin and Kshatriya together lead to the progress of the nation. The welfare, happiness and progress of a state depends on how the king formulates every facet of dharma. As it is only Dharma that helps in the other births. According to Manu-

एक एव सुहृद्धर्मो निधनेऽप्यनुयाति यः।
शरीरेण समं नाशं सर्वमन्यद्धि गच्छति।। (8.17)

In this world, only duty is a friend, that accompanies even after death. Other things perish with the body or are forsaken, but Dharma remains. Manu holds that protection of dharma is only possible through truthful justice, if the knowledge of proofs of dharma is gotten. The science of dharma has three types of knowledge-

प्रत्यक्षं चानुमानं च शास्त्रं च विविधागमम्।
त्रयं सुविदितं कार्यं धर्मशुद्धिमभीप्सता।। (12.105)

One who aspires to understand the actual element of

dharma, must possess due knowledge of obvious proofs (Pratyaksh Pramaan), gaged proofs (Anumaan Pramaan) and scriptural proofs (Shastra Pramaan). Only he can understand the element of dharma (12/106) who can argue on it, in accordance with the tenets of Vedic scriptures and indulge in investigative research. By arguments it is meant, fixing the truth keeping in conformity with the evidence and the Vedas.

To understand dutiful behaviour well and in a succinct manner, Manu says, if Smriti is not apparently helpful in deciding over arguments, in that case, accept the decision of elite people, well conversant with the dharma.

आर्षं धर्मोपदेशं च वेदशास्त्राऽविरोधिना।
यस्तर्केणानुसंधत्ते सः धर्मं वेद नेतरः।। (12.106)
अनाम्नातेषु धर्मेषु कथं स्यादिति चेद्भवेत्।
यं शिष्टा ब्राह्मणा ब्रूयुः स धर्मः स्यादशङ्कितः।। (12.108)

The description of elite people has been clearly given by Manu thus-

धर्मेणाधिगतो यैस्तु वेदः सपरिबृंहणः।
ते शिष्टा ब्राह्मणा ज्ञेयाः श्रुतिप्रत्यक्षहेतवः।। (12.109)

Elite people are those scholars, who have practiced complete celibacy and have thoroughly studied Vedas. On the ground of proofs of Shruti and effortful proofs, they are capable of banning formulations, are follower of Dharma and work for others good.

**Dharma Parishad**

For taking decisions, in consonance with justice and duty Manu has said-

दशावरा व परिषद्यं धर्मं परिकल्पयेत्।
त्र्यवरा वापि वृत्तस्था तं धर्मं न विचालयेत्।। (12.110)

While establishing the Dharmaparishad the king must pay attention on fixing the number of members and examine their competence, essentially. The King must have at least ten erudite scholars or minimum three scholars in composing the Parishad and should not let the system of dharma be flouted.The members of Dharma Parishad ought to be possessing triple education-

आद्यं यत्त्रयक्षरं ब्रह्म त्रयी यास्मिन्प्रतिष्ठिता।
स गुह्योऽन्यस्त्रिवृद्वेदो यस्तं वेद स वेदवित्।। (11.265)
ऋग्वेद विद्यजुर्विच्च सामवेदविदेव च।
त्रयवरा परिषज्ज्ञेया धर्मसंशयनिर्णये।। (12.112)

Manu has instructed regarding superior rule and system of justice, that the king, royal officials, Chief of the forces and the Chief Justice must be learned scholars of the Vedas-

सेनापत्यं च राज्यं च दण्डनेतृत्वमेव च।
सर्वलोकाधिपत्यं च वेदशास्त्रविदर्हति।। (12.100)

The chief of forces, main royal officers, the chief justice, and first and foremost the king, these four must be learned scholars of the Vedas, virtuous, practicing restraint, valiant, just and possess spiritual powers.

त्रैविद्यो हैतुकस्तर्की नैरुक्तो धर्मपाठकः
त्रय श्चाश्रमिणः पूर्वे परिषत्स्याद्दशावरा।। (12.111)

Manu iterates, that the Sabha is adorned by scholars. Such scholars be members of the Sabha, who possess knowledge of the four Vedas, scriptures on justice and the earlier stated Dharmashastra. The Sabha may include celibates, those enjoying worldly pleasures and also Vanprasthas, with their number not less than 10 in any case.

Through these shlokas Manu instructs that, the One who is addressed by three lettered primordial word 'AUM', is the eternal divine root of all, who is possessor of the three Vedic learnings, He has knowledge of all the subjects of the Vedas. For taking righteous decisions on all matters, the scholars who are members of the Parishad, must treat the Rigveda, Yajur Veda and the Sam Veda as the guiding yardstick. Decisions and systems created on their basis, need never be flouted by anyone.

In the following shloka, Manu has treated the duty prescribed by fools as the cause of increasing sins-

एकोऽपि वेदविद्धर्मं यं व्यवस्येद् द्विजोत्तमः।
स विज्ञेयः परो धर्मो नाज्ञानामुदितोऽयुतैः।। (12.113)

According to him, a system formed by millions foolish people, cannot compare with a system formulated by a single (Trividya) scholar of the triple learnings, with in depth knowledge of the Vedas and adhering to Vedic values, which is far superior. Decisions given on conduct, by uneducated, foolish people, ignorant of the Vedas, need not be complied with. It is a famous saying in Sanskrit- 'अन्धैनैव नीयमानाः यथान्धाः'- As those leaning on a blind, fall into a ditch with him, likewise, followers of fools, land in the darkness of foolishness and ignorance, to meet their downfall.

For ruling well and taking decisions righteously, it is necessary that the members be well qualified. Council of Education, Council of Duty, and the Royal Council, may never have ignorant people appointed as their members.

If the Council of Justice prescribed by Manu be compared to the present system of justice, then our head will bow before Manu in reverence, as the Indian judicial systems and parts thereof, are unable to fulfil the assigned obligations. The criminals get out of the witness box and the innocent get inside. Due to unavailability of evidence or at times false evidences are presented, the evidence and the truth gets camouflaged. The truth has to wait for impartial justice, for a lifetime. The state becomes dismal when the judiciary is inflicted with corruption as an infectious disease. The Justice one who is expected to be well conducted, has the Bar Association moving a no confidence motion against him, against the Chief Justice, impeachment proceedings have been seen carried out. This is the bitter truth of the weakness of present judicial system. Holders of power are turning a blind eye towards it, as they are a part of this very system. It will have to be reiterated here that Dharma protects the protector of duty and destroys the one who flouts it. It is an inevitable truth. It is an example of the way the present system is moving towards its downfall.

**Composition of a Strong Committed Parishad**

Like the Brahma Sabha, there is a mention of a Strong Committed Parishad in the Manavdharmashastra. Manu has informed the king of his duty to conclude work and take decisions, for maintaining a strong, stable and successful ruling system, only after consultation of his ministers. A single- minded decision could be detrimental to the interest and welfare of the subjects. Through the consultation of ministers and members of the Council that could be averted from being wrong. By seeking counselling, decisions could be quick, and executed. In the Manavdharmashastra special emphasis has been placed on the character of the ministers and members of the Council and the regulations regarding their qualifications.

मौलाञ्छास्त्रविदः शूराँल्लब्धलक्षान्कुलोद्भवान् ।
सचिवान्सप्त चाष्टौ वा प्रकुर्वीत परीक्षितान् ।। ( 7.54 )

Manu says 'in the self-government, scholars of Vedas and other scriptures, valiants, whose goals and thoughts do not prove futile, such elite and well examined, seven or eight secretaries, superior, dutiful, clever ministers, be appointed by the king. By 'well examined' it means, before appointment the king must ascertain information regarding credentials of his officials, their truthfulness, conduct, area of residence, qualifications and scriptural brilliance. This shloka clearly underlines the need of royal officials and assistants-

अपि यत्सुकरं कर्म तदप्येकेन दुष्करम् ।
विशेषतोऽसहायेन किं तु राज्यं महोदयम् ।। ( 7.55)

It means without assistance it is difficult to perform a simple work for a single person. So, how could the entire affairs of the kingdom be carried out by one person possibly? That is why overburdening the King with the entire administration of the kingdom and expecting him to succeed is not being intelligent.

Regarding the appointment and way of working of officials, assistants and spies Manu says-

तेषामर्थे नियुञ्जीत शूरान्दक्षान्कुलोद्गतान् ।
शुचनाकरकर्मान्ते भीरूनन्तर्निवेशने ।। (7.62)
अनुरक्तः शुचिर्दक्षः स्मृतिमान्देशकालवित् ।
वपुष्मान्वीतभीर्वाग्मी दूतो राज्ञः प्रशस्यते ।। (7.64)

It is expected from the king that he should consult his ministers regularly on matters regarding administration, security, finances and so on. Apart from this, through agents and spies must get information regarding the way of working of his officials, ministers, secretaries, his kingdom and mysterious news of other kingdoms. For spies the word 'Deergh Chakshu' has been used. Manu says that the king ought to appoint adequate number of officials, for completing all the royal tasks.

## Manu instructs regarding division of work-

अमात्ये दण्ड आयत्तो दण्डे वैनयिकी क्रिया ।
नृपतौ कोशराष्ट्रे च दूते संधिविपर्ययौ ।। (7.65)

In the above shloka Manu has divided the work of the kingdom and its officials this way –

Rajan- A bold Rajan will take care of issues of national importance and national level work section directly under his control, like the defence forces and the treasury'.

**Amatya (official)-** The right to impart justice and punish could be delegated to the Amatyas or bold officials, by the king.

**Dandadhikari (Judges)- The right to** maintain discipline, be delegated to the Dandadhikari

**Rajdoot (Ambassadors)-** The formulation of policies for making treaties or oppositions ought to be obligatory for the ambassadors.

In modern democratic countries, the system of ruling, that is in vogue we come across similar division of work, in the form of a hierarchy beginning from the President, the Prime Minister, Home Minister, Foreign Minister, Justices, Police Department, Espionage and Diplomats and so on. It is obvious that the well-organized system of ruling, presented by Manu did not hold relevance for a particular time, but is 'modern' for all times.

## A Just Taxation System

In the purview of Manavdharmashastra, there are instructions for the King and royal officials, that they must do their duty of guarding the subjects primarily. Never overlook the fostering of the people.

मोहाद्राजा स्वराष्ट्रं यः कर्षयत्यनवेक्षया।
सोऽचिराद् भ्रश्यते राज्याज्जीविताच्च सबान्धवः।। ( 7.111)
शरीरकर्षणात्प्राणाः क्षीयन्ते प्राणिनां यथा।
तथा राज्ञामपि प्राणाः क्षीयन्ते राष्ट्रकर्षणात्।। (7.112)

While alerting the King Manu says, a king who is due to attachment or non-thought weakens his kingdom, he along with brothers and relatives gets destroyed and corrupted. Exploiting the subjects is a cause of downfall of his kingdom. A king or his officials who did not adhere to the limitations advised in the scriptures are overpowered by greed and consequently do not protect the subjects and spend the revenue collected as tax, from the subjects, not for their welfare, instead splurge it on their own pleasures, were to be considered lowly.

For running the administration, Manu has presented a duty-bound, just taxation system thus-

यथाल्पाल्पभदन्याद्यं वार्योकोवत्सषट्पदाः।
तथाल्पाल्पो ग्रहीतव्यो राष्ट्राज्ञाब्दिकः करः।। (7.129)

The way leech, calf, and bumble bee, slowly suck the eatable, in the same manner the king ought to charge annual taxes.

With reference to the taxation system, Manu has written this shloka-

योऽरक्षन्बलिमादत्ते करं शुक्लं च पार्थिवः।
प्रतिभागं च दण्डे च सः सद्यो नरकं व्रजेत्।। (8.307)

It means that a king who does not perform the duty of protecting the subjects, still takes one sixth part of the subject's produce in the form of tax, fees, octroi or fine, he remains disturbed in pain.

अरक्षितारं राजानं बलिषड्भागहारिणम् ।
तमाहुः सर्वलोकस्य समग्रमलहारकम् ।। (8.308)

According to Manu the subjects turn against such a ruler, who fails to protect their interests and he becomes a target for criticism in the entire nation.

अनपेक्षितमर्यादं नास्तिकं विप्रलुम्पकम् ।
अरक्षितारमत्तारं नृपं विद्यादधोगतिम् ।। (8.309)

The king who flouts the limitations prescribed by the scriptures, is a non-believer in the voice of the Vedas, over powered by greed, become oblivious of his duty to protect the subjects and instead of people's welfare, uses the tax collected for his own personal selfish interests, meets his downfall pretty fast.

Manu says that, only that king remains stable like Dhruva, who loves to be dutiful, is lover of justice and loves his subjects-

रक्षन्धर्मेण भूतानि राजा वध्यांश्च घातयन् ।
यजतेऽहरहर्ज्ञैः सहस्रशतदक्षिणैः ।। (8.306 )

The King who punishes those who though, committed to be dutiful, to protect the subjects in a just manner, when gets involved in crime, must consider his role as performer of Yagyas daily, involving thousands of alms to be distributed. Meaning thereby, that Raj Dharma, while conducting Yagya is earning the fruits of sacred deeds.

While attributing topmost priority to the welfare of the subjects, Manu has presented a taxation system accepted by all, that is completely just. The king who implements this tax system, and spends the tax received by the subjects in welfare policies, his kingdom prospers and progresses, It can be rightly understood that the national welfare is in the welfare of the people.

For running the administrative system smoothly Manu has instructed that each town must have a secretariat-

नगरे नगरे चैकं कुर्यात्सर्वार्थचिन्तकम् ।
उच्चै स्थानं घोररूपं नक्षत्राणामिव ग्रहम् ।। (7.121)

In each one of the big towns, as among planets the Moon is, likewise, a brilliant secretariat be formed, for thinking over and consultations on issues concerning the kingdom and thereafter, present before the people, for fulfilling the very purpose of the system, which is formation of rules.

The conduct of the royal workers appointed in the Secretariat, invites comment by Manu, who writes (7.122) The chief minister must survey the various offices of the Secretariat from time to time. Information regarding the good qualities and shortcomings of officials related to different departments must be gathered secretively and the erroneous ones be punished and officials with good qualities be appreciated. In this reference there is another shloka-

राज्ञो हि रक्षाधिकृताः परस्वादायिनः शठाः ।
भृत्या भवन्ति प्रायेण तेभ्यो रक्षेदिमाः प्रजाः ।। (7.123)

Usually, royal servants employed to protect the subjects, driven by greed try to extract money and do not abstain from the lowly act of thugi. Manu has instructed the King to protect the subjects from such royal men. Royal men who are greedy and non-dutiful are permitted to be punished by Manu, as he says, 'तेषां सर्वस्वमादाय राजा कुर्यीत्प्रवासनम्' or the royal worker who does not do work assigned for protection, be left bereft of his property by the king and he be duly punished. If the crime is unforgivable then he be cast away from the country, so that other men in royal service dare not through unjust ways and partiality, snatch away people's wealth. Manu has granted a system of enough salary (7.125) to the ministers of all departments, so that they are able to shun greed. Manu has also indicated that the progenies of ministers may not be appointed keeping in with tradition but on the basis of their qualifications for the administrative service.

In the Manu Samhita, pointing towards the duty of the king, it is said-

तत्र स्थितः प्रजाः सर्वाः प्रतिनन्द्य विसर्जयेत् ।
विसृज्य च प्रजाः सर्वा मन्त्रयेत्सह मन्त्रिभिः ।। (7.146)

The King must listen to the grievances of the subjects present and find a satisfactory solution for them. The Jansabha, satisfied with the decision, after being dissolved, must indulge in consultation with the ministers, on issues relating to the royal system and instruct the royal officials to redeem the subjects of their problems.

एवं सर्व विधायेदमितिकर्त्तव्यमानत्मनः ।
युक्तश्चैवाप्रमत्तश्च परिरक्षेदिमाः प्रजाः ।। (7.142)

Thus, the king by fulfilling his duty as formulated, without being care-less, must constantly look after the subjects and make his royal officials also adhere to the duties assigned to them.

**Local Self Government**

Clarifying the subject, how to establish, a secure, well organized, Swashasan, it has been said-

राष्ट्रस्य सङ्ग्रहे नित्यं बिधानमिदमाचरेत् ।
सुसंगृहीत राष्ट्रो हि पार्थिवः सुखमेधते ।। (7.113)

It is the Dharma of the king to always make endeavours for organizing the nation well, take care of its security, control and work for its advancement, as a secure, well controlled and organized rule in a nation, remains happy and progresses.

It is very important from the point of view of national security, controlling centres should be established between two, three or five villages and royal offices be created. Officials be appointed from among pastoral people and the village administrative system be strengthened. In a way it points towards the present Panchayat system. The special creation of locally established self-rule is available in the Manavdharmashastra.

For royal control, Centre office established by Manu, its arrangement index-

1. Central Office in the Capital or the Fort of the King 7.69.76
2. In each town a Secretariat 7.121

3. A main office over hundred villages      7.114.115
4. A main office over twenty villages      7.114.115
5. A main office over 10 villages      7.114.115
6. A main office over 5 villages      7.114.115
7. A main office over two villages      7.114.115

Manu has clearly mentioned about the security, problems and proper rule in the villages that-

ग्रामदोषान्समुत्पन्नान्ग्रामिकः शनकैः स्वयम् ।
शंसेद्ग्रामदशेशाय दशेशो विंशतीशिने ।। 116 ।।
विंशतीशस्तु तत्सर्वं शतेशाय निवेदयेत् ।
शंसेद्ग्रामशतेशस्तु सहस्त्रपतये स्वयम् ।। 117 ।।

In case a problem or defect arises in the village, the Gramadhipati will intimate it to the Dasgraamdhipati, for finding a solution. If he too is not able to alleviate the problem, then the Adhipati of hundred villages be approached with the information. If the Adhipati of hundred villages is unsuccessful, in that state he could contact the Adhipati of a thousand villages for finding a solution.

While talking about the obligations of the Secretary of the Village, Manu in shlok 1189-chapter seven advises, that he ought to collect from the villagers, food stuff, drinking water, and fuel daily, to be deposited with the King. The work of the village system and village officials must be inspected by the King's dear and trustworthy secretaries or ministers, without being lazy. It has been mentioned by Manu in the following mantra-

तेषां ग्राम्याणि कार्याणि पृथक्कार्याणि चैव हि ।
राजोऽन्यः सचिवः स्निग्धस्तानि पश्येदतन्द्रितः ।। 120 ।।

Manu means to say that for running the administration of the Kingdom, inspections must be carried out to check if the work is being done. The inspector must fulfil his obligations speedily and the information provided by him facilitates the King to complete the administrative work.

Manu has narrated the duties of the Gramani, that the Gramani must seek prior approval of the members of the

Sabha while fulfilling his obligations, not in an uncontrolled manner. The Gram Sabha was assembled in the form of a family, a village guild or a village group. This Gram Sabha used to ponder over all questions related to the village or problems faced. Manu says-

यो ग्रामदेशसंघानां कृत्वा सत्येन संविदम्।
विसंवदेन्नरो लोभात्तं राष्ट्राद्विप्रवासयेत्।। (8.219)

It means that if the Gramani, takes a truthful oath before the Gram Community and is later driven by greed, flouts the oath, then the king should turn him out of the country. Manu further says, in shlok 220 of chapter eight that the king ought to charge four golden Mudras, six copper and three hundred and twenty ratti silver from the Gramani as punishment for flouting his oath. As Manu has prescribed a law of punishment for the Gramini flouting his oath, likewise, in the case of controversies regarding the points of boundary, he has made provision of law of punishment for the one perpetrating falsehood. In shlokas from 262 to 266 of eighth chapter Manu advised the King, that the king ought to ascertain the points of boundaries of tilled fields, wells, ponds, gardens and boundaries of houses, in the presence of respectable, dutiful people using them as evidence. If controversies regarding boundaries arise in the village and the villagers speak untruth, then the king ought to punish the perpetrator of falsehood, heavily by Madhyamsahas punishment (heavy fine). By threatening one who snatches away, pond, tilling field, garden, be punished by the King by fining him five hundred panh, in case of usurpation inadvertently, two hundred panh could be fined as punishment and the usurped property be ordered to be returned. If there was a doubt in affixing a boundary, a duty-bound king may keep in mind the interest of the plaintiff and the defendant and then ascertain the boundary. This is the system given in the scriptures. Manu says, 'एषोऽखिलेनाभिहितो धर्मः सीमाविनिर्णये।' For fixing the boundaries, this is the complete dharma.

Above local self rule, village self administration or Panchayat Raj, Manu in various shlokas mentions, that for running the administration of the kingdom properly, establishment of three Sabhas and officials composing it, are of importance. In the present system of ruling, this is being followed for the organization which concludes the Kingdom related issues with the only difference that instead of Sabha, it is called Palika.

1. Vidhan Palika or The Legislature ( Law making parishad)
2. Karya Palika or the Executive ( Officials and workers, giving working form to law and regulations)
3. Nyay Palika   or The Judiciary(Officials working for imparting justice)

**Ashtvidh Karma and Panch Vargas**

In the entire royal duty, Manu has given priority to eight types of deeds and five sections of duty-

कृत्स्नम् चाष्टविधंकर्म पञ्चवर्गं च तत्त्वतः ।
अनुरागापरागौ च प्रचारं मण्डलस्य च ।। **(7.154)**

**Eight types of deeds elucidated by Manu-**

1. To be in the company of acharya ritvik, scholars of the Vedas and learn from them (7.37,38,39,43)
2. Control of senses and giving up vices (7.44,45-53)
3. Appointment of ministers and officials, like Amatyas, assistants, presiding officials and assigning them work (7.54-66)
4. Building forts (70-75)
5. Learning Warfare, and policy of war (7.87,96-100)
6. Removal of obstructions and a just system of punishment (7;111,112,152,124)
7. Payment of salary to workers in accordance to the duty performed. (7. 125-126)
8. Collection of Taxes (7.12,127,128)

**Five Sections**

1. Way of work commencement
2. Arranging for a treasury

3  Country's Time Department
4.  Patronage of scholars
5.  Way of concluding work

Related to minsters Manu has written a shloka about the five parts-

कर्मणमारम्भोपायः पुरुषद्रव्यसंपत्, देशकालविभागः।
विनिपातप्रतीकारः कार्यसिद्धिः इति पञ्चाङ्गे मंत्रः॥

**Affection and Disdain (Anurag and Aparag)**

The King must be informed of the section of his subject, that love and are happy with him and also those, who nurture ill will for him. Here, the two types of subjects stand for people of his own nation and people of other countries.

**Mandal**

With reference to the policy to be adopted in relation to other nations, Manu has described basic nature, known as Mandal (Shloka155-157). For the protection of his nation, the King must have knowledge of 'Mandal' essentially.

**National Protection and International Policy**

While describing the obligations of a ruler to maintain the security of the kingdom and its fort, Manusmriti, (7.63-67) iterates, 'The king for carrying on international relations ought to appoint ambassadors and servants for foreign affairs. By doing so, an eye could be kept on the internal and external affairs'. According to Manu the power of punishment meaning, (elephants, horses, chariots and soldiers on foot or the infantry) is under the chief of defence forces (Senapati). Friendly pacifying activity is also under the power of punishment. The treasury and the nation are under the King's control and treaties and aggression are under the control of the Ambassador. Only those people be appointed delegates, who are well versed in the scriptures, loyal to the kingdom, virtuous, competent, holding knowledge of the place and times, a good personality, fearless and a clever informer. Be a good perceiver of indications and gestures. Be able to understand indications tones changing at the time of speaking, affecting the facial expressions, may be lovely or crude and also gestures conveying anger and other feelings, through the movements of hand and feet. Treaties and aggression (peace or war) is dependent on the delegates or the Ambassador. Thus, Manu has labelled the delegates as fine informers.

Under the international relations, the system of Rajmandal has been discussed at length by Manu, in shloka no.155,156, and 160.he says-

मध्यमस्थ प्रचारं च विजिगीषोश्च चेष्टितम् ।<br>
उदासीन प्रचारं च शत्रोश्चैव प्रयत्नतः ।। (7.155)<br>
एताः प्रकृतयो मूलं मण्डलस्य समासतः ।<br>
अष्टौ चान्याः समाख्याता द्वादश्चैव तु ताः स्मृताः ।। (7.156)<br>
संधि च विग्रहं चैव यानमासनमेव च ।<br>
द्वैधीभावं संश्रयं च षड्गुणांश्चिन्तयेत्सदा ।। (7.160)

Manu opines, that the knowledge of Rajmandal is always essential for a ruler. In international relations diplomacy is the main defence strategy. On this subject he says- There are four propensities of Rajmandal. 1) Medium 2)Craving to conquer 3) Complacent 4) Enemy. Apart from this under the ambit of Rajmandal the King may have eight propensities- 1) Different 2) Ari- Not different 3) Friends with friend 4) Friends with friend of enemy 5) Pashnigrah 6) Agreessive against other than neighbour 7) Pashnigrahsaar 8) Akramak- Aggressive against other than the neighbour, with neighbour's support. Four basic and the other eight propensities, make it twelve in total. The twelve propensities of Rajmandalas already mentioned, have five floating propensities each. 1) Amatya- (Prime Minister) 2) Nation 3) Fort 4) Treasury 5) Punishment. Thus, in total the floating propensities count to 12X5=60. On adding 12 propensities they are a total of 72 propensities in the Rajmandal. Along with knowledge of these, an efficient, courageous, valiant King must keep in mind the protection of the nation, making peace or war, Yan (mobilization), Aasan (Neutrality) and Sanshray (alliance), these additional six qualities have to be inculcated, meaning thereby, the six yardsticks of these policies must be adhered to. A conquering king must always give priority to the interest of his nation while implementing these policies.

While affixing international relations, In chapter seven, Manu has described six subjects of consultation, they have been the basis of ancient Indian diplomacy and statecraft-

1) **Sandhi (Treaty of peace)** : This is a pact between two powerful Kings, under its terms they bind each other to perform certain obligation mutually.

2) **Vigrah (Hostility)** : This is opposite of a treaty. It is nor a state of direct war but is a state of stressed relations. In it diplomatic relations are called off and anti movement the possibility of breaking a war can arise.

3) **Yan or Abhyan(mobilization)** : This is the state of actively making preparations for a war, This activity could be expedited with an aspiration of victory and also for a friend's help.

4) **Asan (Neutrality)** : To maintain a position of impartial view is known as 'asan'. In it one is motivated by a policy of one's protection and defeat of the enemy. Meaning thereby induce enemies to fight amongst themselves, with no detriment to one's own kingdom.

5) **Sanshray ( Subordinate alliances)** : Under this policy a king tormented by his enemy, for grinding his own axe, takes shelter of other powerful kings.

6) **Dvaidibhav (Diplomatic manoeuvring)** : This means a policy wherein the defence forces are divided into two parts, one goes forward to fight and the other remains in the King's supervision.

Manusmriti instructs the King not to leave the battle ground, while fighting against his equal, superior or inferior enemy. Not running from the battle ground, protecting the subjects, serving Brahmins, are welfare activities of a ruler. It is the duty of the King to distribute the wealth obtained on winning a war, amongst the twice born and the underprivileged. A king who collects taxes from his subjects, in accordance with the rules, advocated by the Shruti and Smriti, he alone is dutiful and gets happiness.

Manu has referred to the royal duty of protecting the nation and subjects in the following shlokas-

यस्तु भीतः परावृत्तः संग्रामे हन्यते परैः।
भर्तुर्यद् दुष्कृतं किंचित्तसर्वं प्रतिपद्यते।। (7.94)
राज्ञश्च दद्युरुद्धारमित्येषा वैदिकी श्रुतिः।
राज्ञा च सर्वयोद्धेभ्योदातव्यमपृथग्जितम्।। (7.97)

The main duty of a Kshatriya is to foster the subjects. The King who charges taxes according to the way prescribed in the Shruti and Smriti, from his subjects, he gets happiness. While adhering to this Kshatriya duty, the King ought to-

नित्यमुद्यतदण्डः स्यान्नित्यं विवृतपौरुषः।
नित्यं संवृतसंवायो नित्यं छिद्रानुसार्येः।। (7.102)

Use punishment for imparting justice. He be valiant. He should keep secretive work a secret. Keep an eye on the enemy's activities and their shortcomings. As soon as the opportunity arises must conquer the enemy.

अमायथैव वर्तेत न कथंचन मायया।
बुद्धयेतारिप्रयुक्तां च मायां नित्यं स्वसंवृतः।। (7.104)

While carrying on his duty of war, the King ought never deceive anyone. While focusing on the protection of his own nation, be aware of the possibility of being deceived by the enemy.

नास्य छिद्रं परो विद्याद्विद्याच्छिद्रं परस्य तु।
गूहेत्कूर्म इवाङ्गानि रक्षेद्विवरमात्मनः।। (7.105)

Efficient in the policy of Diplomacy and war, the King must maintain secrecy regarding the internal and external policy of his nation, so that the enemy may not be able to muster enough courage to declare a war. According to Manu, as a turtle keeps his body parts hidden, likewise the king must make his national security system so strong that the enemy may find it impregnable.

Instructing a moralist King, Manu says, the king ought to

make endeavours at the right time, so as to curb the increase in the number of his enemies. He should follow such regulations, that may induce friends be complacent and enemies may not be able to inflict pain on him. The King who understands the good and bad regarding the future, has the competence to take quick decisions, learns lessons from the happenings in the past, in the present and for the future is careful (King cautious in all the three times) in crafting his foreign policy, is never defeated by his enemies.

Where Manu has presented Rajmandal and a sketch of six attributes adorned policy before a diplomatic conqueror King, at the same time he has underlined Manavdharma and the sentiment of friendship, by saying that the King ought to adhere to the duty of war as far as possible. A brave king must take care of those who surrender. Those enemy warriors, whose vehicles get broken and those bereft of their weapons, are injured, are fleeing out of fear, need never be attacked or hit. The King must make all possible endeavours for not letting the state of war arise. First of all he must make efforts for a compromise, but if he finds that the enemy is bent upon waging a war, in that situation, be ready for a war and lift his weapon. On understanding deceitful behaviour of the enemy, he will be treated accordingly. But once out of a state of emergency, the King's practical behaviour ought to be free of deceit. In shloka 223 and 343 of Yagnavalkya Smriti, the composer of Smriti says, that there is no greater duty of the King, than not using the booty amassed on winning a war, for self benefit, but distribute it amongst scholars and benefit of his subjects. Yagnavalkya, also stressed that after the war, in the subjugated kingdom, if the subjects there exhibit discreet, thoughtful behaviour and abide by their family's cultural limitations, in that state, the subjugated kingdom's adminis-tration be carried out by the King who conquered, meaning thereby that the subjugated kingdom be ruled as before. Like Manu, Yagnvalkya writes, that the King must maintain friendly relations with the neighbouring kingdoms as in comparison with gold and land, a friend is considered most superior. The shloka of Manavdharma shastra says-

हिरण्य भूमिसंप्राप्त्या पार्थिवो न तथै धते।
यथा मित्रं ध्रुवं लब्ध्वा कृशमप्यायतिक्षमम्।। (7.208)

Manu does not accept till the end, that a king does not progress as fast by obtaining gold and land, as he does by skilfully involving in doing tasks full of love, dutifulness, far-sightedness and keeping the company of an able friend.

**King Creates An Era or Age (Yuga)**

While presenting the constitutional system of an individual, society, King, nation and war Manusmriti iterates the main seven propensities of conducting the administration of a kingdom-

स्वाम्यमात्यौ पुरं राष्ट्रं कोशदण्डौ सुहृत्तथा।
सप्त प्रकृतयो ह्येताः सप्तांङ्ग राज्यमुच्यते।। (9.294)
तेषु तेषु तु कृत्येषु तत्तदङ्ग विशिष्यते।
येन यत्साध्यते कार्यं तत्तस्मिन् श्रेष्ठमुच्यते।। (9.297)

These seven propensities described by Manu are-
  1) The Lord  2) Minister  3) Fortress  4) Nation
  5) Treasury  6) Punishment  7) Friend

In ruling the kingdom all these seven propensities have a very important role to play. Each propensity has its own importance, and accordingly concludes a task. The utility of each propensity or part connects with one another. Manu treats the kingdom as such a unit, in which all the parts fulfil their obligations, contribute in the consistent progress of the kingdom.

All the seven propensities of the kingdom by doing the work assigned to them, also protect dutifulness. But the first propensity, the 'King' generates power for all the other in carrying on their conduct, in his successful leadership and guidance, the nation reaches its pinnacle of glory. By his deeds the king creates an identity of his time and the conduct of his rule only affixes his age of ruling. Thus, the King has been called creator of an age.

कृतं त्रेतायुगं चैव द्वापरं कलिरेव च।
राज्ञो वृत्तानि सर्वाणि राजा हि युग मुच्यते।। (9.301)

Satyuga, Tretayuga, Dwapar Yuga and the Kaliyuga, are all a consequence of the conduct and behaviours of kings, meaning thereby, as the king would conduct himself, in his kingdom that type of Yuga will emerge, in fact the King only is known as the Yuga, which means the King is the creator of a Yuga. Manu further says-

कलिः प्रसुप्तो भवति स जाग्रद् द्वापरं युगम्।
कर्मस्वभ्युद्यतस्त्रेता विचरंस्तु कृतं युगम्।। (9.302)

When the King goes into a slumber or neglects royal work, then it is 'Kaliyuga'. When he is awake, and performs royal work ordinarily, then it is 'Dwapar Yuga'. When the king and subjects are involved in welfare activities, and the king is always ready to cooperate then it is 'Treta Yuga'. When the King fulfils all his obligations speedily and is keen to know the grievances of his subjects and readily alleviates them to provide happiness to them, then it is 'Satayuga".

**According to Yugas the Chatushpad of Dharma**

चतुष्पात्सकलो धर्मः सत्यं चैव कृते युगे।
नाधर्मेणागमः कश्चिम्मनुष्यान्प्रति वर्तते।। (1.81)

Manu has considered duty to be four footed. In Satyuga, duty is present in the form of sin, knowledge, Yagya, and charity. In Treta Yuga it stays in the form of penance, knowledge, and Yagya, in Dwapar Yuga in Yagya and charity and can be explained thus Kal Yuga only charity is important. Thus, the four components of Dharma go on reducing according to deeds. The said four components can be explained thus-

**Tapa-** (Penance) To be rid of greed and attachment. Practicing self-control, have a feeling of love with everyone spiritually and practicing celibacy are symptoms of Tapa.

**Yagya-** Yagya means doing good to others, this good is done to non-living and living beings with equanimity. Before commencing any task for its success, it is customary to perform Yagya (Homa). For instance, for praying to get rains, performance of Yagya has been granted a scientific basis to it. Which has also been proved by scientific research. It is so ironical that today, for winning a cricket match, winning the election, corrupt political leaders and actors have reduced the duty of Yagya to a mere show.

**Gyan (Knowledge)-** Knowledge refers to study of the Vedas. Through the study of Vedas the awareness of truthful duty is realized. In the scriptures at different instances the mantras mentioned, make it clear that the King's councils and committees, Brahma Sabha, Dharma Sabha, wherein consultations and discussions take place on issues regarding administration, way of conduct, judicial system, its members and present scholars, judges, sermonizers , be scholars of Vedic and other scriptures. Even in Buddhist scriptures it is said, that the king must be possessor of weapons and the scriptural knowledge. As weapons are considered a king's articles of adornment, so are scriptures his adornment of intelligence.

**Daan (Charity)-** This component of duty means, that a part of ones earnestly earned money must be spent for social welfare. According to Manu, 'सर्वेषामेव दानानां ब्रह्म दानं विशिष्टते।' Following this tradition, Dilip, Raghu, Dasharath, Ram , Yayati, Prithu and so many rulers of kingdoms, gave to their distressed subjects foodstuff, clothes and money as alms in charity and provided facilities to the helpless and gained name and fame.

The main purpose of Manu in connecting the way of conduct with Yuga is to put across the fact that a human being's behaviour regulates his life. Since a King is the first citizen, that is why his conduct, nature, personality, know-ledge, controlled regulated life and becomes the inspirational power for his subjects. The way he would behave would be exemplary for his subjects. Good, medium, ordinary and low ruling systems have the national representative, the King mainly responsible for it.

Today's modern Yuga is called Kalyuga for this very reason, that the people responsible for the country's obligetions are corrupt. They do not have a good character. Cheating, deceiving, being crafty forms the foundation of their qualifications. The place of people's welfare has been taken not by self-welfare, but by downright selfishness. Self-welfare is actually a good quality, which elevates a human being spiritually. Leaders deviating from the assigned duties, are completely unaware of the Vedic culture. Their guide for showing the right path, the Manav dharmashastra, is now reduced to add beauty to libraries. It is the need of the hour, that the leaders of the administration, must thoroughly, study then constitution in the form of Manav dharmashastra and contemplate over it, understand and then adhere to it in their conduct.

Manav dharmashastra being the proposed constitution of political science, proposes and lays stress to establish such a state, where selfless politicians discuss people's welfare, where the life of the king is committed to service of his subjects, where sharp, competent and intelligent ones are given importance, where the council of ministers are qualified and committed, where officials have integrity, the council of justice is impartial, the taxation system is not burdening, education is free, teachers are brilliant and intelligent, poor, diseased and homeless, are extended help, the ruling power is decentralized, all pervasive ruling power is secure, where there is social and political unity, Panchayats are active and in a nation so well attributed human beings achieve and experience completeness.

In Manu Samhita, Manu has treated competent admini-stration as the pillar of a successful rule, which is beyond its entire power, and right to inflict punishment, bound by the regulations of duty. The King and the subjects as well are told to be ruled by duty. The ruler is supposed to be such an inspirational power, who while himself following the path of duty, averts everyone from inappropriate conduct and encourage to involve in ethical deeds. An ideal ruler proves to be exemplary before his subjects. 'As the King is, so would be the subjects',(यथा राजा, तथा प्रजा) is an old traditional saying. Manu Smriti proves that a king involved in performance of his duties, immersed in people's welfare, with truthfulness as the driving force, is duty bound and dispenser of justice as a ruler, such a king is invariably followed by his subjects, who adhering to dutifulness, acquire wealth and worldly pleasures, to attain the fruit of redemption or all that is auspicious. Only a truly good ruling system can convert Kalyuga into the golden age.

# Before Conclusion

## 'वादे वादे जायते तत्वबोधः'

On the basis of self- realization and experiences, the nation creates social systems and system of ruling for administrative purposes, they are stably placed on this very democratic principle, **'वादे वादे जायते तत्वबोधः'** But the realization of the element can only happen when we respect one another's opinion. The Indian culture looks up to arguments and counter arguments as realization of the element. Our contention is that the truth is not linear. From various points of view, a truth can be seen, tested and experienced. That is why due to the unity in these diversities, whoever is fully empowered to make complete assessment, is a philosopher. He only is knowled-geable. Democracy gets distorted in a state, where instead of respecting someone else's opinion, there is bending down before it. Bad people with ill pursuits get used to getting their inappropriate demands fulfilled by perpetrating fear and coercive measures, manage to gain prominence in the society like a priest. To avert such a dangerous situation from arising and facing it, scholars have brought out the system of 'refinement of public opinion'. The obligation of refinement of public opinion was handed over to the Sadguru ( Chaste Teacher), Rajguru (Royal teacher), sages. It was said that, apart from the sovereign, having known the sovereign well, well- wishers of the nation, can alone build a healthy public opinion and guide in the right direction. Where the task of public opinion refinement would be on, there the narrowness of thoughts would be broken and a mandal consisting of people with forbearance and self-control will go on expanding. India has always been famous for being the epitome of forbearance.

The first condition of success of democracy is also that, every citizen must give up all preconceived notions about

Dharma and culture and confront its all - pervading, eternal element. They be ready in the forefront to fulfil their duty overwhelmed with national sentiment. As every citizen becomes more and more aware of his obligations, and contribution in the ruling system, he will be driven to fulfil it actively, consequently, will develop more forbearance. But along with forbearance, the principle of the will to conquer is also necessary. Without the feeling of aggrandisement, neither a society can survive, nor can there be development of its life. No human being or society can just live to inhale or exhale, he lives to achieve an ideal, and if need be, to protect that ideal will not deter from putting its life at stake. Those who have the ambition to make their ideals unsurmountable, they only rise above the worldly disappointments and do something commendable. The sages of India have understood along with forbearance, the importance of the will to conquer and aggrandise. On striking a balance between these two propensities only, depends the progress of human beings. All will agree that, he will not be considered rational, or wishful of conquering, who opposes only for the sake of opposition. But that person is superior who is effortful of mutual compatibility and striking a balance. For the present democratic set up this is the biggest challenge 'amidst opinions and differences of opinion finding truth, meaning-fulness, coexistence and support deeds and policies leading to everyone's welfare'.

Today politicians are unable to define duty in its true form, or like Gandhari have their eyes covered for unwanted (unacceptable) sights or are trying to prove something by looking at things with the eyes of others. For material benefits, the concept of 'everything goes,' is gaining strength. Actually, when we use the word 'Dharma' then it includes both economics and political science. Basically 'artha' (finances) are the root of dharma (duty)', because dharma cannot be realized without artha. From this view point, how can that which facilitates dharma be generated through unfair or unethical means? Money generated through unethical means, destroys a human being. This the reason, philosophical sages have made dutifulness, the foundation of fostering of people and a legal royal system, harbinger of people's welfare. Instead of uncontrolled, non-dutiful, unruly freedom, there be support of cultural freedom, wherein there is realization of obligations.

The thought has been strengthened that in the cultural freedom of the nation lies national political freedom, as it is the culture that transmits in the entire body of the nation, as life force. It has its own existence. Like the flow of the river while moving continuously, it maintains its uniqueness intact. Great minds, supporters of self-government, democracy, people's rule, neither accepted the King as the creator of tenets of Dharma, nor gave him the right to explain the rules of dharma. To give counselling to the King and explain the rules to him, there was provision of assembling the Dharma Parishad and parishad of Scholars. For protecting the Dharma the King has been held responsible right from the beginning to the end. One with the right to rule, who for the establishment of Dharma, inspired by dharma, adheres to duty for people, only has been granted the power to punish.

This is the truth that holds good in all the three times, that without the national sentiment no nation can progress, neither has in the past, nor will in the future. For a nation's all round progress a prayer of 'वैभव नेतुमेतत्त्वराष्ट्रम्' has been offered. Attainment of supreme grandeur is possible under two conditions. The first one is that the grandeur be achieved through human pursuits at national level. For it a prayer is offered, 'विजेत्री च नः सहता कार्यशक्तिर्' through united work power, achieving grandeur, is the second compulsory condition. The complete prayer is- While working to fulfil duty, our united power to work, be competent to lead our nation on the road to grandeur, we may succeed. This prayer is the proof of the fact that ancient Indian sages-hermits had on the basis of duty, ordered welfare of the entire subjects and composition of a well-organized national systems. India's ancient scholars have thought of amalgamating 'I' and 'We'. They said,-

'संभूतिं च विनाशं च यस्तद्वेदो भयं सह
विनाशेन मृत्युं तीर्त्वा संभूत्याऽमृतमश्नुते ।'

The basic meaning is that communism and individualism, must go hand in hand to be fruitful. By invoking individualism, the grievances of the individual are alleviated and through communism attainment of immortality is possible. The thought of community is the criterion of nationalism. It ought to be treated as a fine foundation for republican and democratic values. In the present democracy for electing the representatives, the citizen have been granted the right to vote. To vote, is people's obligation and is essential for a clean rule. While voting, if the interest of the nation is foremost, then that will be treated as adhering to dharma, if the interest of the individual is the inspiration behind voting, then it would be treated as non-duty. The ancient Indian thought and thinkers were extra ordinary, for they dropped the thought of 'I' and 'Mine" and inspired to adopt the approach of 'We' and 'Ours'.

To conclude, in the present Indian ruling system and social composition, the ties of oneness that have got loose, they need to be tightened up. For this the sentiment of communism will have to be awakened within-' Flower in a stalk looks more beautiful, its fragrance also spreads only till the time it is not separated from the stalk  This wholesome form (symbol of a nation) of the flower inspires to remain connected with the roots.

विश्वं सुभूतं सुविदत्रं नो अस्तु।

The world should be endowed and prudent prosperous.

\* \* \*

# Books of Reference

1. Rigveda Bhasha Bhashya– Maharshi Dayanand Saraswati. Publisher–Sarvdeshik Arya Pratinidhi Sabha, Maharshi Dayanand Bhawan, Ramlila Maidan, New Delhi-1
2. Yajurveda Bhasha Bhashya–Maharshi Dayanand Saraswati. Publisher–Sarvdeshik Arya Pratinidhi Sabha, Maharshi Dayanand Bhawan, Ramlila Maidan, New Delhi-1
3. Samveda Bhasha Bhashya–Pandit Tulsi Ram Swami. Publisher–Sarvdeshik Arya Pratinidhi Sabha, Maharshi Dayanand Bhawan, Ramlila Maidan, New Delhi-1
4. Atharvaveda Bhasha Bhashya – Khshemkaran Das Trivedi. Publisher–Sarvdeshik Arya Pratinidhi Sabha, Maharshi Dayanand Bhawan, Ramlila Maidan, New Delhi-1
5. Rigvedadi Bhashya Bhoomika–Shrimadayanand Saraswati. Publisher Aarsh Sahitya Prachar Trust, Kharibawali, Delhi-6
6. Rigveda Samhita- Sayan Bhashya, Vaidic Shodh Mandal, Chaukhamba Sanskrit Series (Varanasi)
7. Rigveda Samhita– Padmabhushan Pt. Shripad Damodar Satavlekar- writer, translator and Publisher Swadhyay Mandal (Pardi) Dist. Valsaad, Sitara, Mumbai.
8. Samveda Samhita– Padmabhushan Pt. Shripad Damodar Satavlekar-writer, translator and Publisher Swadhyay Mandal (Pardi) Dist. Valsaad, Sitara, Mumbai.
9. Atharvveda Samhita- Padmabhushan Pt. Shripad Damodar Satavlekar-writer, translator and Publisher Swadhyay Mandal (Pardi) Dist. Valsaad, Sitara, Mumbai.
10. Rigveda Samhita Tamrapatrotkirna Pratikriti, Arsh Sahitya Sansthanam.Shrimaddayanandvedarsh Mahavidyalay 119 Gautamnagar Delhi-49
11. Yajurveda Samhita-Tamrapatrotkirna Pratikriti, Arsh Sahit-ya Sansthanam. Shrimaddayanandvedarsh Mahavid-yalay 119 Gautamnagar Delhi-49
12. Samveda Samhita- Tamrapatrotkirna Pratikriti, Arsh Sahitya Sansthanam.Shrimaddayanandvedarsh Mahavi dy-

alay 119 Gautamnagar Delhi-49
13. Aittireya Brahman--Sayan Bhashya, Travencore University, Sanskrit Series (Trivandrum)
14. Aittiriya Brahman- Poona Sanskaran
15. Taittiriya Brahman-Poona Sanskaran
16. Charak Samhita- Chaukhamba Sanskrit Series (Varanasi)
17. Shatpath Brahman--Asiatic Society of Bengal (Kolkota)
18. Tandaye Brhaman- Asiatic Society of Bengal (Kolkota)
19. Shatpath Brahman– Bhashya ,Swami Sampoornanand Dayanand Sansthan, New Delhi
20. Gopath Brahman– Jeevanand Vidyasagar (kolkota)
21. Aitereyaranyakam– Editor Harinarayan Apte (Poona)
22. Taittireyaranyakam – Editor Harinarayan Apte (Poona)
23. Ashtadhyayi– Panini
24. Aapstambhgriha Sutra–Chaukhamba Sanskrit Series, Varanasi 1972
25. Gautam Dharma Sutra– Shri Gopinath Dixit, Anandashram Mudranalaya, Poona.
26. Ekadashopanishad Bhashya, Dr. Vidyamartandyeya Satyavrat Sidhantalanka (interpreter), Vijaykrishna Lakhanpal (Delhi) Vidyavihar, Dehradun.
27. Manu Smriti (Vishudhh)– Prof Surendra Kumar, publisher Arsha Sahitya Trust, Delhi
28. Manusmriti–Editor and translator Tulsiram Swami. Meerut 1903, publisher Motilal Banarasidas Jawahar Nagar Delhi.
29. Yagyavalkya smriti– Arsha Sahitya Prachar Trust (Delhi) Second Edition 1918
30. Yagyavalkya smriti–Achar Vyahvaar Adhyay-Vishwa Jyoti (Dharmashastra issue) Hoshiyarpur, 1974-75 Second edition.
31. Kautaliya Arthashastra–Translator Udaiveer Shastri, publisher Mehar Chand Laxmandas, Dariyganj Delhi-6 (vol. I, ll & lll)
32. Shukraniti Sar–Swami Jagdishwaranand Saraswati, publisher Rishidevi Rooplal Kapoor dharmarth trust, Ajay

printers Bahalgarh Sonipat, Haryana ,1983

33. Vidurniti- Swami Jagdishwaranand Saraswati, publisher Vijaya kumar Govindram Hasanand, Delhi

34. Valmiki Ramayan– Swami Jagdishwaranand Saraswati, Bhagwati Prakashan, Delhi.

35. Mahabharat–Swami Jagdishwaranand Saraswati, Bhagwati Prakashan, Delhi.

35. Acharya Dinanath Sidhantalankar–-Bharat ki Pracheen Nitiyan, Kitabghar, Delhi, 1976

36. Kashi Prasad Jaiswal--Hindu Rajyatantra (Vol. I), translator-Ram Chandra Verma, Naagri Pracharini Sabha, Kashi, Second Edition 2008

37. Gurudutt-
(i) Prajatantrik Samajvaad, Rajpal and Sons, 1978, Delhi.
ii.Prajatantra athva Varnashram Vyavastha, Shashvat Sanskrit Parishad

38. K.Motwani--Manu Dharmashastra, publisher Ganesh and Co. Ltd.1985.

39. Ta. Shi. Ka. Kannan Kurul Chintan--Tamilveda Tamil Tirrukuralk, Bharatiya Shastron se samya. Publisher Tamil Bhasha Academy, Chennai.

40. Pt. Gangaprasad – Dharma ka Adi srot, Chief Justice Tihri, The founder Head of Religion, Translator- Pt. Harishankar Sharma Arya, Garhwal State, Sahitya Mandal Ltd., Ajmer, Prof.

41. Bharatiyata ke Prabudhh Prahari Pt. Prakashveer Shastri. Smriti Granth Samiti, Editors–Dattatreya Tiwari, Ashok Kaushik, Shiv Kumar Goel. Mayank Printers Delhi, December, 2000

42. Yogendranath Vedant teerth Bagchi– Pracheen Bharat Mei Dandniti (hindi Translation) Shri Durga Dutt Tripathi Shastri, editor- Dr. Shitanshu Shekhar Bagchi, July 1961, (c) Pharma K.L Mukhopadhyaya (Kolkota)

43. Vachaspati Gerole–Vaidic Sahity aaur, Sanskriti, 1969 (Allahabad)

44. Vinayak Rav Abhinandan Granth– Editor in Chief. Vanshidhar Vidyalankaar, (Shashthivarshotsava Samiti) The State of Hyderabad.
45. Shankar Dayal Singh--Samay, Kaal Paristhiti aur Gandhi, Parijat Prakashan, Patna.
46. Shivdutt Gyani–Ved kaleen Samaj, Varanasi, Chaukhambha Vidyabhavan,1967
47. Swami Vivekanand Complete Works, Volume 3, Translation- Surya Kant Tripathi Nirala.
48. Swami Vyomrupanand – Bharatiya Vyakhyaan, Swami Vivekanand publication, Ramkrishna Math Nagpur, 1993 (Eighth edition)
49. Altekar A.S.–
   i. Sources of Hindu Dharma (Solapur) 1952,
   ii. State and Government in Ancient India (Delhi), Motilal Banarsidas ( Fourth Edition),1962, 58
50. Aiyangar S.K.– Hindu India from original sourses, (vol I& ll ) Nag Publication Delhi 1977
51. Aiyangar K.V.R– Rajdharma, Dewan Bahadur Krishna Swami Rao Lectures; University of Madras (Madras) Adyar Library, 1914
52. Aspects of the social and political system of Manusmriti – Radha Kumar Mukherji Lectures– 1946, Lucknow. University of lucknow, 1949
53. Bloomfield. M– The Religion of the Vedas, G.P. Putnam's Sons, New York and London, The Thicker booker press, 1908
54. Bhandarker R.K– Some Aspects of Ancient Hindu Polity tr. by Anand Krishna-(Varanasi) Hindi Prakashan Samiti Kashi Vishvavidyalaya 1974
55. Corpra, P– The Tao of Physics, Weldwood House, 1975
56. Corus, P (Trs) Tao Teh-King of lao. Tzy-Laotzy XXII (Chicago) 1913
57. Duncan J. Derrett M. -
   i. Dharmasastra and Juridical Literature ( A History of

Indian Literature) Vol.4, (Wies Baden) 1933, 1973

ii. Religion Law and the state in India (London) 1968

iii. The concept of Duty in South Asia edited by Flaherty , Vikas Publication House Pvt. Ltd., 1978 , Delhi

58. Dunning, W.A.– A History of political theories, Ancient and Medival P.XIX., New York, The MecMillon Company, London, 1902

59. Gokhale B.G.- Indian political thought through the Ages, Asia publishing House 1952,

60. Ghoshal U.N. –

i. A History of Indian political Ideas (London) colin. M. Brown, Oxford university press, 1959,66

ii. Hindu political theories (London) Oxford university press 1923.

61. Jayaswal K.P.– Hindu polity, vol. I and II, Bangalore printing and publishing co. Itd., 1943 (Bangalore)

62. Kane P.V. – History of DharmaSastra, Bhandarker oriental research Institute 1930-1946 Vol.4 (Poona)

63. Mazumdar R.C. -The Vedic Age; Bhartiya Vidya Bhavan Series-Vol. V

64. Maxmuller F. –

i. The vedas , Indological book house, Delhi ,1969

ii. Upnishadas (I&ll)– Motilal Banarsidas , Delhi, ii. Vol. I & ll  sacrade books of the easter Oxford clarendon Press. 1965

iii. A History of Ancient Sanskrit Literature (Varanasi), Chaukhamba Sanskrit Series, 1968

iv. India What can it Teaches Us, Longmans Green Co. 1892

v. Chips from a German Workshop, ( NewYork) Charles Scribner and co. 1891, 1872, 1966

65. Prasad Beni– Theory of Government in Ancient India, (Allahabad)1928

66. Pret T.B. – Religious Consiousness; (Newyork)1934

67. Sharma R.N.– Ancient India according to Manu (Delhi)

Nag Publication 1980

68. Radhakrishnan S.– The Hindu view of life: (Newyork). George Allen and Unwin Ltd. The Macmillon Co. 1927, 57
69. S. Gopalan– Hindu Social Philosophy, The Radha Krishnan Institute for Advanced Study in Phylosophy, Unviersity Of Madras, 1981
70. Sankhdher M.M – Reflections of Indian Polity (Delhi) MD Gupta Kumar brother 1973
71. Spellman J.W – Political Theory of Ancient India. Oxford Clarendon Press ,1964
72. R.P. Kangle– Kautilya Arthasastra A study, Part III, Motilal Banarsidas
73. Satyaketu Vidyalankar– An extension lectures on Democratic Elements in Ancient Indian Polity, Saraswatisadan, Massooree (UP), at Law College Jaipur, 29th February and1st March 1953, Publisher - The University of Rajputana ,Jaipur
74. Winternitz–A History of Indian literature Vol. II (Calcutta) University of Calcutta 1968
75. Widengrain – Religion Phynominology; Barlin 1969

**Souvenirs , Magazines and Journals**

★ Kalyaan magazine
i) Nitisaar issue , year 37 Jan - Feb. count 1- 2
ii) Veda Kathank Jan- Feb, 1999  year 23 count 1-2, November 1951
Geeta press Gorakhpur
★ Hindustan Varshiki –Times Prakashan, Editor Dattatrey Tiwari (1989-90)
★ Vishvatma – year 12, issue - 7, Nov. 1986
★ Manthan- Deendayal Shodh Sansthan,  triad monthly, issue - 3

★ Shri milind- Year 2012 Sanshodhan Ganga – March-April 2014, issue -2
★ Paropkari– Sarvadeshik Saaptaahik--July 1993, 1991. Paropkarinni Sabha
★ Arya Jagat- 26th January, 1992, 13 February, 2000, 21st June, 1998